TEXTS AND STUDIES

CONTRIBUTIONS TO
BIBLICAL AND PATRISTIC LITERATURE

EDITED BY

J. ARMITAGE ROBINSON B.D.
FELLOW OF CHRIST'S COLLEGE CAMBRIDGE

VOL. II.

No. 2. THE TESTAMENT OF ABRAHAM

THE TESTAMENT OF ABRAHAM

THE GREEK TEXT NOW FIRST EDITED WITH
AN INTRODUCTION AND NOTES

BY

MONTAGUE RHODES JAMES M.A.
FELLOW DEAN AND DIVINITY LECTURER OF KING'S COLLEGE
ASSISTANT-DIRECTOR OF THE FITZWILLIAM MUSEUM

WITH AN APPENDIX CONTAINING
EXTRACTS FROM THE ARABIC VERSION OF

THE TESTAMENTS OF ABRAHAM ISAAC AND JACOB

BY

W. E. BARNES B.D.
FELLOW OF PETERHOUSE

Wipf & Stock
PUBLISHERS
Eugene, Oregon

Wipf and Stock Publishers
199 W 8th Ave, Suite 3
Eugene, OR 97401

The Testament of Abraham
with an appendix containing the Testaments of Abraham,
Isaac, and Jacob by W.E. Barnes
By James, Montague Rhodes
ISBN: 1-59244-890-9
Publication date 9/29/2004
Previously published by Cambridge, 1892

TO

H. J.,   M. E. J.,
   H. E. L.

PREFACE.

THE ancient writings published in this volume have, it is believed, more than one claim on the interest of students. They belong, in the first place, to a class of literature whose importance in the history of both the Jewish and the Christian religion is now amply recognised; namely, the pseudepigraphic. Within the sphere of that literature, they claim kindred with two important groups of books, the apocalyptic and the ethical. In respect of apocalyptic literature, important information is afforded by the Testament of Abraham as to the relationships subsisting between various Visions of the unseen; in particular, both the origin and the wide-spread popularity of the Apocalypse of Paul are illustrated. The ethical group of pseudepigrapha is enriched by the publication of the Testament of Isaac, the relation of which to the *Didache* and to the Testaments of the Twelve Patriarchs will, I hope, be recognised and investigated by others more fully than it has been by myself.

Among the more important points which invite discussion in the Testaments, I would call attention to the occurrence of the weighing of Souls as a feature in the process of judgment, to the suggested influence of the Testament of Abraham upon the Vision of Thurchill, and to the description of the Angel of Death.

It has been possible for me to make use of several unpublished documents of an apocryphal nature. These are, the Latin text of the Apocalypse of Paul, and the Apocalypses of the Virgin, of Sedrach, and of Zosimas. I hope to be able to print the full text of these and of several other similar tracts at no distant date.

PREFACE.

Among matters which I have not discussed in this volume there are two in particular which need to be mentioned here. The first omission is that of ancient accounts of the death of Abraham outside the Testament. There are very few of these, and I have not come across any which seem to be connected with the tract before us. The most noteworthy is that in the Book of Jubilees. In the second place, I had at one time contemplated adding a section on the later history of the tombs and relics of the Patriarchs. This, however, would have led me further afield than I was justified in going, and I need do no more here than refer my reader to the very interesting narrative of the Invention of the three bodies at Hebron in the 13th century, which is printed in the Bollandist *Acta* for March.

My thanks for help rendered in the production of this book are due in the first place to Mr W. E. Barnes, the writer of the Appendix: he has had a difficult task to perform in translating the corrupt text before him; but his excellent performance has very greatly added to the value of this volume. To the Editor of this series I would render my best thanks for his kindness in transcribing a MS of the Testament of Abraham, and for his patient supervision of all the work. To Mr Rendel Harris, for his generous loan of another transcript, and to Professor W. Robertson Smith, for several suggestions and much help incidentally rendered, I also desire to express my gratitude very warmly.

M. R. J.

CONTENTS.

          PAGE

INTRODUCTION
- The MSS 1
- History of the Book 7
- Influence on Later Literature 29
- The two Recensions and the Arabic Version 34
- Christian element in the Testament of Abraham . . . 50
- Thanatos; and the Angelology and Demonology of the Testament 55
- The Speaking Tree 59
- Abraham's unwillingness to die 64
- The weighing of Souls 70
- Abraham's bosom, and the Patriarchs in Paradise . . . 72
- Provenance of the Book 76

TESTAMENT OF ABRAHAM; GREEK TEXT
- Recension A 77
- Recension B 105

NOTES 120

APPENDIX
- Prefatory Note 133
- Extracts from the Arabic Version of the Testaments of Abraham, Isaac, and Jacob 135
- On the Testaments of Isaac and Jacob 155

INDICES
- Index of Greek Words 163
- Index to the Introduction and Notes 164

INTRODUCTION.

THE present edition of the Greek text of the Testament of Abraham in its two recensions is made from nine MSS. Two versions of the book, Roumanian and Arabic, have also been consulted. An account of these authorities will be most appropriately placed at the head of this introduction. The MSS of the Greek text divide themselves into two main classes, those of the Longer, and those of the Shorter Recension. All are late, the oldest belonging perhaps to the 13th century.

MSS of the Longer Recension.

A. Paris, Bibl. Nat. Fonds Grec 770, cent. XIV., written in 1315 by a priest named George. This is a 4to. book, of paper, with 268 ff., written in double columns. The contents are miscellaneous, including various lives of Saints for the months November and December, e.g. SS. Andrew, Nicolas, Barbara, and Anastasia.

The Testament of Abraham occupies ff. 225 b—241 a: it is preceded by S. Chrysostom's Homily on the Expulsion of Adam from Paradise, and followed by the same Father's xiith Homily on Philippians.

Other Apocryphal tracts in the volume are the Gesta Pilati, Story of Joseph of Arimathaea, Anaphora and Paradosis of Pilate, Martyrdom of S. Andrew, S. John's narrative of the Assumption, and Eurippus's Narrative of the Martyrdom of S. John Baptist.

The Codex was used by Tischendorf (*Evang. Apocr.* Ed. II. p. lxxxi.). It is the best MS of the Longer Recension which I have used. I collated it in Sept. 1890.

B. Jerusalem, Cod. S. Sepulcri 66, cent. XV(?). For a full account of the contents of this MS see Mr Rendel Harris's *The Rest of the Words of Baruch*, pp. 27—29. To his kindness I owe a transcript of this MS, which I have found of material importance in the constitution of a text. This copy is closely allied to A; where it differs, its readings are seldom to be preferred.

C. Cod. Bodl. Canonicianus Gr. 19, cent. XV. XVI., on paper, ff. 315.

A miscellany, in which are many Homilies of S. Chrysostom, some of S. Ephraem, a few Lives of Saints for Nov. and Dec. and some Apocryphal matter.

The Testament occupies ff. 128 b—144 b. It is preceded by the Names of the Apostles and Etymology of the Greek letters, and followed by the Revelation of S. Methodius in a form differing from that printed.

Of other Apocryphal matter it contains a fragment of a Narrative of the Assumption (S. John's), Eurippus on S. John Baptist, the Protevangelium, and the Legend of Zosimas. This is, I believe, the only MS of the Testament in England. It seems to be a copy of Cod. E (v. infra). I transcribed it in Nov. 1886.

D. Paris, Bibl. Nat. Fonds Grec 1556, cent. XV. paper, ff. 351, 4to.

It contains Homilies and Lives of Saints, mostly for Nov., Dec. and Jan.

The Testament occupies ff. 22 a—32 b. It is preceded by a Life of S. Nicolas and followed by S. Ephraem's Homily on Joseph.

Of other Apocryphal matter it has: Acts of SS. Andrew and Matthew and Acts of S. Thomas. The uncial fragments of the Acts of SS. Andrew and Matthew published by Tischendorf (*Apocr.* 139), were at one time bound up in this volume, but seem now to have disappeared.

The text of this MS of the Testament is not very good, and shews a tendency to abridgement. I collated it in Sept. 1890.

E. Vienna, Cod. Theol. Gr. 237 (333 in Nessel p. 443) cent. XIII. (?), vellum 8vo. ff. 151.

Homilies and one or two Lives, of S. Euphrosynus, Marinus or Mary, and Alexius.

The Testament (ff. 34 *a*—57 *a*) intervenes between the Life of S. Euphrosynus, and a Homily of S. Chrysostom on Prayer and Fasting. The MS contains the Apocalypse of the Virgin. It was bought at Venice in 1673 from the Abate Domenico Federici. The MS C also came from Venice with the rest of the Canonici MSS, and may have been copied there direct from E, to which it shews the closest similarity, only differing here and there by accidental omission, and more frequently by an increased tendency to itacism. For my knowledge of the text of this MS I am indebted to a transcript kindly made for me by the Editor of this Series, when he was working at Vienna in September, 1890.

F. Paris, Bibl. Nat. Fonds Grec 1313, cent. XV. XVI. 8vo. paper, ff. 364, in a bad hand.

A Miscellany of Homilies and Lives of Saints connected with the winter months, e.g. SS. Andrew, Xenophon, Nicolas, Barbara.

The Testament occupies ff. 32 *b*—38 *b*. It is a mere fragment, ending in § V, and presents a poor text. I collated it in Sept. 1890.

There are one or two errors in the description of this MS in M. Omont's valuable *Inventaire Sommaire*, which it may be well to notice here. (1) The Testament of Abraham is not mentioned at all. (2) The 'Anonymi fragmentum de Adamo' is Tischendorf's 'Apocalypse of Moses' in an abridged form, but complete. (3) The 'Vita Andreae' is the Acts of SS. Andrew and Matthew, and extends, not to f. 173 but to f. 162 *a*; f. 162 *b* is blank, and the space from f. 163 *a*—172 *a* is occupied by a fragment, mutilated at the beginning, of one of the numerous narratives of the Assumption.

Besides the above apocryphal tracts, the volume contains S. John's narrative of the Assumption.

MSS of the Shorter Recension.

A. Paris, Bibl. Nat. Fonds Grec 1613, cent. XV. 8vo. paper, ff. 191.

It contains Homilies and Lives of Saints, e.g. SS. Xenophon, John Calybita, Mary of Egypt, Thomas the Apostle, and John the Almoner.

4 THE TESTAMENT OF ABRAHAM.

The Testament occupies ff. 87 b—96 b. It is preceded by S. Ephraem on Charity and the Second Advent, and followed by S. Chrysostom on the Vanity of Life. This is the best MS of this recension. I transcribed the text in Sept. 1890.

B. Paris, Bibl. Nat. Supplément Grec 162, cent. XIV. 4to. paper, ff. 212, in double columns.

It contains Homilies and Lives of Saints e.g. SS. Mary of Egypt, John Calybita, the Forty Martyrs, George, Nicolas, Barbara.

The Testament occupies ff. 106 b—114 b, and is imperfect, ending in § xiii. The old table of contents in this MS has

περὶ τῆς κοιμήσεως τοῦ πατριάρχου ἀβραάμ [mut. at end.]
διήγησις τοῦ 'Εφραὶμ εἰς τὸν παγκάλον 'Ιωσήφ [gone.]
(S. Chrysostom) τῷ σαββάτῳ τῆς ἀποκρέω εἰς τοὺς κεκοιμημένους [gone.]
τοῦ χρυσοστόμου τῇ κυριακῇ τῆς ἀποκρέω [beginning gone.]

I collated it in September, 1890.

C. Vienna, Cod. Histor. Gr. 126 (p. 175 Nessel), cent. XV. (?), paper, 4to. ff. 137.

Contains Lives of Saints, e.g. SS. Barbara, the Seven Sleepers, Theodore, Nicolas, Susanna.

The Testament occupies ff. 10 b—18 a. A leaf is lost towards the end. It is preceded by the Martyrdom of S. Nicetas the Goth, and followed by some Acts of S. John, printed by Tischendorf. The MS also contains the Rest of the Words of Baruch, the Protevangelium, and the Acts of SS. Peter and Paul.

I was enabled by the good offices of Mr Robinson to obtain an excellent transcript of this MS, made by Dr Rudolf Beer. The text is valuable.

Besides the MSS which have been utilised for the present edition there is one which I have not been able to consult. It is at Montpellier, No. 405 (72 in Omont's *MSS Grecs des Bibliothèques des Départements*), of cent. XV.—XVI. on paper, "petit format," ff. 154. On ff. 61—83 is Διήγησις περὶ τῆς ζωῆς καὶ θανάτου καὶ τῆς φιλοξενίας τοῦ δικαίου 'Αβραάμ...ἔζησε δὲ 'Αβραάμ... The opening words indicate that it is a MS of the Longer Recension. It is preceded by the "Apocalypse of Moses" (v. supra Par. Gr. 1313), and followed by Hymns to the Virgin. The MS also contains the

Revelation of Methodius, the opening words being identical with those of the recension in Canon. Gr. 19. The provenance of the volume is Auxerre; the copyist was Noel de La Brō.

In *Cat. Codd. MSS Angliae*, among Gale's MSS (Pt. iii. p. 187, No. 85) is a *Narratio de Abrahamo*, which may be the Testament. It may, however, also be the Life of S. Abraham the Hermit, which is often described in similar terms, and is a good deal commoner than the Testament, which seems to have given place to it in some collections of lives. Gale's MS did not come to Trinity College; it may be at Leyden. No doubt other copies exist; but at present I have not been able to discover them, nor do I anticipate that very much would be gained by a multiplication of collations.

As to the relations of our available MSS. Those of the Long Recension may be classed as follows: A and B present one and the same form of text, which differs from the others chiefly in its greater fulness. I do not find proof that A is the parent of B. CE shew a rather abbreviated text, and E is obviously very near akin to C. D is still more of an abridgement, but seems to belong to a family not represented by either AB or CE. F is the latest of the MSS, and is quite unimportant.

The text which I have printed of the Long Recension depends more upon A than upon any other single authority. In the *Apparatus Criticus* I have not noted by any means all the variations which occur; those which I have omitted consist in great part of itacisms and of omissions which are obviously accidental. This is more particularly true of the narrative portions of the book: in the Apocalyptic portion I believe my collations to be complete.

The MSS of the Shorter Recension being only three in number do not afford much opportunity of identifying their descent. The Paris MS A gives the fullest and best text here; B shews a tendency to modernise the language and to abridge further, while C takes unwarrantable liberties with the text in at least one place (§ II. III.), which have the effect of confusing the narrative. Their variations are reported with approximate completeness in the *Apparatus Criticus*.

The two Versions of the Testament to which I have had access are not the only ones that exist, nor indeed the only ones

6   THE TESTAMENT OF ABRAHAM.

in print. Of the others, however, I can furnish only scanty particulars.

The Roumanian Version was printed, with an English translation, by Dr Michael Gaster in the Transactions of the Society of Biblical Archaeology, IX. 195—226 (1887), under the name of the Apocalypse of Abraham. The MSS used by him are three in number, of the XVIIIth and XIXth centuries. The title of the book in this version is the most important point connected with it. It runs thus:

"Vieața și moartea parintelui nostru cel drept Avraam, scrisa dupa *Apocalipsi* cu cuvinte frumoase foarte," i.e. "Life and Death of our Father Abraham the Righteous, written according to the Apocalypse in beautiful words."

This is on the whole an abridged and not very faithful form of the Longer Recension. Such details as the "sons of Masek," § II, are omitted. Δρῦς τῆς Μαμβρῆ is always rendered "Dria the Black" μαύρη being read for Μαμβρῆ. The episode of Abraham's wrath against sinners, and the description of Death are much shortened. On the whole this version shews great similarity to the text of the MSS CE. No detail not contained in them appears here.

Dr Gaster's edition of the Roumanian Version was anticipated, it seems, in part by the publication of a fragment of the version by B. P. Hasdeu in *Cuvente den bătrâni* II. 189—94, Bucharest, 1880. A Slavonic version has been printed by Tihonravov in *Pamjatniki Arechennoj Russkoj literatury*, pp. 79—90, Petersburg, 1863. Of neither of these books have I been able to obtain a sight.

The Ethiopic version I cannot discover in a complete form. A copy of the Three Testaments (of Abraham, Isaac, and Jacob) is to be found in MS Eth. 134, of the Bibliothèque Nationale. But here the Testament of Abraham is a mere fragment, beginning in the midst of the trial-scene, where the 'second witness' of the Arabic Version is speaking. From the Arabic Version this in Ethiopic seems to have been made. A copy, which must be much abridged, of all the Three Testaments occupies six leaves in No. 107, of M. D'Abbadie's Ethiopic MSS (*Catalogue raisonné*, p. 119). It is perhaps noteworthy that the MS is a production of the

HISTORY OF THE BOOK. 7

Falashas. The Testaments are here, as in the Arabic, attributed to S. Athanasius.

Of the Arabic Version it is not my purpose to speak in detail now. An examination of its relation to the other authorities will be best reserved to a special section dealing with the topic. It may be said here, that this version only became accessible to me when, after my Greek text had gone to press, Mr Barnes undertook the task of translating it from the Paris MS 31 anc. fonds Arabe, which the French authorities, with their wonted liberality, sent over to the Cambridge University Library. For a complete account of the MS, I would refer the reader to Mr Barnes's Appendix. Its existence was first notified to the world at large by the extract from it printed by M. Zotenberg in his Cat. des MSS Éth. de la Bibl. Nat., à propos of the Ethiopic MS no. 134, of which I have already made mention. These extracts Professor Robertson Smith kindly translated for me, and a further examination of the MS was decided upon.

History of the Book.

Under this head it seems best to include such meagre notices of the existence of our book as are yielded by Patristic Literature. (1) As is often the case when we are dealing with apocryphal books, the bulk of our information consists of a bare mention of the name occurring in lists of such works. There are three principal documents of the kind in Greek, which, though they are not the earliest in date of our available witnesses, we will examine first by way of clearing the ground. Our three documents are (a) the Synopsis of Pseudo-Athanasius[1], (b) The Stichometry of Nicephorus, (c) The List of the Sixty Books. The most recent edition and discussion of these lists is to be found in Zahn's *Gesch. d. NTlichen Kanons* ii. I. 290—318. The Synopsis is, he thinks, a

[1] According to Zahn, the MS from which Montfaucon printed the *Synopsis* has since been lost, and no other is known to exist. I have lately come across a MS in the Library of Eton College (Bl. 5. 13) of cent. XIV. or XV., written by Doukas, the notary of John of Ragusa, Cardinal Bp. of Argos († 1418-19), which contains this Synopsis (f. 1 sqq.). The MS was from 1685 to 1748 the property of the Mauclercs of Vitry, by one of whom, Joh. Hen. Mauclerc, it was presented to the then Librarian of Eton College, Mr Huggett.

production of cir. 500 A.D.; the Stichometry was drawn up at Jerusalem in cir. 850 A.D.; the List of the Sixty Books dates from cir. 600 A.D. Other writers, e.g. Credner and Schürer, have regarded the Stichometry as earlier in date than the Synopsis. But Zahn's reasoning appears to me convincing, and as regards the List of the Sixty Books, it is, I think, demonstrable from internal evidence that it is based on the Synopsis. I append a copy of the three lists, with the view of shewing in what company the work named after Abraham appears. It should be noted that the text of the Stichometry only differs from that of the Synopsis by the addition of the number of στίχοι in each book. It will be remarked further that the List of the Sixty Books omits the item in which we are interested. For this omission I hope to be able to assign a reason. One other note I will add here: Fabricius, *Cod. Pseud. V. T.* i. 402, gives the Stichometry for Abraham as ‚ατ' (1300). This variant is, as Zahn points out, merely a clerical error. The true reading (300) gives us a book rather shorter than the Greek Esther, which has 350 στίχοι.

Ps.-Ath.	Nicephorus.	Sixty Books.
α'. Ἐνώχ.	α'. + στίχοι ‚δω'.	α'. Ἀδάμ.
β'. Πατριάρχαι.	β'. + στίχ. ‚ερ'.	β'. Ἐνώχ.
γ'. Προσευχὴ Ἰωσήφ.	γ'. + στίχ. ‚αρ'.	γ'. Λάμεχ.
δ'. Διαθήκη Μωϋσέως.	δ'. + στίχ. ‚αρ'.	δ'. Πατριάρχαι.
ε'. Ἀνάληψις Μωϋσέως.	ε'. + στίχ. ‚αυ'.	ε'. Ἰωσὴφ προσευχή.
ϛ'. Ἀβραάμ.	ϛ'. + στίχ. τ'.	ϛ'. Ἐλδὰδ καὶ Μωδάδ.
ζ'. Ἐλδὰδ καὶ Μωδάδ.	ζ'. + στίχ. υ'.	ζ'. Διαθήκη Μωσέως.
η'. Ἡλίου προφήτου.	η'. + στίχ. τιϛ'.	η'. Ἀνάληψις Μωσέως.
θ'. Σοφονίου προφήτου.	θ'. + στίχ. χ'.	θ'. Ψαλμοὶ Σολομῶντος.
ι'. Ζαχαρίου πατρὸς Ἰωάννου.	ι'. + στίχ. φ'.	ι'. Ἡλίου ἀποκάλυψις.
ια'. Βαροὺχ, Ἀμβακούμ, Ἐζεχιὴλ καὶ Δανιὴλ ψευδεπίγραφα.	ια'. identical.	ια'. Ἡσαίου ὅρασις.
		ιβ'. Σοφονίου ἀποκάλυψις.
		ιγ'. Ζαχαρίου ἀποκάλυψις.
		ιδ'. Ἔσδρα ἀποκάλυψις.

The entry with which we are especially concerned is the 6th in the first two lists; and the first question which occurs in connexion with it is this: what word are we to supply in order to complete the title? Peter Lambecius, the Vienna librarian quoted by Fabricius *l. c.*, suggested ἀνάληψις, repeating it from the preceding entry. Fabricius himself preferred ψευδεπίγραφα and was for taking the whole of the list of Ps.-Athanasius as one sentence, understanding the word ψευδεπίγραφα with every item after the 'Assumption of Moses.' On the other hand, a reference to the List of the Sixty Books, where the titles are more fully given, shews us that in several instances the word to be supplied is ἀποκάλυψις. This is so in the case of the works attributed to Elijah, Zephaniah, and Zechariah (or Zacharias) and less certainly in the case of 'Baruch'; for probably the 'Apocalypse of Baruch' is alluded to in the 11th entry. The idea that in the case of 'Abraham' the word ἀποκάλυψις must be supplied is favoured by the fact that we know that in the time of Epiphanius an 'Apocalypse of Abraham' existed. I believe, then, that 'Αβραὰμ ἀποκάλυψις is the full title of No. 6 in these lists; and the fact that the Greek MSS of the book here published show a predilection for the term διαθήκη need not militate against an identification of the 'Testament of Abraham' with the 'Apocalypse of Abraham,' if further investigation should seem to point in that direction. For the names 'Testament' and 'Apocalypse' are convertible terms. In the case of the Apocalypse of Adam, Moses, and Isaiah[1], we have positive evidence of this fact, and it is well known that most, if not all, extant 'Testaments' have a large Apocalyptic element. The Testaments of Job and of Solomon come nearest to transgressing this rule, but even they do not actually transgress it.

The second question which occurs to us on an examination of these lists is this: why does the List of the Sixty Books omit the work attributed to Abraham? Is its absence an original feature or a mark of later date?

A glance at the list will shew that it contains fourteen items as opposed to eleven; and of these, five are clearly different from any item in the lists of Ps.-Athanasius and Nicephorus. These items are:

No. 1. Adam.   11. Vision of Isaiah.
    3. Lamech.   14. Apocalypse of Esdras.
    9. Psalms of Solomon.

By 'Adam' we should most probably understand the 'Testament' or 'Apocalypse' of Adam in some form; of 'Lamech' we

[1] The term 'διαθήκη Ἐζεκίου' is applied by Cedrenus (p. 121, ed. Par.) to the 'Ascension of Isaiah.'

never hear elsewhere[1]: the 'Psalms of Solomon' are classed by the other writers among the *Antilegomena* of the Old Testament, which has seemed to me a note of early date. I cannot easily account to myself for their omission of the Vision of Isaiah (= the Ascension of Isaiah) and the Apocalypse of Esdras (= IV. Esdras). I notice, however, in the 'Sixty Books' traces of a rearrangement and corrections of the items in the *Synopsis*, which seems to be distinctly the earlier document of the two. For instance 'Eldad and Medad' is put by the writer of the 'Sixty Books' in a place better suited to the chronological position of the supposed writer, than that assigned to it in the *Synopsis*. Again, the qualifying and probably erroneous words πατρὸς Ἰωάννου attached to the name of Zacharias in the *Synopsis*[2], are omitted in the 'Sixty Books,' and the last entry in the *Synopsis* with its bare list of four names, which 'Nicephorus' understood so little as to be unable to add the Stichometry to them, is replaced in the 'Sixty Books' by the fuller title of a well-known book—the Apocalypse of Esdras. Yet it seems plain that the groundwork of both lists is the same. Nine entries are common to both, and the order of these, but for one transposition (that of Eldad and Medad), is identical. If we suppose that the Synoptic list or its original was known to the later writer, how is it that the entry 'Abraham' has disappeared from the latter's work, and been replaced by the 'Psalms of Solomon'? It must be borne in mind that we have here no addition of a forgotten item; the 'Psalms of Solomon' were known to the author of the *Synopsis*. To place them here, away from their legitimate companions, Wisdom and Ecclesiasticus, was to do violence to the current Byzantine tradition. It seems clear that the substitution was a deliberate one. Why then was it

---

[1] In a very interesting list of Slavonic Apocrypha by E. Kozak (*Jahrb. f. Prot. Theol.* Dec. 1891) a version of the well-known legend of Lamech's murder of Cain occurs as a separate document, under No. 5.

[2] We have very little evidence to go upon in conjecturing the nature of the work attributed to Zechariah. It is not likely to be identical with the writing produced (and possibly written) by the eponymous Zacharias, Abbot of Gerara, on the occasion of the Invention of the body of Zechariah at Eleutheropolis (Sozomen. *Hist. Eccl.* ix. 17). That seems to have been of a haggadic nature. The existence of an Apocalypse of Zephaniah seems to point to the probability that the Zechariah book was an Apocalypse attributed to one of the Old Testament prophets of that name.

made? I answer, first, because the name of Abraham occurs quite out of its chronological place in the *Synopsis;* secondly, because the author of the 'Sixty Books' was very probably not acquainted with any such work; and thirdly, because in his time the 'Psalms of Solomon,' never widely accepted, had come to be regarded as distinctly apocryphal, and could no longer be treated as mere *antilegomena*. Their legitimate chronological place was just that occupied by the entry 'Abraham.' The author of the 'Sixty Books' then had but two easy changes to make. He shifted 'Eldad and Medad' to their proper place, and substituted the 'Psalms of Solomon' for the ill-defined and possibly unknown 'Abraham.'

(2) In connection with these lists we must consider a passage of the Apostolic Constitutions (VI. 16), which, though it does not definitely mention the book before us in so many words, can yet, as it seems to me, be very fairly cited as a witness to its existence when the Constitutions were written. The words—quoted by all writers on pseudepigraphic literature—are these: Καὶ ἐν τοῖς παλαιοῖς δέ τινες συνέγραψαν βιβλία ἀπόκρυφα Μωσέως καὶ Ἐνὼχ καὶ Ἀδὰμ Ἡσαΐου τε καὶ Δαβὶδ καὶ Ἡλία καὶ τῶν τριῶν πατριαρχῶν, φθοροποιὰ καὶ τῆς ἀληθείας ἐχθρά. We are here presented with a list—vaguely expressed and thrown into literary form, but still useful—of O. T. Pseudepigrapha. Some of the items we can recognise at once. We see, for instance, that the Book of Enoch, the Testament (and Assumption) of Moses, the Apocalypse of Elijah, the Ascension of Isaiah, and the Testament or Penitence or Life of Adam must be alluded to. It is not so clear what Apocryphon under David's name is meant: perhaps it was some book resembling the 'History of David' now extant in Carshunic at Paris (Zotenberg, *Cat. MSS Syr.* p. 126).

But there remains one item to be dealt with—τῶν τριῶν πατριαρχῶν. Who are these, and what book was associated with their names? The first question is easily answered. No one but Abraham, Isaac, and Jacob can be meant by the three patriarchs[1], and we are on the way towards answering the second question when we can state that there still exists a book supplying particulars of the last words and the deaths of these three patriarchs, and that one part of this book can be shewn with a great degree of probability to

---

[1] See for instance *Act. Andr. et Matth.* § 16.

12   THE TESTAMENT OF ABRAHAM.

have been known to Origen. A further discussion of the identity of the old book of the Three Patriarchs with the extant Testaments or Apocalypses or Histories of Abraham, Isaac, and Jacob must be deferred for the present.

The evidence of these lists and of the Apostolical Constitutions points to the existence of some book such as the one before us; but it is vague.

Two passages of equal or even greater vagueness must be added which may imply a knowledge of the existence of books attributed to Abraham.

(3) The first is that often-quoted phrase of S. Jerome, *adv. Vigilantium*, wherein he tells his victim that he may if he pleases read "fictas revelationes omnium Patriarcharum et Prophetarum." This sentence is merely rhetorical, of course: but it may mean that Vigilantius had appealed to our book among others. It would more suitably apply to the 'Apocalypse of Abraham' than to the 'Testaments of the Twelve Patriarchs,' but obviously it is language of a kind which cannot be pressed.

S. Jerome knew and cared little about apocryphal literature. 4 Esdras he had never read; his mention (*ad Pammachium*) of *Apoc. Eliae* and *Ascensio Esaiae* is very likely borrowed from Origen; while the only two Old Testament Pseudepigrapha which he really seems to have read are both of them Hebrew books, the 'Little Genesis' and an apocryphal Prophecy of Jeremiah.

(4) The other passage, which seems to me more decisive, is to be found in one of the newly-discovered tracts of Priscillian, edited by the discoverer, Dr Schepss, from the unique MS (of cent. V. or VI.) at Würzburg (Vienna, 1889).

The third tract in this volume is entitled *Liber de Fide et de Apocryphis*: in it Priscillian pleads for the occasional use of non-canonical books. The tract is most unhappily mutilated at the beginning: but much that is interesting is left. We gather from it that the author certainly knew the Book of Enoch (p. 44), 4 Esdras (p. 52), and the Epistle to the Laodiceans (p. 55). And on pp. 45, 46 occurs the following passage:

Quid est quod Tobi sanctus futurae uitae ad filium praecepta disponens, cum quid custodiret ediceret, ait: *Nos fili prophetarum*

HISTORY OF THE BOOK. 13

sumus; Noe profeta fuit et Abraham et Isac et Iacob et omnes patres nostri qui ab initio saeculi profetauerunt? (Tob. iv. 13). Quando in canone profetae Noe liber lectus est? quis inter profetas dispositi canonis Abrahae librum legit? quis quod aliquando Isaac profetasset edocuit? quis profetiam Iacob quae in canone poneretur audiuit? Quos si Tobia legit et testimonium prophetiae in canone promeruit, qualiter, quod illi ad testimonium emeritae uirtutis datur, alteris ad occasionem iustae damnationis adscribitur?

The passage from Tobit is here quoted as the canonical authority to establish the claims of non-canonical books. And Priscillian in his comment upon it seems to me to shew that he actually knew books ascribed to some of the authors mentioned in his text. When he says, 'When was a Book of the prophet Noe ever read *as canonical?* who has read a Book of Abraham among the prophets *of the established canon?*...who ever heard of a prophecy of Jacob as being included *in the canon?*' he seems to me distinctly to imply that there were such books existing *outside* the canon, and that he knew them. The existence of Apocryphal books of Noah seems to be indicated by the frequent references to his preaching before the Flood (e.g. in 1 Clement, 2 Peter, and Sib. Orac. i.; cf. also the Noachian fragments in Enoch). The Book of Abraham I take to be our Testament or Apocalypse; and the Prophecy of Jacob to be, not the Testament of Jacob, but the Prayer of Joseph, which, as the extant fragments shew, contained apocalyptic and mystic utterances of Jacob. I take this view, because I gather, from the way in which Priscillian refers to Isaac that he did not know the Testament of Isaac. Of him he simply says, 'Who has taught that Isaac ever prophesied?' There is no qualifying reference to the canon of Scripture. No such writing as a prophecy of Isaac, whether inside or outside the canon, seems to be known to him. And it is very improbable that the Testaments of Abraham and Jacob were in circulation without that of Isaac: whereas in both Greek and Slavonic the Testament of Abraham has been preserved separately.

(5) The evidence of Epiphanius is the next which confronts us. In speaking of the Sethians (*Haer*. xxxix. 5) he says, Βίβλους δέ τινας συγγράφοντες ἐξ ὀνόματος μεγάλων ἀνδρῶν, ἐξ ὀνόματος

μὲν Σὴθ ἑπτὰ λέγοντες εἶναι βίβλους, ἄλλας δὲ βίβλους ἑτέρας ἀλλογενεῖς οὕτω καλοῦσιν, ἄλλην δὲ ἐξ ὀνόματος Ἀβραάμ, ἣν καὶ ἀποκάλυψιν φάσκουσιν εἶναι, πάσης κακίας ἔμπλεων· ἑτέρας δὲ ἐξ ὀνόματος τοῦ Μωϋσέως, καὶ ἄλλας ἄλλων.

From this we gather the main fact that the Sethians used an Apocalypse of Abraham. What Epiphanius thought of it is of less moment, and we need not attribute much importance to his statement that the book was written in the Sethian interest. That they possessed seven books of Seth and other works, which for some reason they called ἀλλογενεῖς, we do not doubt; but the language throughout is vague, recalling in its earlier clauses the passage of the Apostolic Constitutions quoted above; and if we find other evidence for supposing that a non-Sethian Apocalypse of Abraham existed in early times, we need not hesitate to believe that Epiphanius or his authority is here going too far, and is fathering on the Sethians a book which they may well have used, but which they did not manufacture.

(6) The evidence we seek is furnished by Origen. In his Homilies on Luke (xxxv.), he says, speaking of the 'princeps,' 'iudex,' and 'exactor'; 'Legimus—si tamen cui placet huiuscemodi scripturam recipere—iustitiae et iniquitatis angelos super Abrahami salute et interitu disceptantes, dum utraeque turmae suo eum uolunt coetui uindicare. Quod si cui displicet, transeat ad uolumen quod titulo Pastoris scribitur, et inueniet cunctis hominibus duos adesse angelos: malum, qui ad peruersa exhortatur, et bonum, qui ad optima quaeque persuadet. Scribitur alibi, quod assistant homini siue in bonam siue in malam partem, duplices angeli.' (Cf. Hom. in Luc. xii. Unicuique duo assistunt angeli, alter iustitiae, alter iniquitatis.)

The passage of the *Shepherd* to which Origen refers in both Homilies is *Mand.* vi. 2. δύο εἰσὶν ἄγγελοι μετὰ τοῦ ἀνθρώπου, εἷς τῆς δικαιοσύνης καὶ εἷς τῆς πονηρίας[1]. Throughout the re-

---

[1] With this it is apposite to compare the Latin fragment of the Didache, which begins thus:

Viae duae sunt in seculo, uitae et mortis, lucis et tenebrarum.
In his constituti sunt Angeli duo, unus aequitatis, alter iniquitatis.

The corresponding words to these last in Barnabas are ἄγγελοι τοῦ σατανᾶ.

mainder of this Mandate the phrases ἄγγελος τῆς δικαιοσύνης and ἄγγελος τῆς πονηρίας occur frequently. This fact, coupled with parallels from later Apocalypses, e.g. *Apoc. Pauli* 14 etc., where the word πονηροὶ is uniformly applied to evil angels, would lead us to imagine that here Origen's translator rendered an original πονηρία by 'iniquitas,' although 'malitia,' 'malignus' are commonly the equivalents of πονηρία (-ρός), 'iniquitas' of ἀδικία (or ἀνομία). Further, I cannot as yet discover that the expression ἄγγελος τῆς ἀδικίας is one which occurs in the literature of our subject. The evidence seems to point to the original Greek here having been ἄγγελος τῆς πονηρίας. A word more must be said as to the original form of this passage. The Greek—probably somewhat fuller—does not exist, but similar references are not unfrequent in Origen's works. For the form of quotations 'si cui placet recipere' we may compare the passage in *Tom. v. in Joannem* p. 77, εἰ δέ τις προσίεται κ.τ.λ. where the 'Prayer of Joseph' is being quoted. The word 'interitus' is clearly meant to signify 'destruction' or 'perdition,' not merely 'death,' and must be the rendering of an original ἀπώλεια. The words 'turma' and 'coetus' present more difficulty; but I should conjecture that the original of the former was στῖφος, a word which Severus of Antioch uses in a passage often quoted in Catenae on Jude 9, and on Deut. xxxiv, where he describes an exactly similar scene from the 'Assumption of Moses.'

What is the exact amount of information derivable from this passage? Origen had read a book in which angels of good and evil were represented as contending about the salvation or perdition of Abraham's soul. Does anything in extant legends of Abraham's death bear out this assertion, or help us to any knowledge of the book he used? In the extant 'Testament of Abraham' there is an incident which may well have supplied the groundwork of Origen's quotation. We have there described the trial of a soul whose good and evil deeds were found to weigh equally in the balance. There is in the form of the book which we have no relic of a dispute between good and evil angels; but the part of the book which contains the episode bears traces of extensive working over. Ultimately, *owing to the intercession of Abraham*, the soul in question gains eternal life. It was a suggestion of Dr Gaster, the editor and translator of the Roumanian Version of our

μὲν Σὴθ ἑπτὰ λέγοντες εἶναι βίβλους, ἄλλας δὲ βίβλους ἑτέρας ἀλλογενεῖς οὕτω καλοῦσιν, ἄλλην δὲ ἐξ ὀνόματος 'Αβραάμ, ἣν καὶ ἀποκάλυψιν φάσκουσιν εἶναι, πάσης κακίας ἔμπλεων· ἑτέρας δὲ ἐξ ὀνόματος τοῦ Μωϋσέως, καὶ ἄλλας ἄλλων.

From this we gather the main fact that the Sethians used an Apocalypse of Abraham. What Epiphanius thought of it is of less moment, and we need not attribute much importance to his statement that the book was written in the Sethian interest. That they possessed seven books of Seth and other works, which for some reason they called ἀλλογενεῖς, we do not doubt; but the language throughout is vague, recalling in its earlier clauses the passage of the Apostolic Constitutions quoted above; and if we find other evidence for supposing that a non-Sethian Apocalypse of Abraham existed in early times, we need not hesitate to believe that Epiphanius or his authority is here going too far, and is fathering on the Sethians a book which they may well have used, but which they did not manufacture.

(6) The evidence we seek is furnished by Origen. In his Homilies on Luke (xxxv.), he says, speaking of the 'princeps,' 'iudex,' and 'exactor'; 'Legimus—si tamen cui placet huiuscemodi scripturam recipere—iustitiae et iniquitatis angelos super Abrahami salute et interitu disceptantes, dum utraeque turmae suo eum uolunt coetui uindicare. Quod si cui displicet, transeat ad uolumen quod titulo Pastoris scribitur, et inueniet cunctis hominibus duos adesse angelos: malum, qui ad peruersa exhortatur, et bonum, qui ad optima quaeque persuadet. Scribitur alibi, quod assistant homini siue in bonam siue in malam partem, duplices angeli.' (Cf. Hom. in Luc. xii. Unicuique duo assistunt angeli, alter iustitiae, alter iniquitatis.)

The passage of the *Shepherd* to which Origen refers in both Homilies is *Mand.* vi. 2. δύο εἰσὶν ἄγγελοι μετὰ τοῦ ἀνθρώπου, εἷς τῆς δικαιοσύνης καὶ εἷς τῆς πονηρίας[1]. Throughout the re-

---

[1] With this it is apposite to compare the Latin fragment of the Didache, which begins thus:

Viae duae sunt in seculo, uitae et mortis, lucis et tenebrarum.

In his constituti sunt Angeli duo, unus aequitatis, alter iniquitatis.

The corresponding words to these last in Barnabas are ἄγγελοι τοῦ σατανᾶ.

mainder of this Mandate the phrases ἄγγελος τῆς δικαιοσύνης and ἄγγελος τῆς πονηρίας occur frequently. This fact, coupled with parallels from later Apocalypses, e.g. *Apoc. Pauli* 14 etc., where the word πονηροὶ is uniformly applied to evil angels, would lead us to imagine that here Origen's translator rendered an original πονηρία by 'iniquitas,' although 'malitia,' 'malignus' are commonly the equivalents of πονηρία (-ρός), 'iniquitas' of ἀδικία (or ἀνομία). Further, I cannot as yet discover that the expression ἄγγελος τῆς ἀδικίας is one which occurs in the literature of our subject. The evidence seems to point to the original Greek here having been ἄγγελος τῆς πονηρίας. A word more must be said as to the original form of this passage. The Greek—probably somewhat fuller—does not exist, but similar references are not unfrequent in Origen's works. For the form of quotations 'si cui placet recipere' we may compare the passage in *Tom.* v. *in Joannem* p. 77, εἰ δέ τις προσίεται κ.τ.λ. where the 'Prayer of Joseph' is being quoted. The word 'interitus' is clearly meant to signify 'destruction' or 'perdition,' not merely 'death,' and must be the rendering of an original ἀπώλεια. The words 'turma' and 'coetus' present more difficulty; but I should conjecture that the original of the former was στῖφος, a word which Severus of Antioch uses in a passage often quoted in Catenae on Jude 9, and on Deut. xxxiv, where he describes an exactly similar scene from the 'Assumption of Moses.'

What is the exact amount of information derivable from this passage? Origen had read a book in which angels of good and evil were represented as contending about the salvation or perdition of Abraham's soul. Does anything in extant legends of Abraham's death bear out this assertion, or help us to any knowledge of the book he used? In the extant 'Testament of Abraham' there is an incident which may well have supplied the groundwork of Origen's quotation. We have there described the trial of a soul whose good and evil deeds were found to weigh equally in the balance. There is in the form of the book which we have no relic of a dispute between good and evil angels; but the part of the book which contains the episode bears traces of extensive working over. Ultimately, *owing to the intercession of Abraham,* the soul in question gains eternal life. It was a suggestion of Dr Gaster, the editor and translator of the Roumanian Version of our book, that Origen had made a mistake in his quotation of the Abraham passage. He was really referring to the soul whose fate has just been described, but, by a simple error of memory, he has made Abraham the hero of the incident. I think that this explanation is probably the right one. It has occurred to me that the mistake might have arisen in the following very simple way. Origen has confused two Apocryphal narratives, one relating to the judgment of souls as seen by Abraham, the other telling of the dispute as to the salvation of Moses; the first was found in the 'Apocalypse of Abraham,' the second in the 'Assumption of Moses.' Were we to substitute the name of Moses for that of Abraham in our passage, we should have an exact statement of the leading subject in the latter part of the 'Assumption of Moses.' We have positive information that Origen knew the book (cf. *de Princ.* iii. 2, *Hom. in Jos.* ii. 2), and we have from another source equally good evidence, which shall be given later, that the book contained the episode in question. Under these circumstances it may be asked why we should not at once substitute 'Moyseos' for 'Abrahami' in the text of Origen and let all reference to the latter go by the board. Fortunately, the MSS give no countenance to such a suggestion; and no reason, Biblical or otherwise, that I can see, can be alleged to make an insertion of Abraham's name probable. The Assumption of Moses was a book far better known than most of the kind, and known down to a fairly late date. Sixtus of Siena in the 16th century seems to have had access either to a text of it or to some account of it not known to us. It was, then, far more likely that 'Moyseos' should have replaced an original 'Abrahami,' than that 'Abrahami' should have supplanted 'Moyseos.'

I must now try to shew that the Assumption of Moses contained an episode of contention over souls, which Origen knew and might easily confuse with something in an apocryphal Abrahamic book. There is plenty of evidence for this.

We start with the well-known passage in Jude (9), where 'Michael contending with the devil disputed about the body of Moses.' This has long been recognised as a quotation from the Assumption of Moses. Many MSS of the Epistle have a marginal note to that effect (e.g. Bodl. Auct. E. 5. 9, *Act. Cath.* 30 in Gregory, which has Μωϋcέωc Ἀποκρύφογ), and Origen himself (*de Princ.* iii. 2) tells us that S. Jude made use of the work in his Epistle. Most of our available material comes from Catena-notes on this passage. Of these I may select one or two: most important, as shewing the provenance of the episode, is a passage attributed to Severus of Antioch, from a letter to Thomas Bp of Germanicia, and preserved in various forms, notably in Cramer's Catena *in loc.*, and in the Catena of Nicetas on Deut. xxxiv.

Ἐνταῦθα διὰ σωματικοῦ τύπου προϋπέδειξεν ὁ θεὸς περὶ τὴν ψυχὴν γενόμενόν τι μυστήριον. ἐπειδὴ γὰρ τῆς ψυχῆς χωριζομένης ἀπὸ τοῦ σώματος μετὰ τὴν ἔνθενδε ἀπαλλαγὴν προϋπαντῶσιν αὐτῇ καὶ ἀγγελικαὶ δυνάμεις ἀγαθαὶ καὶ δαιμόνων στῖφος πονηρότατον, ὅπως πρὸς τὴν ποιότητα τῶν ἔργων ὧν ἔπραξεν πονηρῶν τε καὶ ἀγαθῶν ἐπὶ τοὺς προσφόρους τόπους ἢ οὗτοι ἢ ἐκεῖνοι ταύτην ἀποκομίσωσιν φυλαχθησομένην μέχρι τῆς τελευταίας ἡμέρας, καθ' ἣν εἰς κρίσιν πάντες παραστησόμεθα, καὶ ἢ εἰς τὴν αἰώνιον ζωὴν ἢ εἰς τὴν ἀπέραντον φλόγα ἀπαχθησόμεθα, βουλόμενος ὁ θεὸς τοῖς υἱοῖς Ἰσραὴλ καὶ τοῦτο ὑποδεῖξαι διὰ σωματικοῦ τύπου τινός, παρεσκεύασεν ἐν τῇ τοῦ Μωϋσέως ταφῇ φανῆναι ὑπ' ὀφθαλμοὺς αὐτοῖς πρὸς τὴν περιστολὴν τοῦ σώματος καὶ τὴν ἐν τῇ γῇ νενομισμένην κατάθεσιν ἀνθιστάμενον ὥσπερ τὸν πονηρὸν δαίμονα καὶ ἀντιπράττοντα, καὶ τούτῳ τὸν Μιχαὴλ ἀγαθὸν ἄγγελον ὄντα προϋπαντῆσαι καὶ ἀποσοβῆσαι, καὶ μὴ ἐξουσιαστικῶς ἐπιτιμῆσαι, ἀλλὰ τῷ κυρίῳ τῶν ὅλων παραχωρῆσαι τῆς κατ' ἐκείνου κρίσεως καὶ εἰπεῖν Ἐπιτιμῆσαι σοι κύριος, ἵνα διὰ τούτων μάθωσιν οἱ παιδαγωγούμενοι ὥς ἐστί τις ταῖς ψυχαῖς ἀγωνία μετὰ τὴν ἔνθενδε ἀπαλλαγήν, καὶ ὅτι χρὴ διὰ τῶν ἀγαθῶν ἔργων παρασκευάζεσθαι πρὸς τὸ τῆς ἀγγελικῆς ἡμᾶς συμμαχίας μεταλαχεῖν, τῶν δαιμόνων καθ' ἡμῶν ἐπιτριζόντων φθονερὸν καὶ πικρόν. He goes on to say that a cloud of light later surrounded the scene of this vision, and (in the passage as given in the Catena on Deut.) gives his authority for all this. Ταῦτα δὲ ἐν ἀποκρύφῳ βιβλίῳ λέγεται κεῖσθαι λεπτοτέραν ἔχοντι τῆς γενέσεως ἤτοι τῆς κτίσεως ἀφήγησιν. This book is of course the 'Leptogenesis' = Book of Jubilees = Διαθήκη Μωϋσέως. As Rönsch (*das Buch der Jubiläen*, 272) has pointed out, and as a glance at the Lists of Apocrypha given above will shew, the two books of the Διαθήκη and Ἀνάληψις Μωϋσέως were uniformly to

J. 2

be found together, so that Severus might naturally regard the second as an appendix to, or as an integral part of, the first. But this is not the only passage in which Severus treats of the matter; in two other passages, one from the Ἀπολογία τοῦ Φιλαληθοῦς (Nicet. Caten. i. col. 1673) preserved anonymously in Cramer, the other from the συγγράμματα or συντάγματα κατὰ κωδικίλλων Ἀλεξάνδρου, in Nicetas, much of the same phraseology recurs. In the first-named passage a detail is added which serves to fix the 'Assumptio Mosis' as the source. It is said that God shewed the vision τοῖς τότε μικρὰ βλέπουσι καὶ παχύτερον διακειμένοις. Does not this exactly fit what is said of Caleb in the passage of Clement of Alexandria, where he quotes the 'Assumptio' (Strom. vi. p. 679)? Joshua and Caleb see the two forms of Moses, but do not both see alike; ἀλλ' ὁ μὲν καὶ θᾶττον κατῆλθεν, πολὺ τὸ βρῖθον ἐπαγόμενος· ὁ δὲ ἐπικατελθών, ὕστερον τὴν δόξαν διηγεῖτο ἣν ἐθεᾶτο, διαθρῆσαι δυνηθεὶς μᾶλλον θατέρου ἅτε καὶ καθαρώτερος γενόμενος.

I will append lastly a scholium on Jude 9—I believe inedited —from a MS referred to above. (Bodl. Auct. E. 5. 9.)

διὰ τούτου δείκνυσιν ὅτι ἡ παλαιὰ συμφωνεῖ τῇ νέᾳ, ὡς ὑφ' ἑνὸς θεοῦ δεδομένα· ὁ γὰρ διάβολος ἀντεῖχεν θέλων ἀπατῆσαι, λέγων ὅτι Ἐμόν ἐστιν τὸ σῶμα, ὡς τῆς ὕλης δεσπόζων· καὶ ἤκουσεν τὸ Ἐπιτιμῆσαι [κ.τ.λ.] τούτεστιν, ὁ κύριος ὁ πάντων τῶν πνευμάτων δεσπόζων. ἄλλοι δέ, ὅτι βουλόμενος ὁ θεὸς δεῖξαι ὅτι μετὰ τὴν ἔνθενδε ἀπαλλαγὴν, ταῖς ἡμετέραις ψυχαῖς ἀνθιστάμενοι δαίμονες πορευομέναις τὴν ἐπὶ τὰ ἄνω πορείαν, τοῦτο οὖν συνεχώρησεν ὁρᾶσθαι ἐπὶ τῆς Μωσέως ταφῆς. ἐβλασφήμει γὰρ καὶ ὁ διάβολος κατὰ Μωσέως, φονέα τοῦτον καλῶν διὰ τὸ πατάξαι τὸν Αἰγύπτιον. ὁ Μιχαὴλ ὁ ἀρχάγγελος, μὴ ἐνεγκὼν τὴν αὐτοῦ βλασφημίαν, εἴρηκεν αὐτῷ ὅτι Ἐπιτιμῆσαι σοι κύριος ὁ θεός, διάβολε. ἔλεγε δὲ καὶ τοῦτο, ὅτι ἐψεύσατο ὁ θεὸς εἰσαγαγὼν τὸν Μωσῆν ἔνθα ὤμοσεν αὐτὸν μὴ εἰσελθεῖν.

Here a good deal of the matter of Severus is recognisable: and the note seems to me specially interesting as preserving, in Michael's reply, what is probably a literal quotation from the 'Assumptio.' But perhaps enough has been said to shew that at any rate the 'Assumptio' contained some scene of contention between angel and devil, about which language such as that of Origen in the Homily might well be used. It does however seem to me likely that the contention was not one affecting the salvation of Moses, but only as S. Jude tells us concerning the disposition of his *body*. Satan seems to have claimed that at any rate as his property—a murderer could not look for decent burial, but should be cast out of the camp. To set up a claim to the soul of Moses seems almost too great a height of audacity for even Satan to aspire to.

Be this as it may, we can see in the 'Assumptio' a possible source of confusion with 'Abraham.' Let us now examine a passage of Origen in which a similar topic is discussed (*Hom*. v. *in Psalmos*, Vol. XII. 233, ed. Lommatzsch). "Tunc et adiuuabit eos Dominus in tempore tribulationis et eripiet eos et auferet eos a peccatoribus, non solum ab hominibus peccatoribus sedetiam a contrariis potestatibus, uel certe eo tempore, cum anima separatur a corpore, et occurrunt ei peccatores daemones, aduersae potestates, spiritus aëris huius, qui eam uolunt detinere et reuocare ad se, si quid in ea suorum operum gestorumque cognouerint. uenit enim ad unamquamque animam de hoc mundo exeuntem princeps huius mundi et aëreae potestates, et requirunt si inueniant in ea aliquid suum: si auaritiam inuenerint, suae partis est: si iram, si luxuriam, si inuidiam, et singula quaeque eorum similia si inuenerint, suae partis est; et sibi eam defendunt, et ad se eam trahunt, et ad partem eam peccatorum declinant. si uero aliquis imitatus est illum qui dixit: Ecce ueniet princeps mundi huius, et in me non habet quicquam. si se ita aliquis obseruauit, ueniunt quidem isti peccatores, et requirentes in eo, quae sua sunt, et non inuenientes, tentabunt nihilominus ad suam partem uiolenter eum detorquere, sed Dominus eripiet eum a peccatoribus. et forte propterea iubemur cum quodam mysterio etiam in oratione petere, dicentes 'Sed libera nos a malo.'"

The original Greek of this passage is not known to exist: but we find a very similar thought in a Homily of Macarius of Egypt[1]. The document is a very short one (only 18 lines in Migne), and the important parts run as follows.

Ὅταν ἐξέλθῃ ἐκ τοῦ σώματος ψυχὴ ἀνθρώπου, μυστήριόν τι μέγα ἐκεῖ ἐπιτελεῖται. ἐὰν γὰρ ᾖ ὑπεύθυνος ἐν ἁμαρτίαις,

[1] Hom. xxii. ap. Migne, *Patr. Gr.*

ἔρχονται χοροὶ δαιμόνων καὶ ἄγγελοι ἀριστεροί, καὶ δυνάμεις σκότους παραλαμβάνουσι τὴν ψυχὴν ἐκείνην καὶ κρατοῦσιν εἰς τὸ ἴδιον μέρος......καὶ γὰρ τοῖς ἁγίοις δούλοις τοῦ θεοῦ ἀπὸ τοῦ νῦν εἰσὶν ἄγγελοι παραμένοντες, καὶ πνεύματα ἅγια κυκλοῦντα αὐτοὺς καὶ φυλάττοντα, καὶ ὅταν ἐξέλθωσιν ἀπὸ τοῦ σώματος, οἱ χοροὶ τῶν ἀγγέλων παραλαμβάνουσιν αὐτῶν τὰς ψυχὰς εἰς τὸ ἴδιον μέρος, εἰς τὸν καθαρὸν αἰῶνα, καὶ οὕτως αὐτοὺς προσάγουσιν τῷ κυρίῳ.

Compare in this the words τὸ ἴδιον μέρος, suae partis, ἄγγελοι ἀριστεροί, aduersae potestates; and notice that here as in Origen the case of the wicked soul is touched upon first. Possibly Macarius had the passage of Origen before him; but more probably we should recognise that there was a common source from which both writers drew. What was it? Was it the 'Assumptio'? I think not. In that book it is pretty certain that only the individual case of Moses was related: here the description is couched in general terms; we are told what happens to all souls when they go out of the world. There, it was one isolated act in Moses' past life on which Satan grounded his claim, whether to body or soul. Here the souls are represented as undergoing a searching examination at the hands of the powers of darkness. The guiding conception of the passage before us is altogether more developed and represents a later stage of thought than the 'Assumptio' can have done. The writers of the Severian scholia do indeed generalise on the fate of souls but obviously what they say is in the nature of a comment on a text, and is influenced by other sources besides the 'Assumptio.'

If we could find something in Apocalyptic literature which would furnish us with a source for what Macarius and Origen say, and if we could shew further that this source is connected in some way with an Abrahamic apocryphal book, I think we might fairly claim to have found a good explanation for the passage from Origen's Homilies on Luke which forms the text of the present discussion. We find our answer in that enigmatical work which is called the *Apocalypse of Paul*.

Three main sources furnish us with our knowledge of this book. We have first the original Greek, discovered by Tischendorf and edited in the *Apocalypses Apocryphae* 34—69. Secondly we have the Syriac Version, of which Tischendorf has reprinted the English version made by the Rev. Justin Perkins. This contains a good deal more matter than the Greek; and has been usually looked upon as interpolated. Thirdly we have a full Latin Version (as well as multitudes of Latin abridgments) contained so far as I know only in one MS (Paris *Nouv. acq. lat.* 1631 f. 2 *b*—25 *b*), of the eighth century. This was one of the MSS stolen by Libri from Orleans, and sold to Lord Ashburnham. It is fully described in Delisle's *Catalogue des MSS des fonds Libri et Barrois*, p. 108. I transcribed it in September 1890, and it proves to be a most valuable authority for the text, confirming the Syriac in every particular, and shewing that in its present form, the Greek is a shortened text.

Now it must be borne in mind that the Apocalypse of Paul is to a large extent a compilation from earlier works. This can be proved to demonstration. We know when the compilation was made from the Latin version: it was discovered by revelation in Paul's house at Tarsus in the consulship of Theodosius the younger and Cynegius, that is, in 388. A comparison of the book with the extant fragments of the Apocalypse of Peter, with the Ascension of Isaiah, with the Sibylline oracles, Bk. II., and with the recently discovered Sahidic Apocalypse of Zephaniah, will satisfy the most exacting critic that the Pseudo-Paul, in the earlier parts of his work more especially, is a plain plagiarist. If this be once granted, we may proceed to details. The passage concerned consists of §§ 11—18 (pp. 40—48) in Tischendorf's text. Here we have a complete view of the exodus of souls. First, Paul is taken beneath the firmament, and sees the destroying angels, and the angels of God waiting for souls. Then he sees the exodus of a righteous soul and the contention over it. In the Syriac version we have the words "and that soul was bound there: and there was a fight between the good angels and the evil spirits." The soul is then presented to God, and delivered over to Michael to be taken to Paradise. Next is shewn the exodus of a wicked soul. I quote the Latin version here, in order to shew the similarity with Origen. "Cum ergo peruenissent ad potestatem, cum iam ingredi celum abiret, labor impositus est ei super alium laborem: obliuio et susurracio obuiauerunt eam, et spiritus fornicacionis et relique potestates, et dicebant ei 'Vbi perges, misera anima, et audes praecurrere in celo? sustine, ut uideamus si habemus in te peculiaria nostra.'" The soul is presented to God, and delivered to the angel Temeluchus to be tormented. Next is seen a soul which has been in the hands of chastising angels seven days. It denies having sinned, and is confronted with its accusers, convicted and delivered to the angel Tartaruchus, to be kept till the great day.

Here is a defect: in order to be symmetrical and complete, our author should have given us an idea of what happens to a soul which is neither bad nor good. We cannot see any point in the introduction of two wicked souls. The sins of the second and its examination and judgment are more fully dwelt upon, but this gives no clue to the reason for the repetition. Here is a phenomenon which leads us to suspect plagiarism: and when we find later on in the book that Elias and Abraham, Isaac and Jacob are introduced twice over, in different places, our suspicions are confirmed.

This account of the exodus of souls and their judgment is, then, a compilation: and one part of it bears a strong resemblance to the source of Origen and Macarius. Have we any further light, connecting it with Abrahamic books?

The Testament of Abraham is the only Abrahamic apocryph which can help us. It exists in two forms: and both of them help us a little. In the Longer Form we find that Abraham witnessed the trial of a soul whose sins and good deeds were equal, and that by his intercession it was saved. In the Shorter Form we find the same soul introduced; its sins and good deeds weigh equally: but here comes in this extraordinary anomaly, that instead of being prayed for and saved, its sins are investigated and it is condemned: and the accusations against it are those which we find in Pseudo-Paul. This fact can be accounted for very simply. The Shorter Recension has been interpolated from the Apocalypse of Paul. The object of this proceeding was to get rid of some matter which the reviser found objectionable. Full proof of this may be found on a subsequent page (44). That it is the Apocalypse of Paul, and not one of the sources of it which has been used by the reviser, is, I think, clear from the fact that the borrowed phrases are not confined to any one part of the Apocalypse of Paul. On the other hand there is nothing which tends to shew that the writer of the Longer Form copied the Apocalypse of Paul, and yet there is a very considerable similarity of tone.

Now the conjecture which I am about to advance may seem fanciful, but is, I am sure, not extravagant in its demands on our credit. It involves assent to two propositions, one general, the other particular. First, we must be prepared for any amount of borrowing from earlier documents on the part of apocalyptic writers, and indeed early writers in general. Secondly, we must be prepared to allow that the author of at any rate the apocalyptic portion of the Testament of Abraham was a Christian—a Jewish Christian, there can be little doubt, but still a Christian. For a fuller discussion of this topic I must refer my readers to the special section of this Introduction which is devoted to it (p. 50).

That my first postulate is a reasonable one may be seen by any one who will look into the relations between the Apocalypse of S. John and the Book of Daniel, between the Testaments of the XII. Patriarchs and the Book of Jubilees, between the later and earlier Apocalypses of Esdras, or between the Sibylline books of various dates.

My conjecture is that the matter which appears in the passages cited from Origen and Macarius, and borrowed with different degrees of accuracy or audacity by the authors of the Testament of Abraham and the Apocalypse of Paul, comes ultimately from the lost Apocalypse of Peter. That at some future period I may be able to set forth in full my views as to the contents of that work is my earnest desire: at present I must confine myself to a few points.

And, first, it is plain that this lost Apocalypse was an early book and a popular one. The author of the Muratorian fragment and Clement of Alexandria are among our sources of information concerning it: and in their time it stood on the border-line between canonical and apocryphal literature; while in Sozomen's lifetime it was still read publicly in the churches of Palestine on Good Friday. That such a book would exercise a wide influence over later apocalyptic writings we should expect; that it did so influence them may be at once seen from a comparison of the meagre scraps which exist with the Apocalypse of Paul (§ 39, p. 58, § 40, p. 61), and that of Esdras (p. 29, l. 25)[1].

We gather with certainty from these extant fragments that a portion of the book was occupied with a vision of the torments of souls in hell; and we find an almost literal borrowing of one of the torments in the Apocalypse of Esdras, and of its accompanying explanation in that of Paul. Further, if we tabulate the scheme of torments which is found in a group of apocalyptic documents, viz. the two apocalypses mentioned above, together with the 2nd book of the Sibylline oracles (l. 252 sqq.), a Vision contained in the acts of Thomas (ed. Bonnet, p. 39), and the late Apocalypses of John and of the Virgin, we find certain constant elements which strongly favour the idea that the Infernos which all the books present to us have one common origin. We know that in one detail the Apocalypse of Peter furnishes matter to two of them. What more natural than the supposition that it is the source of the constant elements alluded to above? So far we have definite evidence to deal with. The purely conjectural part of my theory lies in this: that I would attribute the original of the account of the exodus of souls and of their trial, which is partially represented both in *Test. Abr.* and *Apoc. Pauli*, to the same source.

All Christian visions of a future state anterior to the time of Gregory the Great, with very few exceptions, and many of those which are later, have common features not directly derivable from canonical sources. I do not mean to say that any one or more features are common to the whole number, but that there are certain salient features, each of which will be found common to several documents. There is no original and new conception save in minor details. Different selections from the same materials are presented over and over again by different writers. Yet when we try to lay our hands on the one starting-point of all these converging lines, we find no one extant book whose date is sufficiently early, or whose reputation and influence can have been

---

[1] The name Temeluchus, quoted above from the Apocalypse of Paul as the name of an angel, is one mark of obligation to the Apocalypse of Peter. Dr Hilgenfeld (*N. T. extz. Can.* p. 73) has recognised that it is the adjective $τημελοῦχος$ misunderstood. This word *only* occurs in a fragment of the Apocalypse of Peter quoted by Clem. Alex. and Methodius.

so considerable as to give any colour to the belief that it was the source of all the later documents. To take an instance: probably the Apocalypse of Zephaniah, now extant in Thebaic, and in a fragmentary condition, is as early as any of our available evidence. It is undoubtedly Christian, and is quoted by Clement of Alexandria (Str. v. p. 586: the passage is not found in the Thebaic fragments): it is, then, certainly Egyptian, and almost certainly a production of the 2nd century. In many details it coincides accurately with the Apocalypse of Paul, especially in its description of the soul's departure. Yet it bears throughout the stamp of a book only written for a limited circle: Clement's quotation is the one reference to it in patristic literature, if we except the mention in the Stichometries, and it is not conceivable that it should ever have been sufficiently widely known to influence later apocalypses to any appreciable extent.

No extant Christian apocalypse ever occupied the position for which we are seeking a claimant; is there any Jewish book which did so? The Book of Enoch undoubtedly set the fashion for all later books which represent the seer as being conducted over unknown regions by angelic guides: but further than this it affords us no help. The Assumption of Moses brings us a step forward: it did indeed, as we have seen, deal with the departure of a soul from the body, but only with a particular instance: there were no general revelations applying to the whole human race. A further step is taken when we come to the Fourth Book of Esdras: here in the 'Missing Fragment' we find some general descriptions of the future state of all souls, descriptions which doubtless did, either mediately or directly, influence later books. But when we seek for an original for our judicial and trial scenes and our Infernos we are still at fault. Moreover when we have got down as far as the Fourth Book of Esdras we have approached a moment when Christian apocalyptic has come into being: when most likely the Apocalypse of John was already written, and when the Apocalypse of Peter, which at one time claimed equal honours with it, had not impossibly been written. It is my belief that in the Apocalypse of Peter alone we have a book which fulfils all the necessary conditions. Received as canonical by more than one Church, mentioned with respect by more than one leading writer, known in Palestine, in Lycia, at Rome[1] and at Alexandria, it and it alone was in a position to exercise a practically unlimited influence over later imitators.

Why then, it will be asked, if all this matter was contained in the Apocalypse of Peter, did not Origen refer to it instead of to an obscure Abrahamic book? The question is a difficult one. I can hardly believe it possible that Origen had no acquaintance with the Petrine work; on the contrary, I believe him to have used it in the Commentary on the Psalms (see p. 19), but it is certain that he nowhere expressly quotes it; and I believe it will be found, if all his quotations from apocryphal writings are collected, that he shews a decided preference for using Old Testament Apocrypha, and that his references to the New Testament apocryphal literature are comparatively very few in number. It may very well be the case that when he found the same matter both in the Apocalypse of Peter and the Testament of Abraham, he preferred to quote the latter as being ostensibly of more venerable antiquity.

To sum up the result of this long and somewhat desultory investigation, it seems to me likely (1) that Origen had seen our Testament of Abraham; (2) that his quotation from it has been affected by confusion with a similar incident in the Assumption of Moses; (3) that Origen and Macarius employed besides these two books a third, which treated of the same topic, the exodus of souls; (4) that this third book was the Apocalypse of Peter; (5) that the Apocalypse of Peter is the ultimate source of the matter which is common to the Testament of Abraham and the Apocalypse of Paul,—the foundation of this last assertion being that the Apocalypse of Paul is demonstrably under obligation to that of Peter, and that it treats of topics also dealt with in the Testament of Abraham.

---

[1] This I do not regard as certain, but as almost certain. The reference in the Muratorian fragment is denied by Zahn. But there is something to be said for the view of Bunsen and Hilgenfeld that Hippolytus used the book. And, further, there is in the tract *de aleatoribus*, which may be a Roman production, an apocryphal quotation which would suit the Apocalypse of Peter according to my view. See § 8, ed. Harnack: Et iterum 'in iudicii dei (die) igne rotante torquebitur.'

HISTORY OF THE BOOK.

During the latter part of this discussion, I have been rather assuming that the book referred to by the various ancient authorities who have been cited is identical with the extant *Testament of Abraham*.

Of this I am myself convinced; but perhaps the best way of convincing others will be to put in tabular form the scraps of information derivable from our authorities, and then to test the extant book by comparing it with them.

We are in possession, then, of the following facts:

1. There existed an Apocryphal book of Abraham, 300 στίχοι in length (*Stichom.*).
2. There existed a book, or set of books, connected with the names of Abraham, Isaac, and Jacob (*Const. Ap.*).
3. The Abrahamic book was called the 'Apocalypse of Abraham' (*Epiph. Stichom.*?).
4. The 'Apocalypse of Abraham' was used by the Sethians, and was 'full of wickedness' (*Epiph.*).
5. An Abrahamic Apocryphal book contained something about a contention over the salvation of a soul (*Orig.*).

It will appear that all save one of these statements are true of the extant book. They shall be treated in order with some short explanations.

1. There exists an Apocryphal book about Abraham not differing widely in length from the old one. But this last matter cannot be pressed, for in its present state the book bears traces of abridgment and rough treatment.
2. There exists, in Arabic and Aethiopic, a set of books about Abraham, Isaac, and Jacob, and the part relating to Abraham is identical with the book just mentioned.
3. A Roumanian version of the Abrahamic book tells us that it is written 'according to' or 'after' the Apocalypse, *sc.* of Abraham. A Slavonic version calls it the 'Apocalypse of Abraham.'
4. This statement, due to Epiphanius, that the Apocalypse of Abraham was used by the Sethians, is the one which we cannot predicate concerning the extant book. The supplementary statement, that it was full of wickedness we may disregard at once: for, if used by the Sethians, any book save the Bible would

28 THE TESTAMENT OF ABRAHAM.

be full of wickedness to the mind of a polemical writer. But one piece of evidence does shew us that the extant book was looked upon as an heretical production. The MS which I consider to give on the whole the best text of our book (Par. Gr. 770) has this marginal note of the 15th or 16th century at the beginning.

αὕτη ἡ διαθήκη ἣν λέγουσιν ἀβραὰμ ἔστιν ὑπὸ αἱρετικῶν συντεθεῖσα ἣν ούκ ὀφείλεις ὁ ἀναγινώσκων πιστεύειν· καὶ γὰρ κελευόμεθα ὑπὸ τῶν ἁγίων ἡμῶν τῆς ἐκκλησίας διδασκάλων· καὶ ἰδὲ εἰς τὸν βλαστάρεα.

The author here mentioned is Matth. Blastares, the compiler of an alphabetical table of the matters contained in the Canons of Councils: I have not found that he mentions the Testament of Abraham, and I have no doubt that what is here thought of is a general injunction against the use of Apocryphal books. But I think the note shews some knowledge on the part of its author that this actual book was not a product of orthodox theology. What the Sethians could have proved from the extant book I do not know; but in it great prominence is assigned to Adam and Abel and Enoch: and Adam and Abel were certainly regarded with veneration by the Sethians. Just this additional point is worth quoting. In the Sethian system Seth apparently was the same as Jesus Christ. In the extant Abraham book Adam is said to resemble either God or Christ (there are various readings) in appearance. Other good reasons (1) that man was made in the image of God, (2) that Christ is the Second Adam, may be assigned, but the fact is worth noting.

5. This is true of the extant book, and a good deal has been already said about it.

As far, therefore, as our ancient external evidence is concerned, we seem to have good reason for believing that the Testament of Abraham as here printed is identical, at any rate in its main outlines, with the book known to Origen and to the author of the Apostolic Constitutions. The very fact of the existence of the work in two recensions and in at least four versions says something in favour of an early date.

And, again, its abrupt transitions from 3rd to 1st person (A § XII) and back again, tell a like story. Corruption and processes of redaction imply a long previous history for the book which undergoes them. The book before us must have been popular, and must be old.

That its popularity was not due in the first instance to its merits as literature will be readily conceded. But either as a vehicle for some novelty in doctrine, or as an appeal to the universal desire to know something of the sacred past and something of the unknown future, it was sure in early times of a kind reception. And once taken to the hearts of the people in any measure, it could not be readily plucked away. We ought, further, to take into account the extreme improbability that a book once fairly popular, as was the old Apocalypse of Abraham, should have been superseded by an entirely new production which also attained such popularity that its text was current in two distinct forms. No; the least we could reasonably say concerning the identity of the old Apocalypse with the extant Testament would be that the latter was a very much mangled *réchauffé* of the former; and to such a verdict I should not very seriously object; only it seems to me probable that all the main features of the old book are preserved to us in the extant one.

And if I am right in this belief, here is another fragment of early popular Christian literature gathered up,—how early, it seems impossible to settle very definitely; but it is later, probably, than the Apocalypse of Peter and earlier than the time of Origen. That it was written in the second century, that it embodies legends earlier than that century, and that it received its present form perhaps in the ninth or tenth century, seems to myself a sufficiently probable estimate. Of the place of its composition I shall have something to say later; at present it will be enough to note that certain indications, e.g. the mention of the weighing of souls, and partly also the terrific presentment of Death, seem to point to Egypt as its birthplace.

Influence of the Testament on Later Literature.

As to the influence of the Testament of Abraham on later literature I do not find it very easy to pronounce. As has been intimated already, I believe it to have been one of several

Apocalypses used by the author of the Apocalypse of Paul; and it is conceivably responsible for the introduction of the 'psychostasy' into mediaeval visions; possibly also some of the numerous liturgical references (see p. 128) may have been influenced by it.

One passage I do find among the numerous Latin visions of the middle ages which recalls in a striking way an episode in the Testament; that, namely, in A § XI, B § VIII, which describes Adam as seated before the gates of Paradise and alternately weeping and laughing, according as he sees the number of lost or of saved souls in the ascendant. Matthew Paris (*Chronica Majora* ed. Luard, Rolls Series, II. 497—511) has preserved the very interesting vision of Thurchill, an Essex labourer. On p. 509 the following passage occurs:

Thurchill, guided by S. Michael, is shewn a tree bearing all manner of fruits: which grows near a spring whence flow four streams. "Sub hac arbore prope fontem requiescebat homo quidam uenustae formae ac gigantaei corporis, qui a pedibus usque ad pectus indutus erat quodam uestimento uarii coloris et mira pulcritudine contexto; ex uno oculo ridere et lugere ex altero uidebatur. Hic, inquit sanctus Michael, est primus parens generis humani Adam, qui per oculum ridentem innuit laetitiam quam habet de filiorum suorum saluandorum ineffabili glorificatione, et per alium lacrimantem denunciat tristitiam quam habet de quorundam filiorum suorum reprobatione et iusto dei iudicio damnandorum. uestimentum quo tegitur, sed nondum ex toto, stola est immortalitatis et uestis gloriae, qua in primaria praeuaricatione fuerat spoliatus. nam ab Abel iusto filio suo usque nunc coepit hanc uestem recuperare per totam filiorum suorum iustorum successionem. et sicut uariis uirtutibus enituerunt electi, ita haec uestis colore uario picturatur. cum uero completus fuerit electorum numerus filiorum, tunc Adam ex toto stola immortalitatis et gloriae uestietur, et sic mundus finem sortietur." Now this may be a case of coincidence in imagination between two Apocalyptic authors, or it may be a trait borrowed from the Testament of Abraham. It is, no doubt, absurd to suppose that an Essex peasant living in the 13th century could have read a Greek Apocalypse. Yet it is quite possible that in this particular case there may have been a literary connexion. For, firstly, we may be pretty certain that in Thurchill's Vision we have a good deal more of what the monks of S. Alban's Abbey imagined than of what Thurchill told them, if he told them anything. The whole document is literary in its form. Mr Wright very strikingly and truly pointed out that in an episode which describes the theatre of Hell, the writer has plainly been influenced by the recollection of the ruined Roman amphitheatre at Verulamium[1]. The Vision, as we have it, was plainly written and embellished at S. Alban's Abbey. Now,—and this is the second and most important consideration—it was precisely at S. Alban's Abbey that a certain amount of knowledge of the Greek Apocryphal literature was current. It was by two men connected with that house, John of Basingstoke and Nicholas the Greek, that the Testaments of the Twelve Patriarchs were translated from Greek into Latin. And I have elsewhere pointed to the very strong probability that the Life of Aseneth was translated into Latin at the same time and place[2]. Certain it is that it first appears in Latin just at the date in question, and that no non-English MS of the full form of the story is known to exist. I have a further suspicion, which I have not yet been able to verify, that the fabulous *Itinerarium Theophili* owes its Latin dress to the same hands. I do not say that the Testament of Abraham was then, or ever, rendered into Latin, but it seems to me a very likely thing that the description of Adam, which seems to occur nowhere else, has made its way into Thurchill's Vision from the Testament, through the medium of some oral report emanating from a Greek scholar at the Monastery.

One Greek mediæval Apocalypse shews undoubted connexion with the Testament, just as one Latin Apocalypse has seemed to do. The document in question is an inedited one: it is only to be found, so far as I know, in one MS, Bodl. Misc. Gr. 56 of cent. xv. f. 92—100, and it is called: τοῦ ἁγίου καὶ μακαρίου Σεδρὰχ λόγος περὶ ἀγάπης καὶ περὶ μετανοίας καὶ ὀρθοδόξων χριστιανῶν καὶ περὶ δευτέρας παρουσίας τοῦ κυρίου ἡμῶν Ἰησοῦ Χριστοῦ.

[1] T. Wright, *Essays on Archaeology* II.
[2] Batiffol, *Studia Patristica*, I. p. 3.

In its present form it is late, corrupt, and confused. The language is full of modern forms, and the whole is a clumsy fusion of two fragments. It begins with a homily on love, ἀγαπητοί, μηδὲν προτιμήσωμεν πλὴν τῆς ἀνυποκρίτου ἀγάπης. Then in f. 93 b of the MS comes a break, thus :—ὅτι μειζότερον τῆς ἀγάπης οὐδέν ἐστιν ἵνα τις τὴν ψυχὴν θῇ ὑπὲρ τῶν φίλων αὐτοῦ· καὶ φωνὴν ἀοράτως ἐδέξατο ἐν ταῖς ἀκοαῖς αὐτοῦ, and from this point to the end we have an Apocalypse, very strongly resembling that of Esdras (of whose name I take Sedrach to be a corruption[1]) as published by Tischendorf (*Apoc. Apocr.*). Both books are the work of a late writer who had read 4 Esdras in Greek; and both books are compilations from various sources, made up at a very late date, perhaps the tenth or eleventh century, and each surviving in a single extremely corrupt copy, Esdras at Paris, Sedrach at Oxford.

The course of the book is briefly this. Sedrach expresses a desire to talk with God face to face. He is carried up ἕως τρίτου οὐρανοῦ and pleads with God for the pardon of man. God finally asks him to number the drops of the sea and the leaves of the trees and so on, as in 4 Esdras, and with this the first episode breaks off. Next, abruptly, as in *Apoc. Esdrae*, God the Father bids the Son take the soul of Sedrach. This the prophet refuses to give up: and in this refusal lies one strong point of similarity to our Testament. I shall have to quote several passages from this section under another head (see p. 66). Sedrach falls to weeping and utters a long (and very corrupt) lament, addressed to the various parts of his body. The next episode shews us Sedrach interceding with God again for man, and begging that God will accept a repentance of three years, then of one year, then of 40 days, on the part of men (cf. Abraham in Gen. xviii.). In this part of the book is a plagiarism from the Testament A §§ XIV, XVIII, thus; καὶ λέγει Σεδράχ πρὸς τὸν ἀρχάγγελον Μιχαὴλ Ἐπάκουσόν μου, προστάτα δυνατέ, καὶ βοήθει μοι καὶ πρεσβεῦσαι ἵνα ἐλεήσει ὁ θεὸς τὸν κόσμον· καὶ πεσόντες ἐπὶ πρόσωπον παρακαλοῦντες τὸν θεὸν [καὶ] εἶπον κ.τ.λ. Michael is never elsewhere mentioned. There follows a short and obscure disquisition on the conditions of

---

[1] It may be noted, however, that Σεδράχ is the LXX. equivalent for Shadrach in the Book of Daniel.

INFLUENCE ON LATER LITERATURE. 33

salvation, and a promise of complete immunity from torment to those who will make mention of Sedrach's name, copy his book, or make a φωταγωγία to him. The conclusion is καὶ λέγει ὁ δοῦλος τοῦ θεοῦ Σεδράχ· "Ἄρτι λάβε τὴν ψυχήν μου, δέσποτα· καὶ ἔλαβεν αὐτὸν ὁ θεὸς καὶ ἔθηκεν αὐτὸν ἐν τῷ παραδείσῳ μετὰ τῶν ἁγίων ἁπάντων· ᾧ ἡ δόξα κ.τ.λ. Besides the clear plagiarism quoted above, and those on p. 66, some shorter passages shew resemblance at least to the Testament. We have for instance τοῦ θανάτου τὴν μνήμην, as in A § IV. p. 81, l. 1, and ἀναμένω αὐτοὺς μετὰ πολλῆς εὐσπλαγχνίας καὶ πολλοὺς ἔτους καὶ πλοῦτος (sic) ἵνα μετανοήσωσιν, as in A § X. p. 88, l. 21. There is, lastly, an allusion to Abraham; δέχομαι αὐτοὺς μετὰ τῶν δικαίων μου ἐν κόλποις Ἀβραάμ.

Another document there is,— one that has exercised no inconsiderable influence over Christian mythology and art,—in which I seem to see traces of the language and thought of the Testament of Abraham. I mean the Greek account of the Assumption of the Virgin which is attributed to S. John (Tischendorf *Apoc. Apocr.* p. 95 sqq.). It is, no doubt, possible that the Marian legend, which was by far the more popular, may have influenced the diction of the Abrahamic, which was no doubt the older; but the resemblances are not in all cases merely resemblances of diction. It will be instructive to note them.

(1) In § 3. The appearance of Gabriel to the Virgin to announce her death and his salutation addressed to her reads like an imitation of the appearance of Michael to Abraham, intentionally assimilated to the account of the Annunciation in S. Luke.

(2) § 3. καταλιποῦσα τὸν κόσμον. Abr. A § VII. p. 84, καταλιπεῖν τὸν κοσμικὸν βίον.

(3) § 5. διὰ τὴν ἄκραν ἀγαθότητά σου. This may be a common phrase, but I am not familiar with it: certainly it recurs in Abr. A XIV. p. 94, l. 29.

Here too the form of the Virgin's prayer to see the Apostles resembles that of Abraham; A § IX. p. 87.

§ 6. διὰ νεφέλης. Abr. A XV. p. 96, l. 6. I lay no stress on the recurrence in both books of the idea of conveyance on a cloud, which the Marian book may quite as well have derived from the Apocryphal Acts of the Apostles. Cf. *Acta Petri et Andreae*, § 1.

(§§ 26, 27 should be compared with the 'Apocalypse of Moses' § 33—36, as also § 38 with *Apoc. Mosis* § 38. There is a good deal of similarity.)

(4) In § 40 the Virgin kisses the hand of Christ, and shortly afterwards dies. Compare Abr. A § xx. p. 103, l. 17.

(5) Christ receives the Virgin's soul in His hands, § 44. So Michael, *l. c.* l. 21.

(6) § 48. Hymns are sung at the tomb for three days, till her body is transferred to Paradise. So in the case of Abraham, *l. c.* l. 23 sqq.

I am not convinced that the Testament of Abraham was the principal or the only document which influenced the form of the Assumption legend; but that that legend was largely modelled on earlier Apocrypha, especially on the Assumption of Moses, I have little doubt.

Similarly, the Egyptian Life of Joseph the Carpenter has been influenced by earlier books: and here again we find points of resemblance to our Testament. The hideous form of death, and the reluctance of Joseph to die, and the presence of Michael at the death-bed, carry us into the same cycle of ideas which we meet with in the Testament, while the parallels between the Testament of Isaac and the latter part of the Joseph story are frequent and striking. I should attribute in this case also some importance to the influence of the Assumption of Moses.

The two Recensions of the Testament: their relation to each other, and to the Arabic Version.

The Testament of Abraham has been preserved in Greek in two distinct recensions, as well as in several versions. Of the versions one only, the Arabic, needs to be treated here.

Now, of the two Greek recensions, the first (which I call A) has this characteristic, that it is somewhat full and verbose; while the second (B), though its language is simpler and probably older on the whole, transposes, and in transposing mutilates and confuses, certain incidents in the story. It is moreover considerably

THE TWO RECENSIONS. 35

shorter than the other recension. With this second recension the Arabic version (Ar.) will be proved to agree in the main.

The object of this section of the Introduction is to set forth as well as may be the relations which these three documents bear to each other and to the primitive form of the book. And a necessary part of this investigation is a survey of the contents of the three documents. Accordingly a somewhat full analysis is here appended, in which those portions of A are italicised which it has in common with B or Ar.

A.	B.	Ar.
§ I. Abraham is 995 years old. His hospitality is described. *God sends Michael to him to bid him prepare for death.*	(As in A.)	(As in A.)
§ II. *M. finds Abr. at Mamre, looking after the ploughing,* with the sons of Masek (=Eliezer) and 12 servants. *Abr. greets M.*, believing him to be a soldier, *and sends for horses for them to ride upon, which M. refuses. They walk to Abr.'s house.*	§ II. M. finds Abr. by the oxen, which are ploughing. Isaac is in his arms. The greeting. Abr. invites M. to lodge with him, lest he be attacked by a wild beast in journeying. M. inquires his name. Abr. tells him how it was changed from Abram to Abraham. M. says he has heard how Abr. entertained angels. The horse is sent for by Abr. and refused. [Here MS C confuses the story by making them ride to the house, when Abr. sends a lad on a horse to fetch some lambs. M. then suggests that they should walk to the fold. See *App. Crit. in loc.*]	M. finds Abr. 'in the sown field.' The greeting. The invitation to lodge, for fear of wild beasts. Eliezer is sent for a horse, which is refused. They walk to the house.
§ III. *On the way they pass a* cypress *tree which speaks. Abr. keeps silence about it.* On their arrival, Isaac notices that the	§ III. The speaking tree is seemingly a tamarisk. The utterance differs from A. It has 300 branches. Arrived at the	The tree is like a tamarisk, with 3 branches. It says, 'Holy, Holy, Holy is He to whom belongs the rule over mankind.'

3—2

36   THE TESTAMENT OF ABRAHAM.

A.	B.	Ar.
stranger is not a human being, and says so to Sarah. He adores M. and is blessed by him. *Abr. sends Isaac for water to wash M.'s feet.* He is moved, *and weeps, Isaac and M. weep. M.'s tears become precious stones,* which Abr. hides in his bosom.	house, Abr. sends for 3 lambs: and washes M.'s feet. His tears are caused by the foreboding that this is the last time that he will wash any stranger's feet.	The water is sent for, the reason for weeping is as in B. The 'precious stones' are omitted. Three of every sort of cattle are sent for.
§ IV. *Abr. bids Isaac make ready the guest-chamber.* This is done, and a table is set. *M. goes out,* on a pretext, *and goes up to heaven. He tells God that he cannot bear to tell Abr. that he must die. God bids him go back, and promises to reveal the matter in a vision,* which M. is to interpret. M. asks how he, being a spirit, is to eat. God promises to send a devouring spirit which will consume the food as if M. were eating it.	§ IV. Sarah hears the weeping, and asks the cause. Abr. tells her it is nothing. She prepares the food. The sun sets, and M. goes up to heaven to adore God, as all angels do at sunset. (The pretext of A is omitted.) After the other angels have gone, M. begs God to reveal to Abr. concerning his death. God bids him return, promising to reveal it to Isaac.	While food is being prepared, M. goes forth in secret and goes up to heaven and begs God to send a vision to Isaac, of Abr.'s death. After Abr.'s hospitality to M. and Gabriel, M. cannot bear to reveal it to him. God consents.
§ V. *M. returns. After supper,* and prayer, *Isaac begs to be allowed to sleep near them, Abr. refuses and Isaac departs.* At the 3rd hour of the night *he awakes, knocks at Abr.'s door, and begs for a last sight of his father. Abr. opens to him. All three weep. Sarah hearing it asks whether M. has brought bad news of Lot. M. tells her that he has not,* and that Isaac's grief is the cause.	§ V. Abr. bids Isaac prepare a chamber for M. (As in A.) § VI. At the 7th hour of the night...(as in A.) but that God has remembered them.	M. returns. The chamber prepared. Isaac's request refused. At midnight he wakes...... Rebekah hears the weeping, and asks if Isaac is dead. When reassured, she asks if there is bad news of Lot, and is told by M. that there is not.

THE TWO RECENSIONS.

A.	B.	Ar.
§ VI. *Sarah recognises from M.'s speech that he is an angel.* She takes Abr. aside and says 'Do you know this man?' Abr. denies it. *Sarah reminds him of the three strangers*, for whom he killed the calf, which, when eaten, came to life again and ran to its dam. This man is one of those strangers. *Abr. agrees and says that he, too, recognised M. when washing his feet.* He then shews the gems which had come from his tears. They agree that some secret thing is to be revealed.	Sarah says, 'Why do you weep when a man of God is here?' Abr. says, 'How know you that he is a man of God?' Sarah answers that she knows him for one of the three strangers. Abr. agrees. Abr. asks what the meaning of the matter is and M. refers him to Isaac.	Rebekah, recognising M. from her parents' reports, blesses him and addresses Abr. as in B. Abr. agrees, and says he recognised M. at the washing of feet. (As in B.)
§ VII. *Abr. bids Isaac relate his dream.* Isaac says '*I saw the sun and moon upon my head, enlightening me. A man brighter than seven suns came out of heaven and took the sun.* As I wept, he came again and took the moon. I besought him to leave it. He said 'Let me take them to the Heavenly King, who wishes for them.' But he left the rays upon me.' M. says, '*You, Abr., are the sun,* Sarah the moon. I am the shining man, and I am come to take your soul.' Abr. declares he will not follow M.	§ VII. (As in A.) Isaac says 'I saw the sun and moon upon my head. A shining man came, took the sun and left the moon. I besought him to leave it, and the sun, moon and stars joined me. The man said 'I am taking it from sorrow to joy,' etc. I said 'Take the rays also.' He said, 'When the 12 hours of the day are over, I will take them all.' Now the sun was like you, my father.' M. says, 'You, Abr., are the sun. Your soul will be taken to heaven, your body remain on earth till 7000 ages are past, and the resurrection comes. Now therefore set your house in order, for your time is come.'	Isaac, bidden to relate his dream, says 'I saw the sun, moon, and stars on my head, giving me light. A shining man came down from heaven. This is he of whom thou wouldst say 'He is the father of all lights.' He took the sun. The moon wept and besought him to leave it. So did the stars, and the sun begged for a respite that he might collect his rays and not leave them behind. Then, O my sister Rebekah, I beheld in my right hand the sun, that it was like my father Abr. and (the moon like) my mother Sarah, and the stars like my servants. And I wept, and the Shining One said 'Weep not, for I take him

THE TESTAMENT OF ABRAHAM.

A.	B.	Ar.
		from sorrow to joy, etc.' And I awoke.' M. said 'It is true,' and all, knowing that Abr. was to die, wept.
§ VIII. M. goes up to heaven, reports the refusal to God. God bids him return to Abr. and remind him of the common lot of men, and of God's mercies to him.		
§ IX. M. reports his message. *Abr. begs him to ask God to allow him, while yet in the body, to see the works of creation.* M. reports the request, and God bids him take Abr. on a cloud, and with angelic chariots, and to shew him the world.	(As in A.) M. promises to ask for permission. § VIII. It is asked and granted.	(As in B.)
§ X. Abr. is shewn the world and the vicissitudes of man's life. *He sees murderers with swords. At his prayer* wild beasts devour them. *He sees adulterers. In like manner, the earth swallows them.* He sees housebreakers: fire consumes them. *God's voice bids M. turn the chariot* and shew Abr. the judgment, *lest he destroy all men, since, never having sinned, he has no pity on sinners.*	(See post, § XII.)	(Entirely omitted.
§ XI. Abr. is taken to the East, to the first gate of Heaven. He sees two ways, narrow and broad, and *two gates, narrow and broad.* Outside, *between these, sits one* like Christ	§ VIII. (contd.). Abr. is taken to the river Oceanus. He sees two gates, narrow and broad. (As in A.)	Abr. is taken to Oceanus. 'And I will speak, even I Abr. I saw two gates,' etc. (As in A.)

A.	B.	Ar.
on a throne, *who alternately weeps and laughs, but weeps 7 times as much as he laughs. Abr. asks M. to explain. He says,* 'The gates are those of salvation and perdition. *The man is Adam who weeps for the loss of souls, and laughs at their salvation.* One soul in 7000 is saved.'	(As in A.)	(As in A.) his weeping exceeded his rejoicing twelve times doubled. (as in A.)
§ XII. 'I saw two fiery *angels driving many souls and beating them with fiery thongs, and one soul was held by an angel.* We followed them to see if any would be saved. Inside the gates they saw a shining man on a crystal table on which was a book 6 cubits thick by 10 broad. On each side was an angel recording. In front was a shining angel with a balance and a fiery angel with a trumpet containing fire. These recorded, weighed, and tested the souls. The angel brought the soul which he held, and its sins and good deeds were looked out in the book. *They weighed equally.* The soul was set in the midst.' § XIII. *M. explains. The judge is Abel.* All souls are judged (1) by Abel, (2) at the second coming by the 12 tribes (or the tribes by the Apostles), (3) by God. The recording angels write	§ IX. Abr. weeps because being a broad man he will not be able to pass through the narrow gate. M. consoles him. They see an angel driving 60,000 souls. They follow and find an angel holding one soul of a woman whose good and bad deeds weighed equally. The others were lost. Abr. asks, and M. explains that the angel is Death. § X. Abr. asks to see the judgment. He is carried on a cloud to Paradise. The soul which they had seen is brought. It asks for mercy. The judge asked 'Why did you kill your daughter?' 'I did not.' The judge calls for the scribe. Two cherubims bring books, and with them comes a great man with 3 crowns, one higher than the rest, called crowns of witness. He has a gold pen. He finds the sins of that soul in the book. The judge	I saw 60,000 souls whom angels drove through the broad gate. M. said, 'Let us follow, and see if any will be saved.' (3rd person). They go, and find one soul whose good and bad deeds were equal, and it was saved. All the rest were lost. (Here the 1st person.) Abr. laments and is consoled, as in B. (He says 'I know not if they will let me enter by the strait gate without suffering torture for 12 years'.) Abr. 'Does God, or their angels, or Death bring souls out of their bodies?' M. 'Death, and Michael[1].' Abr. 'How many die and are born every day?' M. '99999.' A soul is brought to the judge. A man comes forth from behind a curtain and begins declaring the sins of the soul. The soul denies all. God, the Judge, calls witnesses. Three witnesses accuse it of murder and adultery, of luxurious living, and of deceit. It is con-

[1] So the text, corruptly.

A.	B.	Ar.
the good and bad deeds respectively. The weighing angel is Dokiel and the fiery angel Puruel.	accuses the soul of murder and adultery. The soul laments, and is given over to the tormentors.	demned. M. explains that the recorder is Enoch.

§ XIV. The soul in the midst needs but one good deed in order to be saved. At Abr.'s instance, he and M. intercede for it. It vanishes, and M. says *it is saved*. They then intercede for those whom Abr. had destroyed by his prayer (§ X.). Their prayer is heard, as God's voice tells them.

§ XV. *Abr. is now brought back to his house.* Sarah and Isaac and his servants surround him, and M. urges him to make his will and depart. He refuses. M. ascends to heaven, reports the matter to God, and asks for counsel.

§ XVI. God summons Death, who arrives in terror. *God bids him assume a lovely form and go and take Abr.'s soul with all gentleness.* Death adorns himself as an Archangel, and comes to Abr. who is sitting, head on hand, under the oak of Mamre. *Death greets him,* and Abr. takes him for M. *Death tells him who he is,* and Abr., when convinced, refuses to follow him.

§ XI. M. explains. The judge is Abel, the recorder Enoch. At Abr.'s request, M. explains that Enoch was unwilling to record men's sins, but God bade him do so.

§ XII. Abr. is taken into the lower firmament. He sees adulterers. At his prayer they are destroyed by fire. He sees slanderers: they are swallowed up in the earth, and likewise murderers, whom wild beasts devour. God commands that Abr. should be taken home again, seeing he is not long-suffering with sinners. At the 9th hour Abr. returns, and finds that Sarah is dead of grief, and buries her.

§ XIII. When Abr.'s time to die comes, God commands M. to adorn Death in a fair form. Death comes and sits by Abr., and greetings are exchanged. Abr. is afraid; he cannot bear the glory of Death. Death explains why he is so glorious, and who he is.

Abr. is brought back and laid on his bed that he may die. He summons his servants, frees them and makes them a feast. When his time to die comes, God tells M. that Abr. is not to be alarmed. (It is not said that Death adorned himself. Something has dropped out.)

Death comes to Abr. while he is sleeping. Abr. wakes and sees him, and asks who he is, describing his terror and faintness. He calls for Isaac and asks him who the mysterious stranger is. Isaac can see no one. Abr. says he is going to die, and Isaac laments.

THE TWO RECENSIONS.

A.	B.	Ar.
§ XVII. Abr. goes into his house, and into his chamber. Death follows, and will not leave him. *Abr. asks if he always comes in this form.* 'Only to the just: to the ungodly in a frightful shape.' *Abr. begs him to shew his true shape*, God will enable him to bear it.	§ XIV. (As in A.)	Death, being asked, reveals his name and explains the cause of his beauty, as in AB. Abr. asks to see his true form. Death says the servants must depart. Abr. asks if any can die before his time. 'Yes, in times of pestilence, I and my son Atarlimos go forth and slay indiscriminately.'
Death puts on his most awful form and shews 7 dragon-heads and 14 faces, fire, darkness, viper, precipice, [asp,] lion, horned-snake, basilisk, fiery sword, [weapons,] lightning, thunder, sea, torrent, three-headed dragon, poison-cup.	Death shews his hideousness. He has two heads, one of a dragon, because men die of snake-bites, the other of a sword, because men die by that.	Death then grows in height and appears with many faces, some of serpents and some fiery.
7000 *servants die* and Abr. faints.	Abr.'s servants die. Abr. prays, and God raises them.	Eighteen servants die, and all present fall down until M. raises them up, and Death and his son depart to their places.
§ XVIII. Abr., revived, begs Death to resume his beauty. Then he asks how the servants could die. 'Can any die before his time?' 'No; the only marvel is that you survived.' *They intercede for the dead servants, who are restored to life* [*and freed*, MS D].		
§ XIX. Abr. goes up to his chamber. Death follows. Abr., after asking about his authority, demands the interpretation of Death's form. Death says the 7 dragon-heads were the 7 ages of the world. The others stand for different deaths of men.		

THE TESTAMENT OF ABRAHAM.

A.	B.	Ar.
§ XX. *Abr. asks if there is any untimely death.* Death answers that there are 72 kinds of death, but bids Abr. delay no longer. Abr. asks for delay. Isaac, Sarah, and the servants come to him and Abr. becomes faint. Death bids him kiss his hand, and he will feel better. Abr. kisses his hand, and his soul cleaves thereto, and he dies. *M. and a host of angels come, and wrap the soul in a heaven-spun cloth.* On the 3rd day, the body is buried under the oak, the soul adores God. God orders that the soul be taken to Paradise to be with the saints.	After this, M. takes Abr.'s soul, as in a dream, and takes it to heaven. Isaac buries the body by Sarah.	M. takes Abr.'s soul, wraps it in white robes and carries it away in his fiery chariot. The angels meet it and escort it to Paradise. Abr. died on 28 Misri, aged 175. Isaac bewailed him 60 days, and buried him by Sarah, and returning exhorted the freed servants to lead good lives.
Doxology.		*End.*

It will be seen that, while the main outline of the story remains naturally enough the same, the differences between our three forms of it are neither few nor slight. These differences may be conveniently treated under two heads: (i) those which arise naturally from the process of epitomisation; (ii) those which entail a real alteration of the narrative.

To take them in order, we should first refer to the analysis of § II., where it will be seen that the confusion introduced by one of the MSS of Recension B shews that an unskilful redactor has been at work.

Next, let us examine a passage in which the differences are more important,—the vision of Isaac in § VII. of A and B. In A, the course of their vision is this: the sun and moon are on Isaac's head; the Shining One comes twice, and takes first the sun and then the moon, leaving the rays with Isaac. In the interpretation the sun is Abraham, the moon Sarah, the Shining One Michael. The rays are not explained.

In B, the sun and moon are on Isaac's head: the Shining One (who is compared to the 'Father of lights') takes the sun and leaves the rays: the sun, moon and stars join in Isaac's remonstrances. Isaac then asks the Shining One to take the rays, but he refuses to do so until the twelve hours of the day are over. The sun resembles Abraham. The interpretation is much shortened in B. The sun is Abraham, the moon and stars are unexplained, and the Shining One is not mentioned again. But there is an explanation of the mysterious rays, though this again has suffered. Abraham's body, says Michael, is to remain on the earth until the end of 7000 ages, when the resurrection will take place. Evidently then, the rays of the vision, which were to be left with Isaac, answer to the body of Abraham, and the twelve hours of the day correspond to the 7000 ages, the traditional period of the duration of the world. Here too Sarah must be the moon, and the children or servants of Abraham must be the stars. The imagery is plainly derived from the dream of Joseph in Genesis (xxxvii. 9).

The Arabic version (Ar.) presents a marked similarity to B. Here the sun, moon and stars are on Isaac's head; and the Shining One is spoken of as resembling the 'Father of all lights.' He takes the sun. The moon and stars lament, and the sun begs for time to collect his rays and take them with him. The sun resembles Abraham, the moon Sarah, and the stars Isaac's servants. Thus four points common to B and Ar. are absent from A: (1) the mention of the stars, (2) the mention of the 'Father of lights,' (3) the lamentation of the moon and stars, (4) the resemblance of the sun to Abraham.

But no one of these accounts taken by itself is quite full or coherent. It seems to me that the passage is one in which each document supplements its fellows. To take a single instance, in A nothing is said of Sarah's death, but the moon, which represents her in the vision, is removed. In B nothing is said of the removal of the moon, but Sarah's death is related in § XII. Here then the combination of A and B will give us a reasonable and complete account. But both A and B are very plainly abridged.

The Arabic is still more curtailed. It may preserve an original trait in making the sun (and not Isaac as in B) ask that his rays may accompany him. But this is its only contribution; and it attempts no explanation of what is meant by the rays.

The reader will readily multiply for himself instances of omissions in B and Ar. of features prominent in A, and such as can hardly be otherwise than original. Such are, the unwillingness of Abraham to die (omitted by B and Ar.) and the employment of the first person in the Vision of Abraham (present in Ar., absent from B). These omissions I would put down to the epitomiser's credit.

Let us pass to the second class of variations.

The first that requires notice is in § IV. of A and B. In A, Michael goes outside the house on a certain pretext and ascends to heaven. In B, the reason given for his exit is quite different. At sunset, it is said, all angels adore God, and Michael first of them all. It is to fulfil this duty that he goes up to heaven.

In Ar. we read that, while Abraham and Isaac were preparing the supper, Michael went out in secret (?). This evades the difficulty and we have to decide between the claims of A and B to originality. The pretext given in A (ὡς δῆθεν γαστρὸς χρείᾳ ὕδατος χύσιν ποιῆσαι) is so grotesque that I cannot think it was inserted by a later redactor: it even savours of irreverence. That in B, on the other hand, is quite certainly not original: it may be read, *totidem verbis*, in the Apocalypse of Paul (§ 7, p. 38, ed. Tischdf.) ἔτι δὲ μᾶλλον δύνοντος τοῦ ἡλίου· ἐν αὐτῇ γὰρ τῇ ὥρᾳ πάντες οἱ ἄγγελοι ἔρχονται πρὸς τὸν Θεὸν προσκυνῆσαι αὐτῷ. Here we have a very natural phenomenon. The author of B has substituted a detail drawn from another book for one which he disliked in his original.

The most considerable discrepancy, however, is in that part of the book which treats of the judgment of souls (§§ X.—XIV. A, VIII.—XII. B).

The course of events in A is briefly this:

Abraham on his voyage through the air sees various malefactors and at his prayer they are destroyed. At God's command he is taken to Heaven, sees the two gates, the two ways, and Adam. Angels are seen driving lost souls; and one soul is seen whose fate is doubtful. A judgment scene is then described, where Abel is judge, an angel Dokiel weighs souls, another angel Puruel tests them by fire, and two angels act as recorders. The neutral soul is examined and no verdict given. Abraham intercedes for it and subsequently for the sinners whom he had destroyed, and all are saved. It is explained that every soul will be thrice judged, by Abel, by the twelve tribes (or Apostles) and by God. The first person is employed for a moment in this narrative.

In B we have this:

Abraham is taken to the river Oceanus. The two gates and Adam are seen. Abraham is alarmed, and reassured, on the subject of the narrowness of the gate of life. The lost souls are seen, and one soul of a woman whose fate is doubtful. The angel who brings them is Death. The judgment scene, in Paradise, follows. Abel is judge, Enoch is recorder, and two cherubims carry the books of record. The neutral soul is examined and condemned. Abraham is taken to the lower firmament, sees the various sinners, as in A, and destroys them. Then he is taken home. All this narrative is in the third person.

In Ar. we read:

Abraham is taken to the river Oceanus. He sees the two gates and Adam, the lost soul, and the neutral soul, which is saved. Then Abraham's alarm about the gate of life and Michael's reassurance of him are related. A short conversation about Death, and about the number of men who are born and die each day, follows. Next comes the judgment scene. God is the judge, Enoch the recorder, and a soul is examined, confronted with three witnesses, and condemned. Abraham is then taken home. The episode of the sinners destroyed is omitted. The first person is largely employed in this section.

In these three accounts we find certain elements common to all, and certain others common to two of our authorities.

Common to all three are:

1. The two gates and the mention of Adam alternately weeping and laughing.

2. The soul whose sins and good deeds were equal.

Common to two are:

1. Abraham taken to Oceanus (B, Ar.).

2. The introduction of the first person (A, Ar.).
3. The introduction of Death (B, Ar.).
4. Abel as judge of souls (A, B).
5. Enoch as recorder (B, Ar.).
6. A neutral soul is saved (A, Ar.).
7. The examination and condemnation of a soul (B, Ar.).
8. Abraham destroying sinners (A, B).
9. Abraham's alarm about the gate of life (B, Ar.).

In three out of five features, common to B, Ar., we find that they are influenced by a common source, not the original, namely, the Apocalypse of Paul.

(1) Compare Abr. B § VIII., and Ar. ἀνήνεγκεν αὐτὸν ἐπὶ τὸν ὠκεανὸν ποταμόν with *Apoc. Pauli* § 31, p. 57 ἔστησέν με ἐπάνω τοῦ ποταμοῦ τοῦ ὠκεανοῦ, and also § 21, p. 50.

(5) Compare Abr. B § XI. (Cod. B) ὁ ἕτερος...ἐστὶν Ἐνὼχ ὁ μάρτυς τῆς ἐσχάτης ἡμέρας with *Apoc. Pauli* § 20, p. 50 οὗτός ἐστιν Ἐνὼχ ὁ μάρτυς τῆς ἐσχάτης ἡμέρας. This is a marked coincidence of language: but Enoch in *Apoc. Pauli* is not a recorder. This function, however, belongs to him in Jewish tradition.

(7) Compare Abr. B §§ X., XI. with *Apoc. Pauli* §§ 17, 18. In this scene, the Arabic, which substitutes God for Abel as judge of souls, shews a closer likeness to *Apoc. Pauli* than B does.

In the other two traits common to B, Ar., one, the introduction of Death, introduces a plain inconsistency with the latter part of the book, which represents Death not as an ordinary angel but as a terrific being sometimes taking the form of an angel of light. The other, Abraham's alarm about the gate of life, is very probably an original feature, suppressed in A because it seemed ludicrous, just as in B a grotesque trait in § IV. was suppressed.

The two coincidences between A and B are both important, and likely to be original. The defection of the Arabic is to be explained in the first case (Abel as judge) by a reference to the Apocalypse of Paul; in the second case (the destruction of sinners) the episode is merely omitted, having become meaningless in its altered position.

Of the two coincidences between A and Ar. one, the introduction of the first person, is a fresh proof of the originality of A as compared with B; and in the case of the Arabic shews its independence of B in B's present form. The other two Testaments[1] both employ the first person in the sections corresponding to this. The other coincidence, the saving of the neutral soul, is also important. Plainly B must be wrong in condemning it; and not less plainly Ar. must be wrong in its bare and unexplained mention of its salvation, while A gives a good and intelligible motive for the latter, in attributing it to Abraham's intercession.

The most considerable liberty taken with the text is perhaps the shifting of the episode of the destruction of sinners. I cannot but feel that the place assigned to it in A is the only reasonable one. The sinless Abraham is inflamed with righteous indignation at the sight of the wickedness of men, and would at once rid the earth of them. But when he has seen the judgments of God and has realised the exceeding fewness of those that are saved, the reaction takes place, and he does his best to undo the harm he has brought about. That is the reasonable and consistent story in A. In B, after seeing the judgments and the infinitesimal number of the saved, he is none the less ready to swell the numbers of the lost, and is only deterred by God's express command. The story is not a reasonable one: but we can even see why it took its present form in B. The author of that recension thought that the moral of his original was a dangerous one: it seemed imprudent to tell men that, though cut off in the blossom of their sin, they might yet escape punishment through the intercession whether of Abraham or of other righteous men.

It was a better course to omit the whole episode, as Ar. does, than to keep half of it in a wrong place.

Another variation between the documents relates to Sarah.

In A Sarah is alive at the time of Abraham's death.

In B Abraham finds her dead of grief on his return home.

In Ar. Rebekah is substituted for her throughout: but she appears in Isaac's vision as the moon.

A's account disagrees entirely with that in Genesis: and so does that of B, for Sarah died many years before Abraham, and he married Keturah, who seems to have been living at his death. There is, however, in B's view of the matter, a certain similarity

[1] Sc. of Isaac and Jacob; see Appendix.

to the Rabbinic tradition that Sarah almost died of grief when Abraham was away with Isaac on the expedition to Mount Moriah, and that she actually died of joy on suddenly hearing the news of Isaac's rescue from being sacrificed, which was broken to her suddenly by Samael[1]. The substitution of Rebekah for Sarah in Ar. is clumsily done, and is obviously an attempt to harmonise with Genesis.

The concluding sections of the book are much shortened in B and Ar. It is no doubt the case that these same sections are unduly expanded in A, particularly in the description of Death: but the account in A forms a homogeneous whole, while that in B and Ar. is so disproportionately short and so jejune as at once to convey a strong suspicion that something is wanting. In A the death of Abraham is finally brought about by his kissing the hand of Death. To the last he has refused to give up his soul voluntarily: this unwillingness to die will be treated in detail under a separate head; but all that need be noticed here is that the refusal to obey, which constantly recurs in A and finds its climax in Abraham's death, is entirely absent from B and Ar. In this case again I believe that the trait is an original one, and that B and Ar. omit it as being derogatory to Abraham's character. Proof of the antiquity and popularity of the notion will be adduced in the section above alluded to.

In B and Ar. it will be seen that the actual death of Abraham forms a mere appendix to the narrative, and that the purpose of Death's being sent to the patriarch is lost sight of: whereas Abraham's refusal to give up his soul to Michael forms in A the reasonable motive for having recourse to Death.

A word must be said of the matter peculiar to Ar. The desire to harmonise with Genesis is seen in the introduction of Eliezer in § II., as well as in the substitution of Rebekah for Sarah. The additions are: the conversation between Michael and Abraham about the number of deaths and births which take place daily; the introduction of three witnesses in the judgment-scene; Abraham's freeing his servants (occurring also notably in one MS (D) of A); the arrival of Death and the conversation thereon between Abraham and Isaac; the introduction of the son of Death—Atar-

[1] Beer, *Leben Abrahams*, 73.

limos or Pestilence; some details of Isaac's burying of Abraham, and his exhortation to the servants.

Of these, the conversation about Death, and the introduction of Atarlimos may be very likely drawn from current popular mythology: with regard to the latter of the two, it seems to describe the true Egyptian plague[1], and to be an insertion original to this version. The freeing of the servants has, as we see, a slight support in the Greek. The introduction of three witnesses may be referred to the Apocalypse of Paul; the account of the arrival of Death, if original, would shew that both A and B have here been a good deal shortened.

The evidence points to the following conclusions:

A presents us with what is on the whole the fullest, clearest, and most consistent narrative. Its language, however, has been to some extent mediaevalised.

B is an abridgment whose language is on the whole more simple and original than that of A. It omits much, and in several places adulterates the narrative with insertions from the Apocalypse of Paul. It is not an abridgment made from A.

Ar. is an independent abridgment, not made from either A or B, though as a rule more nearly related to B than to A. It, too, shews similarity to the Apocalypse of Paul[2]. It inserts matter not found in A or B, and is shorter than either.

In order to reconstruct the original Testament, we should probably do right in following A in the main, with supplements from B in the Vision of Isaac, and in the account of Abraham's terror at the narrow gate; and we must suppose that something is wanting in all our documents in the account of the judgment-scene in the shape of some dispute over the neutral soul between 'angels of righteousness and angels of iniquity.'

[1] So Professor W. Robertson Smith has suggested to me.

[2] This fact implies that the contamination with the Apocalypse of Paul is due to a common ancestor of B and Ar.

The Christian element in the Testament of Abraham.

In order to determine the extent of the Christian influence which is undoubtedly present in the book, we may begin by collecting such phrases as are unmistakably Christian.

A § I. One MS reads φιλόχριστος for φιλόστοργος.

§ IV. ἀπεχόμενον ἀπὸ παντὸς πονηροῦ (1 Thess. v. 22).
ἐπιβαλῶ τὸ πνεῦμά μου τὸ ἅγιον.

§ VI. δόξα καὶ εὐλογία παρὰ θεοῦ καὶ πατρός.

§ VII. ἐγώ εἰμι Μιχαὴλ ὁ ἀρχιστρ. ὁ παρεστηκὼς ἐνώπιον τοῦ θεοῦ (Luke i. 19, cf. Tobit xii. 14 in *Cod. Sin.* and Rev. viii. 2).

§ X. κλέψαι καὶ θῦσαι καὶ ἀπολέσαι (John x. 10).

§ XI. ἡ μία ὁδὸς στενὴ καὶ τεθλιμμένη καὶ ἡ ἑτέρα πλατεῖα καὶ εὐρύχωρος (Matt. vii. 13).
ἰδέα...ὁμοία τοῦ δεσπότου (v.l. κυρίου ἡμῶν Ἰησοῦ Χριστοῦ).
ἀπάγουσα εἰς τὴν ζωήν...εἰς τὴν ἀπώλειαν (Matt. vii. 14).
πολλοί...ὀλίγοι (*ibid.*).

§ XII. τοῖς βασανισταῖς ἐξέδωκεν (Matt. xviii. 34).
τοῖς σωζομένοις (Acts ii. 4).

§ XIII. ἐν τῇ δευτέρᾳ παρουσίᾳ κριθήσονται (all but one MS ὑπὸ τῶν δώδεκα ἀποστόλων αἱ δώδεκα φυλαὶ τοῦ Ἰσραὴλ) καὶ πᾶσα πνοὴ καὶ πᾶσα κτίσις (Luke xxii. 30).
ὁ ἐπὶ τοῦ πυρὸς ἔχων τὴν ἐξουσίαν (Rev. xiv. 18).
εἴ τινος τὸ ἔργον κατακαύσει τὸ πῦρ (1 Cor. iii. 13—15).

§ XIV. A various reading κύριον ἡμῶν Ἰησοῦν Χριστόν.

§ XVI. ἀοράτου πατρός.

§ XX. τρισάγιον ὕμνον τῷ δεσπότῃ τῶν ὅλων θεῷ,
as well as the doxology and several phrases at the extreme end of the book.

Besides the phrases in this list, which are unmistakably Christian, if not actual quotations from the N. T., there is in A a good deal of what may be called mediaeval matter. The introductory sentences come under this head, and so does much of the speech of God to Michael in § VIII., and the speech of Death to Abraham, and the description of Death. Further, the elaborate greetings which pass between Abraham and Michael, and Abraham and Death, together with the epithets constantly applied to these personages and to God, savour of a late date. All this is what we expect a redactor to furnish, and to a redactor I attribute it.

Next, the vocabulary and grammar contain a certain amount of late forms and constructions. We have εἰπεῖν τινὰ without πρός in § I. etc., ἀπό with an Accusative in § VIII. Of late words we find χαρζαναί § XII., δουλίδες § XVII., ἀνύπαρκτος § XIX, and plenty of the epithets referred to above, ἡλιόρατος ἡλιόμορφος πανιερός and so on.

Again, no MS of A known to me is older than cent. XIII. We cannot reasonably put it in its present form much before cent. IX. or X. though, as I have tried to shew, the groundwork of it, preserved faithfully, I believe, in all its main features, was a book known to Origen and therefore not later than cent. III.; probably as old as cent. II.

How does B compare with A in respect of the features we have noticed? Only one of the expressions quoted from A has a place in B: in § VIII. we read αὐταί εἰσιν αἱ ἀπάγουσαι εἰς τὴν ζωὴν καὶ εἰς τὴν ἀπώλειαν. B has, it is true, one or two N. T. phrases which A has not; e.g. in § XIII. οὐκ ἔστιν ἐκ τοῦ κόσμου τούτου (John xviii. 36), § XII. σπλαγχνίζομαι ἐπί (Mark viii. 2). But on the whole B is far freer from Christianisms of language than A. The language of the narrative throughout is, moreover, simpler and more antique than that of A. In one or two places in B one MS (B) uses the neo-Greek particle ἅς (§ v. p. 109, l. 21 *App. Crit.*) and there are some eccentricities of vocabulary, the most noteworthy being the word ζεῦμα on p. 110, l. 14; but these are exceptions. My impression of the relation of B to A, as elsewhere stated, is broadly this; that B preserves the greatest proportion of the original language, A the greatest proportion of the original story.

To return to the N. T. quotations in A. It will be noticed that they are especially frequent in the Apocalyptic section of the book (§§ X.—XIV.), and that the one in which A and B agree occurs in this same portion. Moreover, it is only in this section that any of the phrases in question form an integral and inseparable part of the text. They can be removed without injury to the sense from every other part of the book: not so can all in the Apocalyptic section. The conception of the two gates and two ways, of the few saved and many lost, appearing in both recensions and greatly emphasised, cannot be divorced from its context. It would seem then, at first sight, that this Apocalyptic section is to some extent Christian or Christianised. And this section is doubtless the kernel of the whole book. The chief object of the original author of it was to give publicity to his views on the judgment of souls. They are peculiar views, and so the redactors of the book have felt: the author of the B-text has revised them so much that he has left little of what we find in A. That the author of the A-text must have removed some glaring heterodoxies we feel almost certain, but cannot so clearly shew.

How far does this presumed Christian influence in the Apocalyptic section extend? Is that section, as it stands in A, a consistent whole? There can be little doubt that the episode of the two gates is founded on the passage of S. Matthew referred to. The actual language of the Gospel is used in both recensions, and it would be doing violence to all probability to look elsewhere for the source of it.

On the two phrases quoted from § XII. little stress can be laid, but with the contents and language of § XIII. we shall do well to acquaint ourselves. The scheme of the judgment of souls there set forth is as follows. Every soul undergoes three judgments. It is first judged by Abel, in virtue of the relation of all men to the father of Abel. Next, at the *Second Coming*, it will be judged by the twelve tribes of Israel (v. l. the twelve Apostles); lastly, at the end of all things, it will be judged by God.

The instruments employed in the first judgment are three: the written records of good and evil actions, the balance which weighs the souls (or actions), and the trumpet full of fire which tests the souls (or actions).

There are certain difficulties here. The greatest lies in the description of the second judgment of souls. All the MSS save one tell us in this place that the twelve Apostles are to be the judges either of the twelve tribes *and* of all the world (BCERo), or simply of all the world (D). When we remember that in Matt. xix. 28 and Luke xxii. 30 the promise is made to the Apostles that they shall in the regeneration sit upon twelve thrones, judging the twelve tribes of Israel, it seems at first sight as if this *must* be the right reading. There is still however something to be said on the other side. The MS evidence is this:

(1) καὶ ἐν τῇ δευτέρᾳ παρουσίᾳ κριθήσονται ὑπὸ τῶν δώδεκα φυλῶν τοῦ Ἰσραήλ, καὶ πᾶσα πνοὴ καὶ πᾶσα κτίσις. A.

(2) καὶ ἐπὶ τὴν δευτέραν παρουσίαν ὑπὸ τῶν ἀποστόλων κριθήσονται αἱ δώδεκα φυλαὶ τοῦ Ἰσρ. καὶ πάσης πνοῆς καὶ πάσης ἄνοις. B.

(3) καὶ ἐν τῇ δευτέρᾳ παρουσίᾳ ὑπὸ τῶν ιβ΄ ἀποστ. κριθήσονται αἱ ιβ΄ φυλαὶ τοῦ Ἰσρ. κ. πᾶσα πνοὴ κ. πᾶσ[α] ἄνθρωπος. CE.

(4) καὶ ἐν τῇ δ. π. ὑπὸ τῶν ιβ΄ ἀποστ. κριθήσεται πᾶσα ἡ οἰκουμένη. D.

Now it seems at once obvious that the reading of *A* may be an instance of omission by homoeoteleuton. An ancestor of *A* might have had

κριθήσονται ὑπὸ τῶν δώδεκα [ἀποστ. αἱ δώδεκα] φυλαί.

At some stage in the transmission the words which I have placed in brackets dropped out and the next scribe altered the senseless ὑπὸ τῶν δώδεκα φυλαί into—φυλῶν. This gives the reading of *A*.

On the other hand, all the remaining MSS agree in placing the verb (κριθήσονται) between ἀποστ. and φυλαί. We are justified in regarding that as its proper place. In that case it disappeared along with the bracketed words from the supposed ancestor of *A*. How came the scribe of *A* to replace it unquestioningly while he allowed the astounding statement about the twelve tribes to stand? Another matter must be remembered, that *A* is easily first in excellence of our MSS.

54   THE TESTAMENT OF ABRAHAM.

But is the reading of *A* quite out of the question on internal grounds? It seems to me not so. For first, the mention of the twelve Apostles introduces an anachronism into the story such as our writer is not elsewhere guilty of. That Abraham should be supposed to know who the twelve tribes of Israel were, is no great demand on our faith. But this allusion to the Apostles has no parallel in the rest of the book. Secondly, the idea of the twelve tribes judging the world would be, I believe, no unfamiliar one to the mind of many Jewish Christians. What would the simple reader of the Apocalypse of S. John gather from that book as to the position of Israel in the future? Are not twelve thousand of each tribe sealed? Do they not dwell on Mount Sion with the Lamb? Are not the "nations" and the "kings of the earth" tributaries to them when the New Jerusalem is established upon earth? The belief that Israel is to rule over the Gentiles is well known and wide-spread. That the Apostles to a certain extent stood for or represented the twelve tribes in the minds of Jewish Christians is no doubt probable. But yet, in the view of the texts already quoted from the Gospels of SS. Matthew and Luke, the interpolation of the Apostles in the case before us would be most obvious and inviting. And to the belief that the mention of them is an interpolation I very strongly incline. The fact that the passage has quite disappeared in B and Ar. seems to me to indicate that their common ancestor has here been maltreating his original because there was something heterodox which had to be got rid of.

But I suspect that further interpolation has taken place in this part of A. In § XII., where the scene is laid before us, we are told shortly the functions of the various personages. The angels on the right and left, it is said, are the recorders of good and evil deeds; the angel with the balance weighs souls; the angel with the fire tests souls. In § XIII. we have first the explanation of Abel and the statement about the triple judgment, all of which is new; and thereon follows a second edition of the explanation of the four angels. The two recording angels are described again as such, in identical terms. Then we read that the angel with the balance is Dokiel, who weighs deeds (not souls), and that the angel with the fire is Puruel, who tests deeds (not souls). Now there is more than one suspicious feature in this passage. First, the angels have punning names, Dokiel from δοκιμάζω, Puruel from πῦρ: secondly, their description is inconsistent with the one previously given: thirdly, there are two most literal quotations from the N. T. close together, one from Rev. xiv. 18, the other from 1 Cor. iii. 15: fourthly, the paragraph from οἱ δὲ δύο ἄγγελοι (p. 92, l. 24) to δοκιμάζονται (p. 93, l. 18) is quite superfluous, though the removal would necessitate the removal of part of Abraham's question at the beginning of § XIII. Some at least of these reasons merit consideration. I do not lay much stress on the matter, but if any part of the judgment scene is non-original, I think it is this.

To conclude: my own deduction from the facts and theories stated in this Introduction is that the Testament was originally put together in the second century by a Jewish Christian: that for the narrative portions he employed existing Jewish legends, and for the apocalyptic, he drew largely on his own imagination. A parallel to this mode of composition is ready to our hand in the Ascension of Isaiah, where the groundwork of the portion which relates the Martyrdom is no doubt Jewish, while the "Vision," as well as other smaller portions of the book, is as clearly Christian. The original compilation was re-edited perhaps in the IXth or Xth century by two different people, and the result of their labours is before us, one being responsible for Recension A, the other for the common original of Recension B and the Arabic Version.

Thanatos; and the Angelology and Demonology of the Testament of Abraham.

Two principal figures from the spiritual world appear in our book, Michael and Thanatos. The functions of the first may be very shortly dismissed. The story of his visit in human form to Abraham, modelled originally perhaps on Gen. xviii., finds its closest parallel in the book of Tobit, to which, be it noted in passing, some modern critics assign an Egyptian origin. In that book, Raphael accompanies the young Tobias on his journey unrecognised, and, when he finally reveals his identity, tells his hosts that during his sojourn with them he had only eaten and drunk in appearance (cf. § v. of the Testament). It is, of course, a mark of God's special favour to Abraham that Michael and not Death is sent in the first instance to take his soul. The figure of Death in our book is far more unusual and striking. Recension B and the Arabic Version introduce him twice, once in the Apocalyptic section where he appears as an angel, and again at the end of the book. In Recension A he figures only in the latter place. This first and incidental mention in B and Ar. I am inclined to regard as an interpolation. It is pointless and abrupt, and the description is inconsistent with what follows. Death, as he appears in the celestial regions, is not distinguishable, it would seem, from other angels, whereas later on in the book, he has to be disguised as an angel before he can approach Abraham. Moreover B and Ar. have, as has been seen (p. 48), dealt most freely with the original document just at this point. But, genuine or not genuine, this first reference to Death is not in any way remarkable. It is his final appearance which throws light on our author's views of him. And they may be shortly stated in these terms. Death is not a good angel; when summoned to appear before God he trembles and quakes. His natural form is a hideous one. When he approaches the righteous this form is modified and becomes beautiful in proportion to the righteousness of the dying man; and in like manner his terrors are intensified by the wickedness of the sinner whose soul he is taking. His natural hideous form is described at length by our writer. The groundwork appears to be the dragon or serpent, with seven heads, which stands for the seven ages of the world, and upon this are heaped all the characteristics of the various violent deaths by which men perish, so that the picture presented to us is that of a constantly changing Protean figure, turning from serpent to wild beast, and again into fire, water, sword, poison-cup, and so forth.

Now, what origin can we most plausibly assign to this tremendous apparition? It is not classical. The winged Thanatos of Greek art and literature, of whom we read in the Alcestis and whom we occasionally see in vase-paintings, has nothing monstrous about him save his wings. The Charon of the Etruscan tomb-paintings is little more than a coarser and more terrific edition of the Greek Death. He too is winged, and in addition is armed with a hammer, and his countenance is frightful; but this is not the monstrous composite form of which we are in search. Lastly, the skeleton, which appears in Graeco-Roman art, takes us no further in the desired direction.

Next, the figure is not of Jewish invention. Only one personage, to my knowledge, at all resembles it. This is the demon Bedargon (Eisenmenger, II. 436), of whom it is said in the *Little Jalkut Rubeni* 116, that he is a hand-breadth broad and has fifty heads and fifty-six hearts. If he strikes a man, the man dies, and if a man strikes him, he dies. This however is an isolated and probably very late fiction. The Jewish Angel of Death has no monstrous characteristics.

But in certain Egyptian Apocrypha we do find resemblances to our Thanatos which are more or less striking. For example, in the *History of Joseph the Carpenter*. The Sahidic version of this (translated by Zoëga and Dulaurier) is fuller than the Arabic. Other Coptic versions may be found in Lagarde's *Aegyptiaca* and Revillout's *Apocryphes Coptes du N. T.* Zoëga and Dulaurier, quoted by Tischendorf in c. xxi., render as follows, "Then I looked to the direction of the southern gate, and saw Death accompanied by Hell as his counsellor, and the Devil, the deceiver from the beginning, and a multitude of monstrous 'Decani' clothed with fire and breathing forth sulphur and flames from their mouths. ...My father Joseph...saw that they were terrible, as when excited by anger and fury against a soul which has just left its body, especially if it be that of a sinner wherein they have found the mark of their own seal." Jesus advanced and routed these spectres, and Death fled and hid behind the door. In the passage corresponding to c. xxiii. Jesus addresses Death thus : "'O thou that comest from the south, enter in and do that which my Father hath commanded thee; but keep Joseph as the apple of thine eyes; for he is my father according to the flesh.' Then Abbaton (=Abaddon) entered in and took the soul of my father Joseph and parted it from the body." Then, as in our book, Michael and Gabriel wrap the soul in a silken cloth and escort it to the heavens.

Again, in the Coptic narrative of the Assumption of the Virgin attributed to S. Evodius (Revillout, op. cit. p. 75—112), we find very much the same ideas. There is, however, no elaborate description of Death. The Apostles are bidden by our Lord to leave the room lest they should see the terrible figure, and as it seems the mere sight of him causes the Virgin's death. She also speaks of his many μορφαί (p. 96).

Some spiritual beings of composite form also appear in the later pages of the *Pistis Sophia*, and noticeably the seven-headed serpent (Lat. transl. p. 99). It is easily intelligible that Egypt should be the quarter from which most of the monstrous shapes of the kind we are discussing made their way into Christian mythology. We can see the tendency plainly enough in art. The country which produced the forms of Thoth and Anubis produced also the Gnostic 'grylli.' In view of the parallels cited from Egyptian Apocrypha, I regard it as in the highest degree probable that Egypt is responsible for the production of the Testament of Abraham, and therefore for the representation of Death which is a prominent feature in it. But in that representation it is possible to recognise another element, the Jewish. The Angel of Death in Jewish mythology, Samael, occupies a very similar position to that of Thanatos in our book. He is an adversary of the race of men, and is practically identified in most cases with Satan. He first brought sin into the world, and delights in inflicting death, the consequence of sin. Yet he is God's minister in this, and is uniformly spoken of as an angel, though an angel hostile to the human race. It may be noted that his name, Samael, which is usually said to mean the 'poison of God,' is well represented in our book by the recurring expression τὸ πικρὸν ποτήριον τοῦ θανάτου.

Of other angels or demons little needs to be said. Of hostile angels we have the recorder of evil and the fiery angels who drive souls; of others the angels Dokiel and Puruel and the recorder of good deeds. Of devils properly so called we hear nothing. This last named feature to my mind is a mark of early date.

The Legend of the Speaking Tree (A § III. B § III.).

This story will be noticed at once as being the most *bizarre* and characteristic episode in the narrative portion of the Testament of Abraham. It will be remembered that the Editor of this series has already made use of it to elucidate and confirm his convincing substitution in the *Passion of S. Perpetua* (c. XI. p. 78), of 'canebant' for 'cadebant' or 'ardebant' of the MSS. The passage to which this emendation applies is in the vision of Saturus, and is a description of the trees in Paradise. The words in question must be quoted here; 'factum est nobis spatium grande, quod tale fuit quasi uiridarium, arbores habens rosae et omne genus flores: altitudo arborum erat in modum cypressi, quarum folia canebant sine cessatione.'

By way of illustration[1], Mr Robinson quotes (Introd. p. 38) the following passages from various sources; (1) a Vision in the History of Barlaam and Josaphat (Boissonade, p. 280) where it is said of the trees of Paradise, τά τε φύλλα τῶν δένδρων λιγυρὸν ὑπήχει αὔρᾳ τινὶ λεπτοτάτῃ: (2) parallels from the Old Testament 1 Chr. xvi. 33, 'Then shall all the trees of the wood sing out at the presence of the Lord': Is. xxxv. 1, 2, 'The desert shall rejoice and blossom as the rose; it shall blossom abundantly, and rejoice even with joy and singing': Is. xliv. 23, 'Break forth into singing, ye mountains, O forest, and every tree therein': (3) the passage under consideration: (4) a phrase from the prayer of Jeremiah in the 'Rest of the words of Baruch' (c. IX., Rendel Harris, p. 62), ηὔξατο εὐχὴν, λέγων· "Ἅγιος, ἅγιος, ἅγιος· τὸ θυμίαμα τῶν δένδρων τῶν ζώντων. The phrase 'sine cessatione' is later on coupled with the *Ter Sanctus*, where it plainly refers to the singing: and the Editor's note on the text gives liturgical parallels. The general drift of Mr Robinson's remarks in this place is to shew that the trees in Paradise were believed to be singing a continual

[1] Mr Robinson has called my attention to the following comment of Primasius on Rev. xxii. 3. In speaking of the leaves of the Tree of Life, he says 'recte folia perpetuae laudis intelligitur cantus.' And some light is thrown on the phrase 'perpetua laus' by a previous comment, which says in reference to the *Trisagion*, 'manente intellectualis creaturae perpetua in coelestibus laude.' The references are Migne *P. L.* LXVIII. 813 D, 930 A.

hymn of praise. The passage from the Testament of Abraham is only incidentally useful. The words which the tree utters begin with the triple "Ἅγιος, and the tree itself resembles those seen by the martyr Saturus in Paradise inasmuch as it is a cypress, and they grew 'in modum cypressi.'

It is desirable to throw more light on this passage in our book: and, with that end in view, we ought first to try and realise what is the exact meaning of the incident; and next we should try and collect parallels to it.

The exact meaning of the episode is, it must be confessed, rather difficult to ascertain: the main lines are plain enough. The tree, which is in Recension A a cypress, and in Recension B an ἐρηκινός, ἐρυκινός, or τρέκινος (probably connected with ἐρείκη, a tamarisk; in Ar. the tree is a tamarisk), utters words, prefaced by "Ἅγιος, and referring obscurely to Abraham's approaching departure to God, or in Recension B, to the fulfilment of Michael's errand: in either case the import of the words is the same; they refer to Abraham's death. Why the tree had 300 branches (as in B), or what is the exact import of the sentence uttered by it in A, it is not so easy to see; but some of the obscurity of the incident must, I think, be ascribed to rough handling by redactors. Parallels to the story are not, so far as I can discover, very abundant. In classical literature we have the oaks of Dodona regarded as the source of oracles. It was from one of these oaks that the branch was cut, which was fixed in the stem of the ship Argo, and gave advice to the Minyae in more than one emergency; e.g. Orph. *Argonautica*, 1160.

ἐκ δ' ἄρα κοίλης
νηὸς ἐπιβρομέουσα Τομαριὰς ἔκλαγε φηγός,
ἥν ποθ' ὑπ' Ἀργῴησι τομαῖς ἡρμόσσατο Παλλάς·
ὧδε δ' ἔφη, θάμβος δὲ περὶ φρένας ἵκετο πάντας.

In the later literature of the Greek world we meet a very striking parallel, as I think, to our story. A famous episode in the Romances of King Alexander relates how he came to Prasiaca where was a sanctuary of the Sun and Moon, and how there were there two trees, one dedicated to each luminary, a male tree for the Sun and a female tree for the Moon. They both spoke with human voices, the former at sunset, the latter at moon-set. Alexander asked them what fate was in store for him, and the tree of the sun made answer that he would be poisoned, and that of the moon, that he would die at Babylon. The earliest source for this story is the Greek Romance of Alexander, ascribed to Callisthenes, his companion, and probably written about A.D. 200. Now Pseudo-Callisthenes (III. 17 ed. Müller) states that the trees of the Sun and Moon were '$\pi\alpha\rho\alpha\pi\lambda\eta\sigma\iota\alpha$ $\kappa\upsilon\pi\alpha\rho\iota\sigma\sigma\text{οις}$.' This phrase is a striking reminder of the 'in modum cypressi' of Saturus' vision. The story is then, that trees resembling cypresses prophesied the death of Alexander: and this story originated at a date sufficiently late to admit easily of contamination from Jewish or Christian mythology.

What meaning can be attached to this coincidence? I believe that the explanation is to be sought in the fact that the cypress was for some reason considered to have been one of the special trees of Paradise[1]. Whether because of the 'incorruptible' nature of its wood, or the preserving properties of the oil derived from it, or the pronounced upward growth of its branches, or for some other reason, I should not care to decide; but such seems to have been the belief. For instance, the western legends of the Cross of Christ uniformly represent the wood of which it was made as having come from Paradise: and one of the trees specified is always the cypress. So again in the Cross-legend as given in a Paris MS of Michael Glycas (cited by Fabric. *Cod. Rend. V. T.* I. p. 428), cypress, pine, and cedar are the three trees which Lot was commissioned by Abraham to fetch from the Nile and to plant by the Jordan. These were afterwards made into the Cross. There is, further, distinct evidence to shew that among the Persians, at any rate, the cypress was specially associated with Paradise. Col. Yule (*Book of Ser Marco Polo*, I. 135), in the course of discussion concerning the *Arbre Sec* or *Arbre Sol* of mediaeval romance, has the following paragraph.

"It will be observed that the letter ascribed to Alexander describes the two oracular trees as resembling two cypress-trees. As such the trees of the Sun and Moon are represented on several

[1] On the Assyrian monuments the Tree of Life almost always resembles the cypress in form.

extant ancient medals, *e.g.* on two struck at Perga in Pamphylia in the time of Aurelian. And Eastern story tells us of two vast cypress-trees, sacred among the Magians, which grew in Khorasan one at Kashmar, near Turshiz, and the other at Farmad near Taz, and which were said to have risen from shoots that Zoroaster brought down from Paradise. The former of these was sacrilegiously cut down by the order of the Khalif Motawakkil, in the 9th century. The trunk was despatched to Baghdad on rollers at a vast expense, whilst the branches alone formed a load for 1300 camels. The night that the convoy reached within one stage of the palace, the Khalif was cut in pieces by his own guards. This tree was said to be 1450 years old, and to measure $53\frac{3}{4}$ cubits in girth......The plane, as well as the cypress, was one of the distinctive trees of the Magian Paradise[1]."

These sentences go far towards establishing the theory that the cypress was in Eastern popular belief a specially celestial tree. It may be suggested, in connexion with them, that the enormous size of the sacred cypress here described, throws some light upon the '300 branches' of the speaking tree in Recension B.

That the trees of Paradise are continually singing seems to be a Mohammedan belief. In the *résumé* of Mohammedan descriptions of Heaven which Sale gives in his Preliminary Discourse to the Koran (section IV.) this is mentioned; 'even the trees themselves will celebrate the divine praises with a harmony exceeding whatever mortals have heard.' In Wolff's *Muhammedanische Eschatologie* (p. 197) this is reported as a tradition of Ali, and therefore probably of Persian origin, according to Professor Robertson Smith. The voice of these trees is not an articulate one.

Not to be omitted in this connexion are the traditions which represent the trees of Eden as being able to speak. The treatise *Aboth d. R. Nathan* (c. i), edited by Dr S. Schechter, to whose kindness I owe this reference, says that when the serpent was about to touch the Tree of Knowledge, in order to prove that

---

[1] The source of this legend appears to be Firdosi, or Vullers' *Fragmente über die Religion Zoroasters*, 71, 113. At least this last is the book quoted by Spiegel *Erânische Alterthumskunde*, I. 703; who gives the same legend with a few additional details. This reference I owe to the kindness of Professor Robertson Smith.

THE SPEAKING TREE.

God's prohibition was unnecessary, the Tree spoke and said, 'Wicked one, touch me not,' at the same time quoting a verse of the 36th Psalm, 'Let not the foot of pride come against me, and let not the hand of the ungodly cast me down.' Again, a Mohammedan legend quoted by Weil (*Biblische Legende d. Muselm.* 19—28) represents the tree Talh (the *mauz*, or the acacia) as crying out against Adam and Eve when they were trying to hide themselves from God in the garden.

The different passages here quoted seem to me to establish the existence of certain beliefs in the East. (*a*) The cypress is a distinctive tree of Paradise. (*b*) Certain cypresses gave oracles, and in one instance prophesied approaching death. (*c*) The trees of Paradise praise God and sometimes speak with human voices. And these beliefs are united in the story before us.

In conclusion, I must notice one or two other instances of speaking trees.

Once again we find such a phenomenon in a legend of Patriarchal times. In the unedited Ethiopic treatise, the 'Book of the Mysteries of Heaven and Earth' by Abba Bahayla Mikhael, which in the 17th century was mistaken for the Book of Enoch, and transcribed by Michael Vansleb, there is mention of the wanderings of Joseph, who, while going to his brethren in Dothan, lost his way. A tree spoke to him and warned him of the plot against his life. (Zotenberg, *Cat. MSS. Éth. Paris*, p. 138.) The function of the tree here is rather like that of the speaking cypress, but until the treatise is better known, we cannot settle whether there has been borrowing from the Testament of Abraham.

Again, in the Targum Sheni on Esther[1], to which Dr Schechter has referred me, a number of trees are made to speak and give their reasons why Haman should not be hanged upon them. Here however we find ourselves nearing the region of poetry. There is no popular belief in the speech of trees implied: the proper parallels to such a passage are Jotham's parable in Judg. vii. and the parable of king Jehoahaz in 2 K. xiv. 9.

It has not been my aim to make any exhaustive list of passages which speak of 'tongues in trees'; these notes are merely intended

---

[1] See the English translation in Clark's *Foreign Theological Library, Comm. on Esther*, by Dr P. Cassel, *Appendix*, p. 336.

to throw light on one particular legend; and in this I hope I have succeeded.

Abraham's unwillingness to die.

This feature, so prominently present throughout Recension A of the Testament, is, very noticeably, quite absent from B and the Arabic. Are we here dealing with an addition on the part of A, or an omission on the part of B? The concurrence of the Arabic with B is not, to my mind, a matter of importance; for I have already adopted the view that the Arabic and B have a common ancestor.

I believe the trait to be original. The omission of it is due, as I think, to motives of reverence. It was thought derogatory to the character of Abraham that he should exhibit an unmanly fear of death. In at least one other place (see p. 44) B is found to have substituted a patch from the Apocalypse of Paul for a detail which seems grotesque and irreverent. It might indeed be argued with some plausibility that the theme of the fear of death is one which very late writers have dwelt upon with relish. The proofs of this will be adduced: but the range of documents which introduce this motive seems to me too considerable to allow of the supposition that in our book the trait is not original. As usual, the citation of parallel instances will form the staple of what I have to say on the subject. To this I will proceed at once.

I find similar episodes in the following documents:

1. *Historia Josephi Fabri Lignarii,* ed. Tischendorf, *Evang. Apocr.* 122.

2. *Apocalypsis Esdrae,* ed. Tischendorf, *Apoc. Apocr.* 24.

3. *Homilia Sedrach* in Cod. Bodl. Misc. Gr. 56, saec xv. f. 92. See above, p. 32.

4. *De Vita et Morte Mosis libri III*, translated from Hebrew into Latin by Gilbert Gaulmyn of Moulins, and reprinted by Fabricius (separately), and by Gfrörer, *Prophetae veteres Pseudepigraphi,* 1840, p. 303.

Two of these three documents deal especially with the death of Moses. Other Hebrew forms of the same legend are to be found in Jellinek's *Beth-ha-Midrasch*. There is no doubt some connexion between these books and the Assumption of Moses.

5. A modern Greek ballad printed by Sakellarios, Κυπριακά, ed. 2, vol. II.

1. *Historia Josephi.* Joseph's fear of death appears most prominently in c. xiii., where he prays that Michael may assist him at his last hour.

'For great terror and bitter sadness come upon all bodies at the day of their death, whether they be male or female, tame or wild beasts, even all that creepeth upon the earth or flieth in the heaven: in a word, all creatures under heaven wherein is the breath of life are shaken with horror, with great fear and excessive weakness, when their souls depart from their bodies.'

In c. xvi. he pronounces woes upon all the parts of his body for their sins. 'Of a truth,' he adds, 'that same fearful hour is now upon me, which came to my father Jacob, when his soul departed from his body.' However, he does not, like Abraham, refuse to obey the decree of God.

2. *Apocalypsis Esdrae*, p. 31. τότε ἦλθεν φωνὴ πρός με· Δεῦρο τελεύτα, Ἐσδράμ, ἀγαπητέ μου· δὸς τὴν παρακαταθήκην. καὶ εἶπεν ὁ προφήτης· Καὶ πόθεν τὴν ψυχήν μου ἔχετε ἐξενεγκεῖν; καὶ εἶπον οἱ ἄγγελοι· Διὰ τοῦ στόματος ἔχομεν ἐκβαλεῖν αὐτήν. καὶ εἶπεν ὁ προφήτης· Στόμα πρὸς στόμα ἐλάλουν τοῦ θεοῦ, καὶ οὐκ ἐξέρχεται ἔνθεν. The dialogue goes on: Διὰ ῥινῶν σου... Esdras; Αἱ ῥῖνές μου ὠσφράνθησαν τὴν δόξαν τοῦ θεοῦ. Angels; Διὰ τῶν ὀφθαλμῶν σου... Esdras; Οἱ ὀφθαλμοί μου ἴδον τὰ ὀπίσθια τοῦ θεοῦ. Angels; Διὰ τὴν κορυφήν σου... Esdras; Μετὰ Μωσῆ καὶ ἐν τῷ ὄρει ἐπεριπάτησα, καὶ οὐκ ἐξέρχεται ἔνθεν. Angels; Διὰ τῶν ἀκρωνύχων σου... Esdras; Καὶ οἱ πόδες μου ἐν τῷ θυσιαστηρίῳ περιεπάτησαν. The angels return unsuccessful. The Son is sent. He says: Δὸς παρακαταθήκην ἣν παρεθέμην σοι· ὁ στέφανός σοι ἡτοίμασται. Esdras; Κύριε, ἐὰν ἄρῃς τὴν ψυχήν μου ἀπ' ἐμοῦ, τίς σοι λείψει δικάζεσθαι (= λοιπὸν δικάσεται) ὑπὲρ τοῦ γένους τῶν ἀνθρώπων; God says: Δεῦρο τελεύτα. Esdras weeps and says: Οἴμμοι, οἴμμοι, ὅτι ὑπὸ σκωλήκων μέλλω ἀναλίσκεσθαι. κλαύσατέ με, πάντες οἱ ἅγιοι καὶ δίκαιοι... ὅτι εἰς τὸ τρύβλιον τοῦ ᾅδου εἰσῆλθον, and so forth.

3. *Homilia Sedrach.* In addition to other points of connexion with the Testament, this book, as has been said, contains the episode of a refusal to die. It is introduced quite suddenly: καὶ εἶπεν ὁ θεὸς τὸν υἱὸν αὐτοῦ τὸν μονογενῆ· (so *Esdr.* p. 31) Ὕπαγε, λάβε τὴν ψυχὴν τοῦ ἠγαπημένου μου Σεδρὰχ, καὶ ἀποθοῦ αὐτὴν ἐν τῷ παραδείσῳ. λέγει ὁ μονογενὴς υἱὸς τὸν Σεδράχ· <Δός μοι τὴν παρακαταθήκην[1]> ἣν παρέθετο ὁ πατὴρ ἡμῶν ἐν τῇ κοιλίᾳ τῆς μητρός σου ἐν τῷ ἁγίῳ σου σκηνώματι ἐκ βρέφους. λέγει Σεδράχ· Οὐ δίδωμί σοι τὴν ψυχήν μου. λέγει αὐτὸν ὁ θεός· Καὶ διὰ τί ἀπεστάλην ἐγὼ καὶ ἦλθον ὧδε, σὺ δέ μοι προφασίζεις; ἐγὼ γὰρ ἠγγέλθην παρὰ τοῦ πατρός μου μὴ ἀναισχύντως λάβω τὴν ψυχήν σου· εἰ <δὲ> μὴ, δός μοι τὴν ποθεινωτάτην ψυχήν σου. καὶ εἶπεν Σεδρὰχ τὸν θεόν· Καὶ πόθεν μέλλεις λαβεῖν τὴν ψυχήν μου, καὶ ἐκ ποίου μέλους; καὶ λέγει αὐτὸν ὁ θεός· Ἡ ψυχή σου οὐκ οἶδας ὅτι χορηγεῖται ἐν μέσῳ τῶν πνευμόνων σου κ.τ.λ.... καὶ οἵαν ὥραν μέλλει ἐξέρχεσθαι, ἀρχὴν σπάρναται καὶ συνάζεται ἀπὸ τῶν ἀκρωνύχων καὶ ἀπὸ πάντων μελῶν, καὶ ἔστι μεγάλη ἀνάγκη τοῦ χωρισθῆναι ἀπὸ τοῦ σώματος καὶ ἀποσπασθῆναι τῆς καρδίας. Then Sedrach utters a lamentation over the members of his body. As will be noticed, his question whence the soul is to be taken is also that of Esdras; but it is not answered. Some of the conversation here quoted suggests that the Son was not the original *dramatis persona.* ὁ θεὸς is far less suitable than ὁ θάνατος. But the whole thing is so wretched a patchwork that nothing is too bad to be original.

4. *De Vita et Morte Mosis.* Of these three tracts the *Vita Mosis* contains nothing to the purpose; the other two, *De Morte Mosis,* deal almost entirely with the unwillingness of the prophet to submit to God's decree.

In the first tract, *de Morte,* the following passages seem to be to the point;

(*a*) Gfrörer, p. 318. Igitur cum Mosem mori oportuit, Deus illum sic allocutus est: Appropinquauerunt dies tui ad moriendum. cui Moses: Domine, post tot susceptos labores mihi mortem nuntias: omnino ego uiuam.

(*b*) p. 322. Moses says: Sed quid homines dicent? illi *pedes,* qui coelos calcarunt, *manus* quae legem susceperunt, *os* quod Dei

---
[1] Supplied from *Esdr.* p. 31.

audire et reddere uoces meruit, misericordiam consequi non poterit; quanto magis aliis difficilem.

(c) p. 331. Tunc uero Deus Samaeli mortem Mosis mandauit; ille laetissimus animo ad saeuitiam obfirmato, ensem accinctus, et irarum plenus ad eum contendit... *Samael*. Venit tibi summa dies, da mihi animam tuam. *Moses*. Quis te huc misit? *Sam*. Qui orbem creauit et animas, quas omnes potestati meae ab orbe condito tradidit. Samael returns unsuccessful and is sent again: Moses smites him with his rod and he flees a second time. God eventually takes away the soul of Moses with a kiss.

In the second recension of the story, which differs from the first mainly by its greater wealth of comment on the narrative, we have passages essentially the same as the two last: p. 359, Respondit Deus (Samaeli): Omnes isti similes Mosis non fuerunt; sed quomodo animam eius auferes? an per *faciem*? illa mihi in os locuta est: *Et locutus est Deus ad Mosem a facie in faciem*: an per *manus*? illae leges acceperunt; an per *pedes*? hi caliginem qua obductus sum calcauerunt et usque ad me peruenerunt: *Accessit Moses ad caliginem in qua erat Deus*. nihil in omnia eius membra potes. *Samael*. Permitte tamen ut animam eius auferam. *Deus*. Aufer. Then follows the passage resembling (c).

Before I quote the last authority on my list, it seems proper to draw attention to the extreme similarity which exists between these passages of the Moses-legend and the Apocalypses of Esdras and Sedrach. The reader may have noticed that the passage quoted from Esdras on p. 65 is couched in language which is really only appropriate to Moses. Esdras asserts that he has spoken face to face with God, that he has inhaled the perfume of His glory, that he has seen His hinder parts, and has walked in 'the mount.' The words $\mu\epsilon\tau\grave{a}$ $M\omega\sigma\hat{\eta}$ in this clause are a clumsy attempt at verisimilitude.

Again, Esdras asks who will be left to intercede for men if he is taken: Moses repeatedly alludes, in both recensions of the legend, to his intercession for Israel. Further, Moses pronounces a woe against various parts of his body: (p. 330) Vae manibus meis, quae fructus terrae melle et lacte fluentis non decerpent, et palato, quod non gustabit. Cf. p. 357. A similar lamentation

5—2

expanded to a great length, occurs in Sedrach, as well as in *Hist. Josephi*, xvi.

Compare, again, the enumeration of the blessings in store for Moses (pp. 324, 328) with the phrase, which occurs more than once in Esdras, ὁ στέφανός σοι ἡτοίμασται.

It appears probable to me that both Esdras, Sedrach, and the Moses-legend draw from a common source here; and this source I think was most likely the Assumption of Moses. No other ancient book, or certainly none whose name has survived, treated in detail of the last moments of Moses; and that the Assumption of Moses existed down to a very late date is plain, e.g., from Sixtus Senensis (ap. Fabric. *Cod. Pseud. V. T.* II. 128): possibly it may be extant even now in Slavonic[1].

In the Mohammedan mythology we find an episode resembling that in the Moses and Ezra legends, where the soul refuses to make its exit by the several parts of the body on the ground of their being sanctified in different ways. Wolff, *Muhamm. Eschat.* 30, "When God wishes to summon the soul of a man, the Death-angel comes to his mouth in order to take the soul thence. The praise of God issues from his mouth and says: 'Thou hast no path by way of me for from hence was God praised'... The angel returns to God and reports it. God says, 'Take the soul from another part.' He comes to the hand. Here he is met by the good deeds; and so at the feet; these say, 'We have visited the sick.' The ear says, 'I have hearkened to the Koran.' The eye, 'I have read the scriptures.' God bids the angel write His name on his hand and show it to the man, and the soul leaps forth at sight of the name, and parts without bitterness." This is understood to happen generally in the case of believers, and is not the account of an incident which happened to one particular person. It seems likely that the Mohammedan tradition is here dependent upon Jewish sources.

5. The ballad in question is a Cypriote one (Sakellarios, Κυπριακά, ed. 2, vol. II., p. 29). It is in the form of an acrostic, a dialogue between a man and Χάρος or Death: the title is Ἄσμα τὸ Ἀλφάβητον τοῦ Χάρου.

[1] See *Jahrb. f. Prot. Theol.*, Dec. 1891, No. 14 in Kozak's list of Slavonic Apocrypha.

After an invocatory prayer, the dialogue begins.

In l. 36 the man complains of his sufferings (cf. Abr. A § xx. p. 103).

βάρος πολλύ μ' ἐφόρτωσες, χάροντα, 's τὸ κεφάλι,
καὶ τὴν καργιάν μου κέντησες κὴ ἔχω μεάλην ζάλην.

l. 65. Death says he has the balance of mercy in his hand, wherewith he will weigh the soul.

Ζύϊν (ζυγίον) βαστῶ 's τὸ χέριν μου τῆς ἐλεημοσύνης
γιὰ (διὰ) νὰ ζυάσω τί 'καμες κὴ ἐσοὺ νὰ μὲν (μὴ) 'πομείνης.

In l. 99 the man invokes Michael: 'Michael is writing your sentence.' In l. 116 Death says (cf. Abr. A § xx. p. 103), ὁ κύριος ἐπρόσταξε 'πίσω νὰ μὲν σ' ἀφήσω. Many other remonstrances and prayers for a little respite follow, and constitute the bulk of the poem. But finally, in l. 173, we read

ὁ ἄγγελος μὲ τὴν ψυχὴν 's τοὺς οὐρανοὺς ἐπῆεν,
κὴ ἐππέσαν προσκυνήσασι Χριστόν μας τὸν σωτῆρα.
ὁ δικαιότατος κριτὴς ὥρισε νὰ τὴν βάλουν
's τὸν τόπον τῆς ἀμανατῶν καὶ πεὸν νὰ μὲν την 'βκάλουν.

'The angel went to heaven with the soul and they fell and worshipped Christ our Saviour. The most just judge ordained that they should put the soul into its place immediately, and remove it no more' until the last day. Cf. the conclusion of Abr. A. But we must refrain from going deeper into the mediaeval and modern literature of the subject. It would not be difficult to find parallels in some of the numerous dialogues between Soul and Body (cf. *Poems of Walter Mapes*, Cam. Soc.). The Dances of Death are founded on the same idea, and so are many old ballads, such as that of 'Death and the Lady' (Chappell's *Popular Music of the Olden Time*, I. 164). It will be understood, I hope, that in these citations of parallels I do not wish to imply that there is in every case a literary connexion with the Testament of Abraham. Such a connexion may very probably exist where the last moments of some individual prophet or saint are being narrated; but where the image is one of general application, I do not seek to press the resemblance. The theme of the fear of death is one which must of necessity occur to men of all nations and in all times. One particular way of treating it has been my subject in this short excursus.

The weighing of Souls.

The subject of the weighing of souls, or as it may be conveniently called, the ψυχοστασία, is one which comes before us in the Testament of Abraham. It is not the fact that such are weighed, actually; but one of the angels who is present at the judgment scene is represented as holding a balance in his hand; and is directed to weigh the righteous and evil acts of one soul in his balance. The subject is an interesting one. It was ably treated by M. Alfred Maury in some articles in the 1st volume of the *Revue Archéologique* (1844), pp. 235, 291; see also p. 647, and Vol. II. p. 707. (See also some remarks in *Archaeologia* XXIII. 315.) Dr Friedr. Wiegand, in his pamphlet *Der Erzengel Michael*, Stuttgart 1886, p. 38 sqq., gives Maury's chief results, and adds something to them. Both these writers dwell mainly on the iconographic side of the matter, on which line, interesting though it is, I do not propose to follow them very far. The point to which I wish to give prominence is that the Testament of Abraham is the first Apocalyptic document which brings the idea of the balance and the weighing of good and evil deeds before us in concrete form. In dealing with a conception of this nature we have usually two alternatives presented to us. We may take the idea to have originated in a metaphor and to have become solidified in the popular mind with a concrete belief, or we may suppose that the popular mind first figured this process of judgment to itself by means of a familiar image, and that subsequently more elevated intelligences etherealised the existing belief and treated it merely as a convenient means of expressing abstract truths. Thus the man who first said 'God weighs actions' may have believed that God actually took a pair of scales and weighed them, while subsequent writers treated the words as not literally true, but as conveying a true idea: on the other hand, the originator of the expression may have meant that our actions are known to God and would be judged by Him, while his hearers figured to themselves the existence of a heavenly balance, and a literal weighing of the good against the bad.

THE WEIGHING OF SOULS. 71

Now, as to the particular belief, the first traces of it are found in Egypt: and of Egyptian mythology it may be broadly said that instead of being a spiritual religion in course of decay, it is, as we know it, a savage religion in course of being spiritualised. Such, at least, seems to be the conclusion to which the students of to-day are coming. Probably then in Egypt, this belief arose from the almost inevitable comparison between the two processes of weighing and of judging. In the few passages in the Old Testament which imply the same thought, it is clearly shewn that no more than a metaphor is intended. In other words, the myth is becoming spiritualised. Among the passages alluded to are Job xxxi. 6, Dan. v. 27, Ps. lxii. 9, Prov. xvi. 2. Compare also 4 Esd. iii. 34, and vii. 59, in the first of which passages there is a more overt and less allusive use of the image. The rider on the black horse in Rev. vi. 5, to whom a pair of scales is given, cannot be brought into connexion with this cycle of ideas. He is merely the angel of famine, and carries the scales in token of the scarcity of food.

From the metaphorical language of the Bible we pass to the material ideas of later Apocalypses, and foremost among them stands this of Abraham. A doubtful allusion in the Apocalypse of Paul, for it is hardly more, occurs in that portion of Paul which shews connexion with Abraham. And up to the present I have failed to detect any clear description of the Psychostasy in the Apocalyptic literature proper, save one in a Coptic Apocalypse, of which Oscar von Lemm has given us some scanty particulars in his *Bruchstücke Sahid. Bibelübersetzung*, p. viii. (see also the *Proceedings of the Leyden Oriental Congress*, I. 143[1]).

The chief developments are to be found in isolated Visions of the Middle Ages: on these an excellent essay by Wagner in *Romanische Forschungen* may be consulted; some pertinent passages are quoted in Maury's articles. But in almost all the documents which relate to the matter, one remarkable difference from the presentation in Abraham is to be noticed. The later documents and monuments uniformly introduce the accusing Satan,

---

[1] He seems to have read a translation of it at the Oriental Congress in Leyden, but it has not been yet published. My attempts to obtain further light upon this book have not been crowned with success as yet.

as a party in the case; he generally tries by foul means to depress the scale in his favour.

In the Mohammedan mythology, as given in Wolff's *Muhamm. Eschatologie* 140, the weighing of souls is a process which takes place at the day of judgment. Each man has his sins recorded on forty-nine enormous rolls. In the case of a believer, a leaf no bigger than an ant's head, inscribed with the confession of faith, will outweigh all these. The tradition, which dwells chiefly upon the enormous size of the heavenly balance, purports to come from Ibn 'Abbâs.

Abraham's bosom: the Patriarchs in Paradise.

There is no mention of Abraham's bosom, save in the concluding lines of Recension A, which are most probably not in their original form. Yet in various parts of the book there are hints of the belief. For instance, it is said (B, IV.) '$\sigma\grave{v}$ $\gamma\grave{a}\rho$ $\dot{\epsilon}\xi$ $\dot{a}\rho\chi\hat{\eta}s$ $\dot{\epsilon}\pi o \acute{\iota}\eta\sigma as$ $a\grave{v}\tau\grave{o}v$ $\dot{\epsilon}\lambda\epsilon\epsilon\hat{\iota}v$ $\psi v\chi\grave{a}s$ $\pi\acute{a}v\tau\omega v$ $\dot{a}v\theta\rho\acute{\omega}\pi\omega v$.' This phrase has, I think, its bearing not only on the subsequent intercession of Abraham for sinners, but on the belief that in the next world Abraham would, like Adam, Abel, and Enoch, exercise a distinct function in regard to souls. Moreover the three occasions on which Abraham intercedes for others, namely for a soul under judgment, for the sinners whom he had killed, and for the 7000 servants who died, point in the same direction. The model on which they are drawn is obviously the intercession of Abraham for the Cities of the Plain in Gen. xviii., and this event no doubt had its share in shaping the belief that Abraham cared for righteous souls, and that they dwelt in 'Abraham's bosom.'

Now as to 'Abraham's bosom.' The manner of the mention of it in S. Luke (xvi.) implies the familiarity of the hearers with the idea: but I believe I am right in saying that the Jewish literature of early times throws but little light on the subject. Such writers as Lightfoot, Schoettgen, and Eisenmenger, cite instances of the occurrence of the phrase, but do not give any elaborate explanation of it: and indeed none such seems to be necessary. The passage quoted by most commentators from Josephus (4 Macc. xiii. 16) affords as good a key to the underlying thought as can be desired. There the Maccabean martyrs are represented as saying ' οὕτως παθόντας ἡμᾶς Ἀβραὰμ καὶ Ἰσαὰκ καὶ Ἰακὼβ ὑποδέξονται εἰς τοὺς κόλπους αὐτῶν, καὶ πάντες οἱ πατέρες ἐπαινέσουσιν.' And in the parable, Lazarus is received into Abraham's bosom as being a true son of Abraham, alike by descent and by character. We should guard against the interpretation assigned to the words by many, who interpret them as meaning that Lazarus sits with Abraham at the feast of Paradise, reclining on his bosom, much as S. John lay on our Lord's bosom at the Last Supper. No doubt the view referred to is due in part to the recollection of the words, ' they shall *sit down* with Abraham, and Isaac, and Jacob in the kingdom of heaven' (Matth. viii. 11).

Jewish views as to Abraham's position and functions in the other world are not without their bearing on this expression. According to the treatises of *Erubhin* (19 a) and *Bereshith Rabba* (c. 48) Abraham sits at the gate of Hell and suffers none to enter therein who has in any way proved worthy of his descent from the father of the faithful (Beer, *Leben Abrahams* 89). The position selected for Abraham recalls that of Adam in the Testament of Abraham, and his functions are not dissimilar to those implied in our Lord's Parable. For other not essentially different stories see Eisenmenger, II. 286, 340 etc.

In the very curious Vision of S. Barontus (of Pistoia, cir. 700), edited in the Bollandist Acta, March 25, on p. 570, we have an interesting reference to Abraham's bosom. "Ut autem uenimus inter Paradisum et infernum, uidi ibi uirum senem, pulcherrimum aspectu, habentem barbam prolixam, in alta sede quietum sedentem. Et ego ut uidi coepi ad eum inclinato capite caute interrogare quis esset ipse potens et tam magnificus uir. At illi conuersi ad eum dixerunt: Ipse est Abraham pater noster, et tu Frater oportet te semper Dominum rogare ut cum te a corpore iusserit migrare in sinu ipsius Abrahae te faciat quietum habitare."

In Christian Art 'Abraham's bosom' is not unfrequently represented in two connexions: (*a*) in early compositions illustrating the Last Judgment; e.g. on the West Portal of S. Trophime at Arles (xiith cent.), and on the North Portal of Rheims Cathedral (xiiith cent.); (*b*) in illustrations of the Parable of Dives and Lazarus; e.g. on the West Front of Lincoln Cathedral (xi—xiith cent.); in a window at Bourges in the North Choir aisle (xiiith cent.); and in a series of engravings by Martin Heemskerck (xvith cent.).

A certain amount of material is still to be collected, regarding the position of the Patriarchs after death. Very important, as shewing the intercessory functions of the Patriarchs, is a passage from the Coptic Apocalypse of Zephaniah.

Apoc. of Zeph. (ed. Stern, *Zeitschr. f. Aegypt. Sprache*, 1886, p. 121). A fragment begins with the end of a prayer for those in torment. It proceeds: 'And when I saw them, I spake to the angel which talked with me, and he answered; "These are Abraham, Isaac and Jacob. At a certain hour every day they come forth with this great Angel. He bloweth his trumpet toward Heaven, and there is an echo upon the earth. All the righteous hear the sound and come hither to the West, while they entreat the Lord Almighty daily for all them that are in these torments."'

Apoc. Pauli. There are two passages in this book which treat of the patriarchs in Paradise: a fact to which I have referred before as shewing the clumsiness of its compilation. I shall quote the passages from the inedited Latin version, for both are shortened in the Greek, and the second does not appear in the Syriac.

(*a*) Cf. § 27 in the Greek. "Iterum adsumpsit me et tulit me ad aquilonem ciuitatis et duxit me ubi erat flumen uini, et uidi illic Abraam, Hisaac, et Iacob, Lot et Iop et alios sanctos, et salutauerunt me: et interrogaui et dixi Quis est hic locus, domine? Respondit angelus et dixit mihi Omnes qui susceptores peregrinorum sunt, cum exierint de mundo, adorant primum dominum[1] deum et traduntur Michaelo et per hanc uiam inducuntur in ciuitatem; et omnes iusti salutant eum sicut filium et fratrem et dicunt ei Quoniam seruasti humanitatem et susceptionem peregrinorum, ueni, aereditatem abe in ciuitatem domini dei nostri: unusquisque iustus secundum proprium hactum accipiet in ciuitate bona dei."

Here is set forth the reward of φιλοξενία, which is, as I have said, the key-note of the first part of the Testament of Abraham.

(*b*) § 47 in Greek. Adhuc ea loquente uidi tres uenientes a

[1] See below, p. 126.

longe pulcros ualde speciae Christi, et imagines eorum fulgentes (et *or* sicut) angelos ipsorum, et interrogaui Qui sunt hii, domine ? Et dixit mihi Nescis eos ? Et dixi Nescio, domine. Et respondit Hii sunt patres populi Abraham, Hysaac, et Iacob. Et uenientes iuxta salutauerunt me et dixerunt Aue Paule dilectissime dei et hominum : beatus est qui uim sustinet propter dominum. Et respondit mihi Abraham (et) dixit Hic est filius meus Hysaac, et Iacob dilectissimus meus, et cognouimus dominum et secuti sumus eum : beati omnes qui crediderunt uerbo tuo ut possint hereditare regnum dei per laborem abrenunciacione et sanctificatione et humilitate et caritate et mansuetudine et recta fide ad dominum : et nos quoque abuimus deuocionem ad dominum quem tu praedicas testamento ut omnes (omni) anime credencium ei adsistamus et ministremus sicut fratres ministrant filiis suis.

speciae Christi recalls the description of Adam (A, XI.) ὁμοία τοῦ δεσπότου, which may be not independent of this. The obvious reason for the likeness of the Patriarchs to our Lord is that they were his ancestors.

patres populi, Gk. οἱ προπάτορες οἱ δίκαιοι.

After *dilectissime dei* there is a gap in the Greek extending to about eight lines of the Latin.

The concluding lines of the extract shew that the Patriarchs exercised protection over the souls of *believers*: a Christian adaptation of the old Jewish idea.

The *Acta Andreae et Matthiae* (Tisch. *Acta Apocr.* p. 145) contain an account of the temporary resurrection of the 'Three Patriarchs' from their graves at Mamre, when our Lord sent a stone Sphinx to call them in order to confute the Jewish Highpriests. In the same book, p. 147, the disciples of Andrew see a vision of Paradise, and the Three Patriarchs are there.

So again they appear with other saints in the fragmentary Coptic Apocalypse of Bartholomew (Tisch. *Apoc. Apocr.* xxv.) at a scene of the pardoning of Adam. And in S. John's Narrative of the Assumption (l. c. p. 111) they are seen by the Apostles.

Provenance of the Book.

The following reasons lead me to believe that our book was written in Egypt:

1. It is first mentioned by Origen. This, though worth noting, cannot be pressed.

2. There is a resemblance in the representation of Michael to the story of Raphael in the Book of Tobit, which is very probably of Egyptian origin.

3. The representation of Death agrees very closely with those found in the Egyptian Apocryphal books (see p. 57).

The same remark applies to

4. The conducting of Abraham round the creation (see p. 122).

5. The wrapping of Abraham's soul in a cloth by Michael (p. 57).

6. The idea of the weighing of souls is found in this book. It is a prominent feature in Egyptian mythology; and the only other Apocalypse belonging to the earlier literature in which it occurs is a Coptic one (see p. 71).

7. The idea of recording angels, prominent in this book, finds very close parallels (*a*) in the Egyptian Book of the Dead, where it is connected with the weighing of souls, (*b*) in the Coptic Apocalypse of Zephaniah (see p. 129).

8. It is the verdict of those who have examined the Arabic Version that this latter was probably made in Egypt.

Α.

ΔΙΑΘΗΚΗ ΑΒΡΑΑΜ.

I. Ἔζησεν Ἀβραὰμ τὸ μέτρον τῆς ζωῆς αὐτοῦ, ἔτη ἐννακόσια ἐνενήκοντα πέντε, πάντα δὲ τὰ ἔτη τῆς ζωῆς αὐτοῦ ζήσας ἐν ἡσυχίᾳ καὶ πραότητι καὶ δικαιοσύνῃ, πάνυ ὑπῆρχε φιλόξενος ὁ δίκαιος· πήξας γὰρ τὴν σκηνὴν αὐτοῦ
5 ἐν τετραοδίῳ τῆς δρυὸς τῆς Μαμβρῆ, τοὺς πάντας ὑπεδέχετο, πλουσίους καὶ πένητας, βασιλεῖς τε καὶ ἄρχοντας, ἀναπήρους καὶ ἀδυνάτους, φίλους καὶ ξένους, γείτονας καὶ παροδίτας, ἴσον ὑπεδέχετο ὁ ὅσιος καὶ πανίερος καὶ δίκαιος καὶ φιλόξενος Ἀβραάμ. ἔφθασεν δὲ καὶ ἐπὶ τοῦτον τὸ
10 κοινὸν καὶ ἀπαραίτητον τοῦ θανάτου πικρὸν ποτήριον, καὶ τὸ ἄδηλον τοῦ βίου πέρας. προσκαλεσάμενος τοίνυν ὁ δεσπότης θεὸς τὸν ἀρχάγγελον αὐτοῦ Μιχαὴλ εἶπεν πρὸς αὐτόν· Κάτελθε, Μιχαὴλ ἀρχιστράτηγε, πρὸς Ἀβραάμ, καὶ εἰπὲ αὐτὸν περὶ τοῦ θανάτου, ἵνα διατάξεται περὶ τῶν
15 πραγμάτων αὐτοῦ· ὅτι ηὐλόγησα αὐτὸν ὡς τοὺς ἀστέρας

ABCD
EFR

A=Par. Gr. 770. B=Cod. Hierosol. S. Sep. 66. C=Cod. Bodl. Canon. Gr. 19. D=Par. Gr. 1556. E=Cod. Vind. Theol. Gr. 237. F=Par. Gr. 1313. R=Roumanian Version.

Tit. Διαθ. τοῦ ὁσίου π̄ρ̄ς ἡμ. δικαίου πατριάρχου Ἀ. Διαλύων δὲ καὶ θανάτου πέραν, τὸ πῶς δεῖ ἕκαστος ἐτελεύτησεν εὐλ. A; Διήγησις καὶ διαθ. τοῦ δικ. καὶ πατριάρχου Ἀ. Δηλοῖ δὲ καὶ τὴν πεῖραν τοῦ θανάτου αὐτοῦ εὐλ. δεσπ. B; Ἡ διαθ. τοῦ ὁσ. π̄ρ̄ς ἡμ. καὶ δικ. Ἀ. δυαλύον δὲ καὶ τὴν τοῦ θαν. πειρ. εὐλ. C; λόγος ἐκ τοῦ βίου καὶ τῆς διαθ. τοῦ δικ. καὶ φιλοξένου Ἀ. D; Ἡ—θανάτου πόρον as C + τὸ πῶς δὴ ἕκαστος τελευτᾷ ἄνος. δεσπ. εὐλ. E; Διήγ. περὶ τῆς ζωῆς καὶ τοῦ θαν. τοῦ δικ. Ἀ., τὸ πόσ ἐδιετάχθη τῆς ζωῆς καὶ τῆ(ς) φυλοξενίας αὐτοῦ καὶ πὸς ἐδιελέγετο μετὰ τοῦ ἀγγέλου καὶ μετὰ τὸν θάνατον εὐλ. δ. F; for R cf. Introd.

2 ἐννακόσ.—πέντε] 999 years A; 95 F; 175 DER   10 ποτήριον] μυστήριον B   14, 15 ἵνα—πραγ.] om B

78   THE TESTAMENT OF ABRAHAM.

ABCD
EFR

τοῦ οὐρανοῦ, καὶ ὡς τὴν ἄμμον τὴν παρὰ τὸ χεῖλος τῆς
θαλάσσης· καὶ ἔστιν ἐν εὐπορίᾳ βίου πολλοῦ καὶ πραγμάτων πολλῶν, καὶ ὑπάρχει πλούσιος πάνυ· παρὰ πάντων
δὲ δίκαιος ἐν πάσῃ ἀγαθωσύνῃ, φιλόξενος καὶ φιλόστοργος
ἕως τέλους τῆς ζωῆς αὐτοῦ· σὺ δὲ, ἀρχάγγελε Μιχαὴλ, 5
ἄπελθε πρὸς τὸν Ἀβραὰμ, τὸν ἠγαπημένον μου φίλον, καὶ
ἀνάγγειλον αὐτῷ περὶ τοῦ θανάτου αὐτοῦ, καὶ πληροφό-
ρησον αὐτὸν ὅτι Μέλλεις ἐν τῷ καιρῷ τούτῳ ἐξέρχεσθαι
ἐκ τοῦ ματαίου κόσμου τούτου καὶ μέλλεις ἐκδημεῖν ἐκ τοῦ
σώματος καὶ πρὸς τὸν ἴδιον δεσπότην ἐλεύσῃ ἐν ἀγαθοῖς. 10
II.   ἐξελθὼν δὲ ὁ ἀρχιστράτηγος ἐκ προσώπου τοῦ
θεοῦ κατῆλθεν πρὸς τὸν Ἀβραὰμ ἐπὶ τὴν δρῦν τὴν
Μαμβρῆ, καὶ εὗρεν τὸν δίκαιον Ἀβραὰμ ἐπὶ τὴν χώραν
ἔγγιστα, ζεύγη βοῶν ἀροτριασμοῦ παρεδρεύοντα μετὰ τοὺς
υἱοὺς Μασὲκ καὶ ἑτέροις παισὶν τὸν ἀριθμὸν δώδεκα· 15
καὶ ἰδοὺ ὁ ἀρχιστράτηγος ἤρχετο πρὸς αὐτόν· ἰδὼν δὲ ὁ
Ἀβραὰμ τὸν ἀρχιστράτηγον Μιχαὴλ μηκόθεν ἐρχόμενον, δίκην στρατιώτου. εὐπρεπεστάτου, ἀναστὰς τοίνυν ὁ
Ἀβραὰμ ὑπήντησεν αὐτῷ καθότι καὶ ἔθος εἶχεν, τοῖς
ἐπιξένοις πᾶσιν προϋπαντῶν καὶ ὑποδεχόμενος· ὁ δὲ ἀρχι- 20
στράτηγος προχαιρετίσας αὐτὸν εἶπεν· Χαῖρε, τιμιώτατε
πάτερ, δικαία ψυχὴ ἐκλεκτὴ τοῦ θεοῦ, φίλε γνήσιε τοῦ
ἐπουρανίου. εἶπεν δὲ Ἀβραὰμ πρὸς τὸν ἀρχιστράτηγον·
Χαῖρε, τιμιώτατε στρατιῶτα, ἡλιόρατε καὶ πανευπρεπέ-
στατε ὑπὲρ πάντας τοὺς υἱοὺς τῶν ἀνθρώπων· καλῶς 25
ἥκεις· τούτου χάριν αἰτοῦμαι τῆς σῆς παρουσίας πόθεν
ἥκεν τὸ νέον τῆς ἡλικίας σου; δίδαξόν με τὸν σὸν ἱκέτην,
πόθεν καὶ ἐκ ποίας στρατιᾶς καὶ ἐκ ποίας ὁδοῦ παρα-
γέγονεν τὸ σὸν κάλλος; ὁ δὲ ἀρχιστράτηγος ἔφη· Ἐγὼ,
δίκαιε Ἀβραὰμ, ἀπὸ τῆς μεγάλης πόλεως ἔρχομαι· παρὰ 30
τοῦ μεγάλου βασιλέως ἀπεστάλην διαδοχὴν φίλου αὐτοῦ
γνησίου κομιζόμενος, ὅτι καὶ αὐτὸν ὁ βασιλεὺς προσκα-
λεῖται. καὶ ὁ Ἀβραὰμ εἶπεν· Δεῦρο, κύριέ μου, πορεύθητι

2 εὐπορίᾳ] ἐμπ. ACDEF   4 φιλόστοργος] φιλόχριστος A   17 μη-
κόθεν] ἀπὸ μακρόθεν CE   24 ἡλιόρατε—πανευπρ.] om CE   26 ἥκεις]
ἔοικας AE; ἔηκας C; ἥκας BDR (?)   27 ἥκεν] ἡκαινὴ B; αἵηκεν (-ας E) CE;
ἔοικεν A   31 διαδοχήν] διὰ δοχὴν C   32 κομιζόμ.] ἀποκομίζομαι AD;
ἐπικομίζομαι CE

RECENSION A.

μετ' ἐμοῦ ἕως τῆς χώρας μου. καὶ φησὶν ὁ ἀρχιστρά- ABCD
τηγος· Ἔρχομαι. ἀπελθόντες δὲ ἐν τῇ χώρᾳ τοῦ ἀροτρι- EFR
ασμοῦ ἐκαθέσθησαν πρὸς ὁμιλίαν. εἶπεν δὲ Ἀβραὰμ τοῖς
παισὶν αὐτοῦ τοῖς υἱοῖς Μασέκ· Ἀπέλθατε εἰς τὴν ἀγέλην
5 τῶν ἵππων καὶ ἐνέγκατε δύο ἵππους εὐμενεῖς καὶ ἡμέρους
δεδαμασμένους ὅπως ἐγκαθεσθῶμεν ἐγώ τε καὶ ὁ ἄνθρωπος
οὗτος ὁ ἐπίξενος. καὶ εἶπεν ὁ ἀρχιστράτηγος· Μὴ, κύριέ
μου Ἀβραάμ, μὴ ἐνέγκωσιν ἵππους, ὅτι ἀπέχομαι τούτου,
τοῦ μὴ καθίσαι ἐπὶ ζώου τετραπόδου ποτέ· μὴ γὰρ ὁ
10 ἐμὸς βασιλεὺς οὐκ ἦν πλούσιος ἐν ἐμπορίᾳ πολλῇ, ἔχων
ἐξουσίαν καὶ ἀνθρώποις καὶ κτήνεσιν παντοίοις; ἀλλ' ἐγὼ
ἀπέχομαι τούτου, τοῦ μὴ καθίσαι ἐπὶ ζώου τετραπόδου
ποτέ· ἀπέλθωμεν οὖν, δικαία ψυχή, πεζεύοντες ἕως τοῦ
οἴκου σου μετεωριζόμενοι. καὶ εἶπεν Ἀβραάμ· Ἀμὴν,
15 γένοιτο.

III. ἀπερχομένων δὲ αὐτῶν ἀπὸ τοῦ ἀγροῦ πρὸς τὸν
οἶκον αὐτοῦ, κατὰ τῆς ὁδοῦ ἐκείνης ἵστατο δένδρον κυπά-
ρισσος· καὶ κατὰ πρόσταξιν τοῦ θεοῦ ἐβόησεν τὸ δένδρον ἀν-
θρωπίνῃ φωνῇ, καὶ εἶπεν· Ἅγιος, ἅγιος, ἅγιος κύριος ὁ θεὸς
20 ὁ προσκαλούμενος αὐτὸν τοῖς ἀγαπῶσιν αὐτόν. ἔκρυψεν
δὲ Ἀβραὰμ τὸ μυστήριον, νομίσας ὅτι ὁ ἀρχιστράτηγος
τὴν φωνὴν τοῦ δένδρου οὐκ ἤκουσεν. ἐλθόντες δὲ πλησίον
τοῦ οἴκου ἐν τῇ αὐλῇ ἐκαθέσθησαν· καὶ ἰδὼν ὁ Ἰσαὰκ
τὴν πρόσωψιν τοῦ ἀγγέλου εἶπεν πρὸς Σάρραν τὴν
25 μητέρα αὐτοῦ· Κυρία μου μῆτερ, ἰδοὺ ὁ ἄνθρωπος ὁ καθε-
ζόμενος μετὰ τοῦ πατρός μου Ἀβραὰμ υἱός οὐκ ἔστιν ἀπὸ
τοῦ γένους τῶν κατοικούντων ἐπὶ τῆς γῆς. καὶ ἔδραμεν
Ἰσαάκ, καὶ προσεκύνησεν αὐτὸν καὶ προσέπεσεν τοῖς
ποσὶν τοῦ ἀσωμάτου· καὶ ὁ ἀσώματος ηὐλόγησεν αὐτὸν
30 καὶ εἶπεν· Χαρίσεταί σοι κύριος ὁ θεὸς τὴν ἐπαγγελίαν
αὐτοῦ ἣν ἐπηγγείλατο τῷ πατρί σου Ἀβραὰμ καὶ τῷ
σπέρματι αὐτοῦ, καὶ χαρίσεταί σοι καὶ τὴν τιμίαν εὐχὴν
τοῦ πατρός σου καὶ τῆς μητρός σου. εἶπεν δὲ Ἀβραὰμ
πρὸς Ἰσαὰκ τὸν υἱὸν αὐτοῦ· Τέκνον Ἰσαάκ, ἄντλησον ὕδωρ

4 ἀγέλην] ἀγωγὴν B   6 δεδαμασμ.] δεδεμένους B   8 ἀπέχομαι]
ἀπέσχομαι (ἀν- A) AB   9—13 μὴ γὰρ—ποτέ] om CDER   19, 20 κ̅ς̅ ὁ θ̅ς̅
ὁ προσκ.—ἀγ. αὐτόν] "The Lord God calls thee" R   20 αὐτὸν (pri.)]
ἑαυτὸν ACE, om B   22 ἐλθόντες] ἐλθὼν AB   28 αὐτὸν κ. προσέπ.] om B

ABCD EFR ἀπὸ τοῦ φρέατος καὶ ἔνεγκέ μοι ἐπὶ τῆς λεκάνης ἵνα νίψωμεν τοῦ ἀνθρώπου τούτου τοῦ ἐπιξένου τοὺς πόδας, ὅτι ἀπὸ μακρᾶς ὁδοῦ πρὸς ἡμᾶς ἐλθὼν ἐκοπίασεν. δραμὼν δὲ Ἰσαὰκ εἰς τὸ φρέαρ ἤντλησεν ὕδωρ ἐπὶ τῆς λεκάνης καὶ ἤνεγκεν πρὸς αὐτούς· προσελθὼν δὲ Ἀβραὰμ ἔνιψεν τοὺς πόδας τοῦ ἀρχιστρατήγου Μιχαήλ· ἐκινήθησαν δὲ τὰ σπλάγχνα τοῦ Ἀβραὰμ καὶ ἐδάκρυσεν ἐπὶ τὸν ξένον. ἰδὼν δὲ Ἰσαὰκ τὸν πατέρα αὐτοῦ κλαίοντα, ἔκλαυσεν καὶ αὐτός· ἰδὼν δὲ ὁ ἀρχιστράτηγος αὐτοὺς κλαίοντας συνεδάκρυσεν καὶ αὐτὸς μετ' αὐτῶν, καὶ ἔπιπτον τὰ δάκρυα τοῦ ἀρχιστρατήγου ἐπὶ τῆς λεκάνης εἰς τὸ ὕδωρ τοῦ νιπτῆρος, καὶ ἐγένοντο λίθοι πολύτιμοι· ἰδὼν δὲ ὁ Ἀβραὰμ τὸ θαῦμα καὶ ἐκπλαγεὶς ἔλαβεν τοὺς λίθους κρυφαίως καὶ ἔκρυψεν τὸ μυστήριον, μόνος ἔχων ἐν τῇ καρδίᾳ αὐτοῦ.

IV. εἶπεν δὲ Ἀβραὰμ πρὸς Ἰσαὰκ τὸν υἱὸν αὐτοῦ· Ἄπελθε, υἱέ μου ἀγαπητέ, εἰς τὸ ταμεῖον τοῦ τρικλίνου καὶ καλλώπισον αὐτό· στρῶσον δὲ ἡμῖν ἐκεῖ δύο κλινάρια, ἕνα ἐμὸν καὶ ἕνα τοῦ ἀνθρώπου τούτου τοῦ ἐπιξενισθέντος ἡμῖν σήμερον· ἑτοίμασον δὲ ἡμῖν ἐκεῖ δίφρον καὶ λυχνίαν καὶ τράπεζαν ἐν ἀφθονίᾳ παντὸς ἀγαθοῦ· καλλώπισον τὸ οἴκημα, τέκνον, καὶ ὑφάπλωσον σινδόνας καὶ πορφύραν καὶ βύσσον· θυμίασον πᾶν τίμιον καὶ ἔνδοξον θυμίαμα, καὶ βοτάνας εὐόσμους ἐκ τοῦ παραδείσου ἐνέγκας πλήρωσον τὸν οἶκον ἡμῶν· ἄναψον λύχνους ἑπτὰ διελαίους ὅπως εὐφρανθῶμεν, ὅτι ὁ ἀνὴρ οὗτος ὁ ἐπιξενισθεὶς ἡμῖν σήμερον ἐνδοξότερος ὑπάρχει βασιλέων καὶ ἀρχόντων, ὅτι καὶ ἡ ὅρασις αὐτοῦ ὑπερφέρει πάντας τοὺς υἱοὺς τῶν ἀνθρώπων. ὁ δὲ Ἰσαὰκ ἡτοίμασεν πάντα καλῶς· παραλαβὼν δὲ Ἀβραὰμ τὸν ἀρχάγγελον Μιχαήλ, ἀνῆλθεν ἐν τῷ οἰκήματι τοῦ τρικλίνου, καὶ ἐκαθέσθησαν ἀμφότεροι ἐπὶ τὰ κλινάρια, μέσον δὲ αὐτῶν προῆγε τράπεζαν ἐν ἀφθονίᾳ παντὸς ἀγαθοῦ. ἐγερθεὶς οὖν ὁ ἀρχιστράτηγος ἐξῆλθεν ἔξω, ὡς δῆθεν γαστρὸς χρείᾳ ὕδατος χύσιν ποιῆσαι, καὶ ἀνῆλθεν εἰς τὸν οὐρανὸν ἐν ῥιπῇ ὀφθαλμοῦ καὶ ἔστη ἐνώπιον τοῦ θεοῦ, καὶ εἶπεν πρὸς αὐτόν· Δέσποτα κύριε, ἵνα

12 πολιτ.] ἀτίμητοι ἤγουν πολύτιμοι B   18 ἐπιξενισθ.] ἐπιξενωθέντος B
20 ἀφθονίᾳ] εὐθυνία CE   23 ἐνέγκας] ναύκας CE   33 χρείᾳ ὕδατος χύσιν] χρείαν ποιήσασθαι CE

RECENSION A. 81

γινώσκῃ τὸ σὸν κράτος ὅτι ἐγὼ τὴν μνήμην τοῦ θανάτου ABCD
πρὸς τὸν δίκαιον ἄνδρα ἐκεῖνον ἀναγγεῖλαι οὐ δύναμαι, ὅτι EFR
οὐκ εἶδον ἐπὶ τῆς γῆς ἄνθρωπον ὅμοιον αὐτοῦ, ἐλεήμονα,
φιλόξενον, δίκαιον, ἀληθινόν, θεοσεβῆ, ἀπεχόμενον ἀπὸ
5 παντὸς πονηροῦ πράγματος· καὶ νῦν γίνωσκε, κύριε, ὅτι
ἐγὼ τὴν μνείαν τοῦ θανάτου ἀναγγεῖλαι οὐ δύναμαι. ὁ δὲ
κύριος εἶπεν· Κάτελθε, Μιχαὴλ ἀρχιστράτηγε, πρὸς τὸν
φίλον μου Ἀβραὰμ, καὶ ὅτι ἐὰν λέγῃ σοι, τοῦτο καὶ ποίει.
καὶ ὅτι ἐὰν ἐσθίῃ, ἔσθιε καὶ σὺ μετ' αὐτοῦ· ἐγὼ δὲ ἐπι-
10 βαλῶ τὸ πνεῦμά μου τὸ ἅγιον ἐπὶ τὸν υἱὸν αὐτοῦ Ἰσαὰκ,
καὶ ῥίψω τὴν μνήμην τοῦ θανάτου αὐτοῦ εἰς τὴν καρδίαν
τοῦ Ἰσαὰκ, ἵνα καὶ αὐτὸς ἐν ὀνείρῳ θεάσηται τὸν θάνατον
τοῦ πατρὸς αὐτοῦ, καὶ Ἰσαὰκ δὲ ἀναγγελεῖ τὸ ὅραμα, σὺ
δὲ διακρινεῖς· καὶ αὐτὸς γνώσεται τὸ τέλος αὐτοῦ. καὶ ὁ
15 ἀρχιστράτηγος εἶπεν· Κύριε, πάντα τὰ ἐπουράνια πνεύματα ὑπάρχουσιν ἀσώματα, καὶ οὔτε ἐσθίουσιν οὔτε πί-
νουσιν· καὶ οὗτος δὲ ἐμοὶ τράπεζαν παρέθετο ἐν ἀφθονίᾳ
πάντων ἀγαθῶν τῶν ἐπιγείων καὶ φθαρτῶν· καὶ νῦν, κύριε,
τί ποιήσω; πῶς διαλάθωμαι τοῦτον, καθήμενος ἐν μιᾷ
20 τραπέζῃ μετ' αὐτοῦ; ὁ δὲ κύριος εἶπεν· Κάτελθε πρὸς
αὐτὸν, καὶ περὶ τούτου μή σοι μελείτω· καθεζομένου γὰρ
σοῦ μετ' αὐτοῦ ἐγὼ ἀποστελῶ ἐπί σε πνεῦμα παμφάγον,
καὶ ἀναλίσκει ἐκ τῶν χειρῶν σου καὶ διὰ τοῦ στόματός
σου πάντα τὰ ἐπὶ τῆς τραπέζης· καὶ συνευφράνθητι μετ'
25 αὐτοῦ ἐν πᾶσιν· μόνον τὰ τοῦ ὁράματος διακρινεῖς καλῶς
ὅπως ἂν γνώσεται Ἀβραὰμ τὴν τοῦ θανάτου δρεπάνην,
καὶ τὸ τοῦ βίου ἄδηλον πέρας, καὶ ἵνα ποιήσῃ διάταξιν
περὶ πάντων τῶν ὑπαρχόντων αὐτοῦ, ὅτι ηὐλόγησα αὐτὸν
ὑπὲρ ἄμμον θαλάσσης, καὶ ὡς τοὺς ἀστέρας τοῦ οὐρανοῦ.
30 V. τότε ὁ ἀρχιστράτηγος κατῆλθεν εἰς τὸν οἶκον τοῦ
Ἀβραὰμ καὶ ἐκαθέσθη μετ' αὐτοῦ ἐν τῇ τραπέζῃ, Ἰσαὰκ
δὲ ὑπηρέτει αὐτοῖς· τελεσθέντος δὲ τοῦ δείπνου ἐποίησεν
Ἀβραὰμ τὴν κατὰ ἔθος εὐχήν, καὶ ὁ ἀρχάγγελος ηὔχετο
μετ' αὐτοῦ, καὶ ἀνεπαύσαντο ἕκαστος εἰς τὴν κλίνην ABCDER
F def.

2—6 ὅτι οὐκ—δύναμαι] om AB by homoeoteleuton   18 ἐπιγ. κ. φθ.] ἐπιγείων παρέχουσι B; ἐπιφθαρτῶν C; ἐπιγ. φθαρτῶν ADE (A ἀφθάρτων)   33 καὶ
ὁ ἄγγελος ὁμὲς F ends thus   34 ἀνεπαύσαντο] AD (-ατο D); ἀνέπεσεν
CE; ἔπεσεν B

J.   6

αὐτοῦ. εἶπεν δὲ Ἰσαὰκ πρὸς τὸν πατέρα αὐτοῦ· Πάτερ, ἤθελα κἀγὼ ἀναπαῆναι μεθ' ὑμῶν ἐν τῷ τρικλίνῳ τούτῳ, ἵνα ἀκούσω κἀγὼ τὰ διαλεγόμενα ὑμῶν· ἀγαπῶ γὰρ ἀκούειν τὴν διαφορὰν τῆς ὁμιλίας τοῦ παναρέτου ἀνδρὸς τούτου. εἶπεν δὲ Ἀβραάμ· Οὐχί, τέκνον, ἀλλὰ ἄπελθε ἐν 5 τῷ σῷ τρικλίνῳ καὶ ἀναπαύσαι ἐν τῇ κλίνῃ σου, ἵνα μὴ γινώμεθα ἐπιβαρεῖς τῷ ἀνθρώπῳ τούτῳ. τότε Ἰσαὰκ λαβὼν τὴν εὐχὴν παρ' αὐτῶν, καὶ εὐλογήσας, ἀπῆλθεν ἐν τῷ ἰδίῳ τρικλίνῳ καὶ ἀνέπεσεν ἐπὶ τὴν κλινὴν αὐτοῦ· ἔρριψεν δὲ ὁ θεὸς τὴν μνήμην τοῦ θανάτου εἰς τὴν καρδίαν 10 τοῦ Ἰσαὰκ ὡς ἐν ὀνείροις· καὶ περὶ ὥραν τρίτην τῆς νυκτὸς διυπνισθεὶς Ἰσαὰκ ἀνέστη ἀπὸ τῆς κλίνης αὐτοῦ καὶ ἦλθεν δρομαίως ἕως τοῦ τρικλίνου ἔνθα ὁ πατὴρ αὐτοῦ ἦν κοιμώμενος μετὰ τοῦ ἀρχαγγέλου. φθάσας οὖν Ἰσαὰκ πρὸς τὴν θύραν ἔκραζεν λέγων· Πάτερ Ἀβραάμ, ἀναστὰς 15 ἄνοιξόν μοι ταχέως, ὅπως εἰσέλθω καὶ κρεμασθῶ ἐν τῷ τραχήλῳ σου καὶ ἀσπάσωμαί σε πρὶν ἢ σε ἀροῦσιν ἀπ' ἐμοῦ. ἀναστὰς οὖν Ἀβραὰμ ἤνοιξεν αὐτῷ· εἰσελθὼν δὲ Ἰσαὰκ ἐκρεμάσθη ἐπὶ τὸν τράχηλον αὐτοῦ, καὶ ἤρξατο κλαίειν φωνῇ μεγάλῃ. συγκινηθεὶς οὖν τὰ σπλάγχνα ὁ 20 Ἀβραὰμ ἔκλαυσεν καὶ αὐτὸς μετ' αὐτοῦ φωνῇ μεγάλῃ· ἰδὼν δὲ ὁ ἀρχιστράτηγος αὐτοὺς κλαίοντας, ἔκλαυσεν καὶ αὐτός· Σάρρα δὲ ὑπάρχουσα ἐν τῇ σκηνῇ αὐτῆς ἤκουσεν τοῦ κλαυθμοῦ αὐτῶν καὶ ἦλθεν δρομαία ἐπ' αὐτούς, καὶ εὗρεν αὐτοὺς περιπλακομένους καὶ κλαίοντας· καὶ εἶπεν 25 Σάρρα μετὰ κλαυθμοῦ· Κύριέ μου Ἀβραάμ, τί ἐστιν τοῦτο ὅτι κλαίετε; ἀνάγγειλόν μοι, κύριέ μου, μὴ οὗτος ὁ ἀδελφὸς ὁ ἐπιξενισθεὶς ἡμῖν σήμερον φάσιν ἤνεγκέν σοι περὶ τοῦ ἀδελφιδοῦ σου Λώτ, ὅτι ἀπέθανεν, καὶ διὰ τοῦτο πενθεῖτε οὕτως; ὑπολαβὼν δὲ ὁ ἀρχιστράτηγος εἶπεν πρὸς 30 αὐτήν· Οὐχί, ἀδελφὴ Σάρρα, οὐκ ἔστιν οὕτως ὡς σὺ λέγεις· ἀλλὰ ὁ υἱός σου Ἰσαάκ, ὡς ἐμοὶ δοκεῖ, ὄνειρον ἐθεάσατο,

---

7 ἐπιβ. τῷ ἀνθρ.] ἐπιβαρὺς τοῦ A ; παρενοχλεῖς τὸν B; ὑποβαρεῖς τοῦ CDE 8 καὶ εὐλ.] om ACDER   20 Here a long section is omitted by CDER but contained in AB. The text of CDER is as follows: τράχηλον τοῦ πατρὸς αὐτοῦ καὶ ἤρξατο κλαίειν φωνῇ μεγάλῃ· καὶ ἔκλαυσεν Ἀβραάμ. ἰδὼν δὲ ὁ ἀρχιστρ. κλαίοντας ἔκλαυσεν καὶ αὐτὸς μετ' αὐτῶν· καταλιπὼν δὲ Ἀ. λέγει (see p. 83, l. 30).

καὶ ἦλθεν πρὸς ἡμᾶς κλαίων, καὶ ἡμεῖς τοῦτον ἰδόντες τὰ ABCDER
σπλάγχνα συνεκινήθημεν, καὶ ἐκλαύσαμεν.

VI. ἀκούσασα δὲ Σάρρα τὴν διαφορὰν τῆς ὁμιλίας
τοῦ ἀρχιστρατήγου, εὐθὺς ἐγνώρισεν ὅτι ἄγγελος κυρίου
5 ἐστὶν ὁ λαλῶν· συννεύει οὖν ἡ Σάρρα τὸν Ἀβραὰμ τὰ
πρὸς τὴν θύραν ἔξω ἐλθεῖν, καὶ λέγει αὐτῷ· Κύριέ μου
Ἀβραάμ, σὺ γινώσκεις τίς ἐστιν οὗτος ὁ ἀνήρ; εἶπεν δὲ
Ἀβραάμ· Οὐ γινώσκω. εἶπεν δὲ Σάρρα· Ἐπίστασαι,
κύριέ μου, τοὺς τρεῖς ἄνδρας τοὺς ἐπουρανίους τοὺς ἐπι-
10 ξενισθέντας ἐν τῇ σκηνῇ ἡμῶν παρὰ τὴν δρῦν τὴν Μαμβρῆ
ὅτε ἔσφαξας τὸν μόσχον τὸν ἄμωμον καὶ παρέθηκας αὐτοῖς τράπεζαν· δαπανηθέντων δὲ τῶν κρεάτων, ἠγέρθη
πάλιν ὁ μόσχος καὶ ἐθήλαζεν τὴν μητέρα αὐτοῦ ἐν ἀγαλ-
λιάσει· οὐκ οἶδας, κύριέ μου Ἀβραάμ, ὅτι καὶ καρπὸν κοι-
15 λίας ἐξ ἐπαγγελίας ἡμῖν ἐδωρήσαντο τὸν Ἰσαάκ; ἐκ γὰρ
τῶν τριῶν ἁγίων ἀνδρῶν ἐκείνων οὗτός ἐστιν ὁ εἷς ἐξ
αὐτῶν. εἶπεν δὲ Ἀβραάμ· Ὦ Σάρρα, τοῦτο ἀληθὲς εἴρη-
κας· δόξα καὶ εὐλογία παρὰ θεοῦ καὶ πατρός· καὶ γὰρ
ἐγὼ τῇ ὀψὲ βραδείᾳ, ὅτε ἔνιπτον τοὺς πόδας αὐτοῦ ἐν τῇ
20 λεκάνῃ τοῦ νιπτῆρος εἶπον ἐν τῇ καρδίᾳ μου· Οὗτοι οἱ
πόδες ἐκ τῶν τριῶν ἀνδρῶν εἰσὶν οὓς ἔνιψα τότε. καὶ
τὰ δάκρυα αὐτοῦ ὀψὲ ἐν τῷ νιπτῆρι πίπτοντα ἐγένοντο
λίθοι τίμιοι. καὶ ἐκβαλὼν ἐκ τοῦ κόλπου αὐτοῦ δέδωκεν
αὐτὰ τῇ Σάρρᾳ, λέγων· Εἰ ἀπιστεῖς μοι, νῦν θέασαι ταῦτα.
25 λαβοῦσα δὲ αὐτὰ ἡ Σάρρα προσεκύνησεν καὶ ἠσπάσατο
καὶ εἶπεν· Δόξα τῷ θεῷ τῷ δεικνύοντι ἡμῖν θαυμάσια·
καὶ νῦν γίνωσκε, κύριέ μου Ἀβραάμ, ὅτι ἀποκάλυψίς
τινος ἔργου ἐστὶν ἐν ἡμῖν, κἄν τε πονηρὸν κἄν τε
ἀγαθόν.

30 VII. καταλιπὼν δὲ Ἀβραὰμ τὴν Σάρραν εἰσῆλθεν ἐν
τῷ τρικλίνῳ καὶ εἶπεν πρὸς Ἰσαάκ· Δεῦρο υἱέ μου ἀγαπητέ, ἀνάγγειλόν μοι τὴν ἀλήθειαν, τί τὰ ὁραθέντα καὶ
τί πέπονθας ὅτι οὕτω δρομαίως εἰσῆλθες πρὸς ἡμᾶς; ὑπολαβὼν δὲ Ἰσαὰκ ἤρξατο λέγειν· Εἶδον ἐγώ, κύριέ μου,
35 τῇ νυκτὶ ταύτῃ τὸν ἥλιον καὶ τὴν σελήνην ὑπεράνω τῆς

11 ὅτε—παρέθ.] θήσαντες ὑμεῖς παρέθ. A   12 ἠγέρθη] εἰσῆλθεν A
14 ἴδες A   18 εὐλογ.] δόξα εἰ καὶ κρίνει B   19 ὀψὲ βραδὺ B ; ὄψει βραδείᾳ
A   27 ἀποκάλυψις—ἡμῖν] ἀποκάλυψιν τινὸς ἔργου ὑμῖν A

ABCDER κεφαλῆς μου, καὶ τὰς ἀκτῖνας αὐτοῦ κυκλοῦντα καὶ φωταγωγοῦντά με· καὶ ταῦτα οὕτως ἐμοῦ θεωροῦντος καὶ ἀγαλλιωμένου, εἶδον τὸν οὐρανὸν ἀνεῳγότα, καὶ εἶδον ἄνδρα φωτοφόρον ἐκ τοῦ οὐρανοῦ κατελθόντα ὑπὲρ ἑπτὰ ἡλίους ἀστράπτοντα· καὶ ἐλθὼν ὁ ἀνὴρ ὁ ἡλιόμορφος ἐκεῖνος ἔλα- 5
βεν τὸν ἥλιον ἀπὸ τῆς κεφαλῆς μου, καὶ ἀνῆλθεν εἰς τοὺς οὐρανοὺς ὅθεν καὶ ἐξῆλθεν· ἐγὼ δὲ ἐλυπήθην μεγάλως ὅτι ἔλαβεν τὸν ἥλιον ἀπ' ἐμοῦ· καὶ μετ' ὀλίγον ὡς ἔτι ἐμοῦ λυπουμένου καὶ ἀδημονοῦντος, εἶδον τὸν ἄνδρα ἐκεῖνον ἐκ δευτέρου ἐκ τοῦ οὐρανοῦ ἐξελθόντα· καὶ ἔλαβεν ἀπ' ἐμοῦ 10
καὶ τὴν σελήνην ἐκ τῆς κεφαλῆς μου· ἔκλαυσα δὲ μεγάλως καὶ παρεκάλεσα τὸν ἄνδρα ἐκεῖνον τὸν φωτοφόρον καὶ εἶπον· Μή, κύριέ μου, μὴ ἄρῃς τὴν δόξαν μου ἀπ' ἐμοῦ, ἐλέησόν με καὶ εἰσάκουσόν μου· καὶ κἂν τὸν ἥλιον ἄρας ἀπ' ἐμοῦ, κἂν τὴν σελήνην ἔασον ἐπ' ἐμέ. αὐτὸς δὲ εἶπεν· 15
Ἄφες ἀναληφθῆναι αὐτοὺς πρὸς τὸν ἄνω βασιλέα, ὅτι θέλει αὐτοὺς ἐκεῖ. καὶ ἦρεν αὐτοὺς ἀπ' ἐμοῦ, τὰς δὲ ἀκτῖνας ἔασεν ἐπ' ἐμέ. εἶπεν δὲ ὁ ἀρχιστράτηγος· Ἄκουσον, δίκαιε Ἀβραάμ· ὁ ἥλιος ὃν ἑώρακεν ὁ παῖς σου, σὺ εἶ, ὁ πατὴρ αὐτοῦ· καὶ ἡ σελήνη ὁμοίως ἡ μήτηρ αὐτοῦ Σάρρα 20
ὑπάρχουσα· ὁ δὲ ἀνὴρ ὁ φωτοφόρος ὁ ἐκ τοῦ οὐρανοῦ καταβὰς, οὗτός ἐστιν ὁ ἐκ τοῦ θεοῦ ἀποσταλεὶς, ὁ μέλλων λαβεῖν τὴν δικαίαν σου ψυχὴν ἀπό σου. καὶ νῦν γίνωσκε, τιμιώτατε Ἀβραὰμ, ὅτι μέλλεις ἐν τῷ καιρῷ τούτῳ καταλιπεῖν τὸν κοσμικὸν βίον καὶ πρὸς τὸν θεὸν ἐκδημεῖν. 25
εἶπεν δὲ Ἀβραὰμ πρὸς τὸν ἀρχιστράτηγον· Ὦ θαῦμα θαυμάτων καινότερον! καὶ λοιπὸν σὺ εἶ ὁ μέλλων λαβεῖν τὴν ψυχήν μου ἀπ' ἐμοῦ; λέγει αὐτῷ ὁ ἀρχιστράτηγος· Ἐγώ εἰμι Μιχαὴλ ὁ ἀρχιστράτηγος ὁ παρεστηκὼς ἐνώπιον τοῦ θεοῦ, καὶ ἀπεστάλην πρός σε ὅπως ἀναγγείλω 30

1 κυκλ. κ. φωτ.] κλητὰς καὶ φωταγουγοῦντας CE   4 ὑπὲρ ἑπτὰ ἡλ.] ὑπὲρ ἐξ ηλιου A; ὑπὲρ πάσας ἡλίους B   6—11 καὶ ἀνῆλθεν—κεφαλῆς μου] om B by homœot. 14 ἐλέησον—εἰσάκ. μου] om A   16—18 ἄφες—ἐπ' ἐμέ] ἄφες ἀρτίως ἀναληφθέντος αὐτοῦ ἀπ' ἐμοῦ τοὺς δὲ ἀκτῖνας αὐτὸν ἔασεν A; ἄφες ἀναληφθῆναι αὐτοὺς ἐκεῖ καὶ ἦρεν αὐτοὺς ἀπ' ἐμοῦ καὶ τὰς ἀκτ. αὐτοῦ B; ἄφες αὐτοὺς ἀπελθεῖν ὅτι θέλει αὐτοὺς ὁ ἄνω βασ. D   20 ὁμοίως] om B   21 ὑπάρχουσα] om B; ὑπῆρχεν CE   25 κόσμον καὶ τὸν βίον B; κόσμον CE   29 ὁ παρεστ. —κῡ] BD; ἀρχιστ. κῡ ACE

σοι τὴν τοῦ θανάτου μνήμην· καὶ εἶθ' οὕτως ἀπελεύσομαι ABCDER
πρὸς αὐτὸν καθὼς ἐκελεύσθημεν. καὶ εἶπεν Ἀβραάμ· Νῦν
ἔγνωκα ἐγὼ ὅτι ἄγγελος κυρίου εἶ σύ, καὶ ἀπεστάλης
λαβεῖν τὴν ψυχήν μου· ἀλλ' οὐ μή σοι ἀκολουθήσω· ἀλλ'
5 ὅπερ κελεύει[ς] ποίησον.

VIII. ὁ δὲ ἀρχιστράτηγος ἀκούσας τὸ ῥῆμα τοῦτο,
εὐθέως ἀφανὴς ἐγένετο· καὶ ἀνελθὼν εἰς τὸν οὐρανὸν ἔστη
ἐνώπιον τοῦ θεοῦ καὶ ἀνήγγειλεν πάντα ὅσα εἶδεν εἰς τὸν
οἶκον Ἀβραάμ· εἶπεν δὲ καὶ τοῦτο ὁ ἀρχιστράτηγος πρὸς
10 τὸν δεσπότην ὅτι Καὶ τοῦτο λέγει ὁ φίλος σου Ἀβραάμ
ὅτι Οὐ μή σοι ἀκολουθήσω, ἀλλ' ὅπερ κελεύει[ς] ποίησον·
ἀρτίως δέσποτα παντοκράτωρ, εἴ τι κελεύει ἡ σὴ δόξα καὶ ἡ
βασιλεία ἡ ἀθάνατος; εἶπεν δὲ ὁ θεὸς πρὸς τὸν ἀρχιστράτηγον Μιχαήλ· Ἄπελθε πρὸς τὸν φίλον μου Ἀβραὰμ ἔτι
15 ἅπαξ καὶ εἶπε αὐτῷ οὕτως· ὅτι Τάδε λέγει κύριος ὁ θεός σου,
ὁ εἰσαγαγών σε ἐν τῇ γῇ τῆς ἐπαγγελίας, ὁ εὐλογήσας σε
ὑπὲρ τὴν ἄμμον τῆς θαλάσσης καὶ ὑπὲρ τοὺς ἀστέρας τοῦ
οὐρανοῦ, ὁ διανοίξας μήτραν Σάρρας τῆς στειρώσης καὶ
χαρισάμενός σοι καρπὸν κοιλίας ἐν γήρει τὸν Ἰσαάκ· Ἀμὴν
20 λέγω σοι ὅτι εὐλογῶν εὐλογήσω σε καὶ πληθύνων πλη-
θυνῶ τὸ σπέρμα σου, καὶ δώσω σοι πάντα ὅσα ἂν αἰτήσῃς
παρ' ἐμοῦ, ὅτι ἐγώ εἰμι κύριος ὁ θεός σου, καὶ πλὴν ἐμοῦ
οὐκ ἔστιν ἄλλος· σὺ δὲ τί ἀνθέστηκας ἀπ' ἐμοῦ καὶ τί ἐν
σοὶ λύπη, ἀνάγγειλον· καὶ ἵνα τί ἀνθέστηκας ἀπὸ τὸν
25 ἀρχάγγελόν μου Μιχαήλ; ἢ οὐκ οἶδας ὅτι οἱ ἀπὸ Ἀδὰμ
καὶ Εὔας πάντες ἀπέθανον; καὶ οὐδεὶς ἐκ τῶν προφητῶν
τὸν θάνατον ἐξέφυγεν· καὶ οὐδεὶς ἐκ τῶν βασιλευόντων
ὑπάρχει ἀθάνατος· οὐδεὶς ἐκ τῶν προπατόρων ἐξέφυγεν
τὸ τοῦ θανάτου μυστήριον· πάντες ἀπέθανον, πάντες ἐν τῷ
30 ᾅδῃ κατηλλάξαντο, πάντες τῇ τοῦ θανάτου δρεπάνῃ συλ-
λέγονται· ἐπὶ δέ σε οὐκ ἀπέστειλα θάνατον, οὐκ εἴασα

1 ἀπελεύσομαι—ἐκελεύσθημεν] ἀπελευσόμεθα πρὸς τὸν ἄνω (πάντων E) βασιλέα CE   2 ἐκελεύσθημεν] ἐκέλευσέν μοι A   4 σοι] σει A; σε BCDE
4, 5 ἀλλ'—ποίησον] ὅπερ νῦν κελ. ποιήσων A; δι' ὅνπερ κελεύεις ποιῆσαι B; om
CDE : txt from l. 11 where AB omit   18—24 ὁ διανοίξας—ἀνάγγειλον]
om CDE   26 καὶ οὐδεὶς—θαν.] ἐξέφυγεν] om ACDE   28, 29 οὐδεὶς—
μυστήριον] om B   28 προπατ.] πατέρων AE   29 μυστ.] κειμήλιον
ADE   30, 31 πάντες τῇ—συλλέγ.] πάντας ἡ κ.τ.λ. συλλέγεται B; om CDE

ABCDER νόσον θανατηφόρον ἐπελθεῖν σοι· οὐ συνεχώρησα τῇ τοῦ
θανάτου δρεπάνῃ συναντῆσαί σοι, οὐ παρεχώρησα τὰ τοῦ
ᾅδου δίκτυα συμπλέξαι σε, οὐκ ἠθέλησά ποτέ τινι κακῷ
συναντῆσαί σε· ἀλλὰ πρὸς παράκλησιν ἀγαθὴν τὸν ἐμὸν
ἀρχιστράτηγον Μιχαὴλ ἐξαπέστειλα πρός σε, ἵνα γνώσῃς 5
τὴν ἐκ τοῦ κόσμου μετάστασιν, καὶ ποιήσῃς διάταξιν περὶ
τοῦ οἴκου σου, καὶ περὶ πάντων τῶν ὑπαρχόντων σοι, καὶ
ὅπως εὐλογήσῃς τὸν Ἰσαὰκ τὸν υἱόν σου τὸν ἀγαπητόν.
καὶ νῦν γνώρισον ὅτι μὴ θέλων λυπῆσαί σε ταῦτα πε-
ποίηκα. καὶ ἵνα τί εἶπας πρὸς τὸν ἀρχιστράτηγόν μου 10
ὅτι Οὐ μή σοι ἀκολουθήσω; ἵνα τί ταῦτα εἴρηκας; καὶ
οὐκ οἶδας ὅτι ἐὰν ἐάσω τὸν θάνατον καὶ ἐπέλθῃ σοι, τότε
ἂν εἶχον ἰδεῖν κἂν ἔρχῃ κἂν οὐκ ἔρχῃ;

IX. λαβὼν δὲ ὁ ἀρχιστράτηγος τὰς παραινέσεις τοῦ
κυρίου κατῆλθεν πρὸς τὸν Ἀβραάμ· καὶ ἰδὼν αὐτὸν ὁ 15
δίκαιος ἔπεσεν ἐπὶ πρόσωπον εἰς τὸ ἔδαφος τῆς γῆς ὡς
νεκρός, ὁ δὲ ἀρχιστράτηγος εἶπεν αὐτῷ πάντα ὅσα ἤκουσεν
παρὰ τοῦ ὑψίστου· τότε οὖν ὁ ὅσιος καὶ δίκαιος Ἀβραὰμ
ἀναστὰς μετὰ πολλῶν δακρύων προσέπεσεν τοῖς ποσὶν
τοῦ ἀσωμάτου καὶ ἱκέτευεν λέγων· Δέομαί σου, ἀρχιστρά- 20
τηγε τῶν ἄνω δυνάμεων, ἐπειδὴ κατηξίωσας ὅλως αὐτὸς
πρὸς ἐμὲ τὸν ἁμαρτωλὸν καὶ ἀνάξιον δοῦλόν σου καθε-
κάστην ἔρχεσθαι, παρακαλῶ σε καὶ νῦν, ἀρχιστράτηγε,
τοῦ διακονῆσαί μοι λόγον ἔτι ἅπαξ πρὸς τὸν ὕψιστον, καὶ
ἐρεῖς αὐτῷ ὅτι Τάδε λέγει Ἀβραὰμ ὁ οἰκέτης σου ὅτι 25
Κύριε, κύριε, ἐν παντὶ ἔργῳ καὶ λόγῳ ὃ ᾐτησάμην σε εἰσήκουσάς μου, καὶ πᾶσαν τὴν βουλήν μου ἐπλήρωσας· καὶ
νῦν, κύριε, οὐκ ἀνθίσταμαι τὸ σὸν κράτος, ὅτι κἀγὼ γινώσκω ὅτι οὐκ εἰμὶ ἀθάνατος ἀλλὰ θνητός· ἐπειδὴ οὖν τῇ σῇ
προστάξει πάντα ὑπείκει καὶ φρίττει καὶ τρέμει ἀπὸ προσ- 30

1, 2 οὐ συνεχώρ.—συναντ. σοι] om B   2, 3 οὐ παρεχώρ.—συμπλέξαι σε]
om CDE   3 ᾅδου] θανάτου B   3, 4 σε] σοι AB (bis)   4 παράκλησιν]
παράταξιν B   9 καὶ νῦν—πεποίηκα] om CDE   12, 13 τότε—οὐκ ἔρχῃ]
τότε ἴδῃς...ἔρχεσαι B ; τότε ἰδεῖν ἔχεις CE : om D   14—17 τὰς παραιν.—
ἀρχιστρ.] om B   15—17 καὶ ἰδὼν—νεκρὸς] ἔπεσεν δὲ Ἀ. εἰς τ. πόδας τοῦ
ἀρχιστ. Μιχ. CE ; καὶ ἰδὼν αὐτὸν ἔπεσεν Ἀ. D   19, 20 προσέπεσεν—ἀσωμ.
καὶ] om BCDE   26, 27 εἰσήκουσάς μου καὶ πᾶσαν] ἐποίησας καὶ ἔδωκάς μοι
κατὰ τῆς καρδίας μου καὶ πᾶσαν A   30 ὑπείκει] ὑπείκηνται A; ὑπήκει B;
ἐπίχη C (-κη E); ὑπακούει D

ὥπου δυνάμεώς σου, κἀγὼ δέδοικα, ἀλλὰ μίαν αἴτησιν αἰ- ABCDER
τοῦμαι παρὰ σοῦ· καὶ νῦν, δέσποτα κύριε, εἰσάκουσόν μου
τῆς δεήσεως, ὅτι ἔτι ἐν τούτῳ τῷ σώματι ὢν θέλω ἰδεῖν
πᾶσαν τὴν οἰκουμένην καὶ τὰ ποιήματα πάντα ἃ διὰ
5 λόγου ἑνὸς συνέστησας, δέσποτα, καὶ ὅτε ἴδω ταῦτα, τότε
ἐὰν μεταβῶ τοῦ βίου ἄλυπος ἔσομαι. ἀπῆλθεν οὖν πάλιν ὁ
ἀρχιστράτηγος καὶ ἔστη ἐνώπιον τοῦ θεοῦ καὶ ἀνήγγειλεν
αὐτῷ πάντα, λέγων· Τάδε λέγει ὁ φίλος σου Ἀβραάμ, ὅτι
Ἤθελον θεάσασθαι πᾶσαν τὴν οἰκουμένην ἐν τῇ ζωῇ μου,
10 πρὸ τοῦ ἀποθανεῖν με. ἀκούσας δὲ ταῦτα ὁ ὕψιστος,
πάλιν κελεύει τὸν ἀρχιστράτηγον Μιχαὴλ καὶ λέγει αὐτῷ·
Λάβε νεφέλην φωτὸς, καὶ ἀγγέλους τοὺς ἐπὶ τῶν ἁρμάτων
τὴν ἐξουσίαν ἔχοντας, καὶ κατελθὼν λάβε τὸν δίκαιον
Ἀβραὰμ ἐπὶ ἅρματος χερουβικοῦ καὶ ὕψωσον αὐτὸν εἰς
15 τὸν αἰθέρα τοῦ οὐρανοῦ ὅπως ἴδῃ πᾶσαν τὴν οἰκουμένην.

X. καὶ κατελθὼν ὁ ἀρχάγγελος Μιχαὴλ ἔλαβεν τὸν
Ἀβραὰμ ἐπὶ ἅρματος χερουβικοῦ καὶ ὕψωσεν αὐτὸν εἰς
τὸν αἰθέρα τοῦ οὐρανοῦ καὶ ἤγαγεν αὐτὸν ἐπὶ τῆς νεφέλης
καὶ ἑξήκοντα ἀγγέλους καὶ ἀνήρχετο ὁ Ἀβραὰμ ἐπὶ ὀχή-
20 ματος ἐφ' ὅλην τὴν οἰκουμένην· καὶ θεωρεῖ Ἀβραὰμ τὸν
κόσμον καθὼς εἶχεν ἡ ἡμέρα ἐκείνη, ἄλλους μὲν ἀροτριῶν-
τας, ἑτέρους ἁμαξηγοῦντας, ἐν ἄλλῳ δὲ τόπῳ ποιμαινεύ-
οντας, ἀλλαχοῦ ἀγραυλοῦντας, καὶ ὀρχουμένους καὶ παί-
ζοντας καὶ κιθαρίζοντας, ἐν ἄλλῳ δὲ τόπῳ παλαίοντας καὶ
25 δικαζομένους, ἀλλαχοῦ κλαίοντας, ἔπειτα καὶ τεθνεῶτας ἐν
μνήματι ἀγομένους· εἶδεν δὲ καὶ νεονύμφους ὀψικευομέ-
νους· καὶ ἁπλῶς εἰπεῖν, εἶδεν πάντα τὰ ἐν κόσμῳ γινόμενα,
ἀγαθά τε καὶ πονηρά. διερχόμενος οὖν ὁ Ἀβραὰμ εἶδεν
ἄνδρας ξιφηφόρους, ἐν ταῖς χερσὶν αὐτῶν κρατοῦντας ξίφη
30 ἠκονημένα, καὶ ἠρώτησεν Ἀβραὰμ τὸν ἀρχιστράτηγον·

4—6 καὶ τὰ ποιήμ.—ἔσομαι] καὶ οἵ τη ἐτούμε μετὰ πάντα καὶ νῦν ἐὰν μετα-
στῷ τοῦ βίου ἀλήπτως ἔσωμαι (C)E   8—10 λέγων—ἀποθανεῖν με] καθὰ
ἤκουσεν περὶ τοῦ Ἀβρ. B ; om CE ; ἃ παρὰ τοῦ Ἀ. ἤκουσεν D   16—20 ἔλαβεν
—οἰκουμένην] ἔλαβεν τὸν Ἀ. ἐπὶ ὀχήματος ἐφ' ὅλην τ. οἰκ. B   20 θεωρεῖ]
ἑώρα A   20, 21 καὶ θεωρ.—τὸν κόσμον] om CDE   22 ἁμαξηγοῦντας B (-ιγ-) ;
ἅμα ἐξηγοῦντας A ; ἁμαξιξήτουντας C ; ἁμαξοξυγοῦντας D ; ἁμάξας ἡγοῦντας E
ἐν ἄλλῳ—ποιμ.] om CDE   23, 24 καὶ ὀρχ.—κιθαρίζ.] om B   24 καὶ
κιθαρίζ.] om CDE   παλαίοντας] ἀπολαβόντας D   25, 26 τεθν.—ὀψικ.]
om B   26, 27 ὀψικ.—εἰπεῖν] om D   27 εἰπεῖν] om CE   εἶδεν] om B

ABCDER Τίνες εἰσιν οὗτοι; καὶ εἶπεν ὁ ἀρχιστράτηγος· Οὗτοί εἰσιν
κλέπται, οἱ βουλόμενοι φόνον ἐργάζεσθαι καὶ κλέψαι καὶ
θῦσαι καὶ ἀπολέσαι. εἶπεν δὲ Ἀβραάμ· Κύριε, κύριε,
εἰσάκουσον τῆς φωνῆς μου καὶ κέλευσον ἵνα ἐξέλθωσιν
θηρία . τοῦ δρυμοῦ καὶ καταφάγωσιν αὐτούς. καὶ ἅμα 5
τῷ λόγῳ αὐτοῦ ἐξῆλθον θηρία ἐκ τοῦ δρυμοῦ καὶ κατέφαγον αὐτούς· καὶ εἶδεν εἰς ἕτερον τόπον ἄνδρα μετὰ γυναικὸς
εἰς ἀλλήλους πορνεύοντας, καὶ εἶπεν· Κύριε, κύριε, κέλευσον ὅπως χάνῃ ἡ γῆ καὶ καταπίῃ αὐτούς. καὶ εὐθὺς ἐδι-
χάσθη ἡ γῆ καὶ κατέπιεν αὐτούς· καὶ εἶδεν εἰς ἕτερον 10
τόπον ἀνθρώπους διορύσσοντας οἶκον καὶ ἁρπάζοντας ἀλ-
λότρια πράγματα, καὶ εἶπεν· Κύριε, κύριε, κέλευσον ἵνα
κατέλθῃ πῦρ ἐξ οὐρανοῦ καὶ καταφάγῃ αὐτούς. καὶ ἅμα
τῷ λόγῳ αὐτοῦ κατῆλθεν πῦρ ἐκ τοῦ οὐρανοῦ καὶ κατέφαγεν αὐτούς. καὶ εὐθέως ἦλθεν φωνὴ ἐκ τοῦ οὐρανοῦ 15
πρὸς τὸν ἀρχιστράτηγον, λέγων οὕτως· Κέλευσον, ὦ Μιχαὴλ ἀρχιστράτηγε, στῆναι τὸ ἅρμα, καὶ ἀπόστρεψον τὸν
Ἀβραάμ, ἵνα μὴ ἴδῃ πᾶσαν τὴν οἰκουμένην· ἢν γὰρ ἴδῃ
πάντας τοὺς ἐν ἁμαρτίᾳ διάγοντας, ἀπολέσει πᾶν τὸ ἀνά-
στημα· ἰδοὺ γὰρ ὁ Ἀβραὰμ οὐχ ἥμαρτεν, καὶ τοὺς ἁμαρ- 20
τωλοὺς οὐκ ἐλεᾷ· ἐγὼ δὲ ἐποίησα τὸν κόσμον, καὶ οὐ θέλω
ἀπολέσαι ἐξ αὐτῶν οὐδένα, ἀναμένω δὲ τὸν θάνατον τοῦ
ἁμαρτωλοῦ, ἕως τοῦ ἐπιστρέψαι καὶ ζῆν αὐτόν· ἀνάγαγε δὲ
τὸν Ἀβραὰμ ἐν τῇ πρώτῃ πύλῃ τοῦ οὐρανοῦ, ὅπως θεάσηται ἐκεῖ τὰς κρίσεις καὶ ἀνταποδόσεις, καὶ μετανοήσῃ 25
ἐπὶ τὰς ψυχὰς τῶν ἁμαρτωλῶν ἃς ἀπώλεσεν.

XI. ἔστρεψεν δὲ ὁ Μιχαὴλ τὸ ἅρμα καὶ ἤνεγκε τὸν
Ἀβραὰμ ἐπὶ τὴν ἀνατολὴν ἐν τῇ πύλῃ τῇ πρώτῃ τοῦ
οὐρανοῦ. καὶ εἶδεν Ἀβραὰμ δύο ὁδούς· ἡ μία ὁδὸς στενὴ
καὶ τεθλιμμένη καὶ ἡ ἑτέρα πλατεῖα καὶ εὐρύχωρος <καὶ 30

1 οὗτοι (pr.)]+ἀσώματε CE   5—7 καὶ ἅμα—αὐτούς] καὶ εὐθὺς ἐγένετο
οὕτως B; om CE   8 εἰς ἀλλήλους] om CE   9, 10 καὶ εὐθ.—αὐτούς]
CDE (ἐσχίσθη D); om AB   11 ἀνθρ. διορ.] ἀνοὺς δύο ῥίπτοντας A; ἀνοὺς
δύο ὀρυσσομένους B; ἀνθρ. διορύγοντας CE; ἄνδρας διορύσσοντας D   13—
15 καὶ ἅμα—αὐτούς] om BCDE   18 B has ἵνα μὴ ἴδῃ· εἶδεν δὲ πολλὰς
ψυχὰς etc. (p. 89, 1. 5) omitting ten lines.   22 ἀναμένω δὲ] ἀναμ. γὰρ CE;
ἀλλ' ἀναμ. D   23 ζῆν αὐτὸν] ζῆσαι A   25 τὰς κρίσεις κ. ἀντ.] τὴν κρίσιν
κ. ἀντ. CDE   27 Μιχ.] ἀρχιστρ. CE; ἀρχάγγ. D   28 ἐπὶ τὴν ἀνατ.] om D
ἐπὶ τὴν ἀνατ.—Ἀβρ.] om A by homœoteleuton   29, 30 corrupt. The

εἶδεν ἐκεῖ δύο πύλας· μία πύλη πλατεῖα>, κατὰ τῆς πλα- ABCDER
τείας ὁδοῦ, καὶ μία πύλη στενὴ κατὰ τῆς στενῆς ὁδοῦ·
ἔξωθεν δὲ τῶν πυλῶν τῶν ἐκεῖσε τῶν δύο, ἴδον ἄνδρα
καθήμενον ἐπὶ θρόνου κεχρυσωμένου· καὶ ἦν ἡ ἰδέα τοῦ
5 ἀνθρώπου ἐκείνου φοβερά, ὁμοία τοῦ δεσπότου· καὶ ἴδον
ψυχὰς πολλὰς ἐλαυνομένας ὑπὸ ἀγγέλων καὶ διὰ τῆς
πλατείας πύλης εἰσαγομένας, καὶ ἴδον ἄλλας ψυχὰς ὀλίγας
καὶ ἐφέροντο ὑπὸ ἀγγέλων διὰ τῆς στενῆς πύλης. καὶ ὅτε
ἐθεώρει ὁ θαυμάσιος ὁ ἐπὶ τοῦ χρυσοῦ θρόνου καθήμενος
10 διὰ τῆς στενῆς πύλης ὀλίγας εἰσερχομένας, διὰ δὲ τῆς
πλατείας πολλὰς εἰσερχομένας, εὐθὺς ὁ ἀνὴρ ἐκεῖνος ὁ
θαυμάσιος ἥρπαξεν τὰς τρίχας τῆς κεφαλῆς αὐτοῦ καὶ τὰς
παρειὰς τοῦ πώγωνος αὐτοῦ καὶ ἔρριψεν ἑαυτὸν χαμαὶ
ἀπὸ τοῦ θρόνου κλαίων καὶ ὀδυρόμενος· καὶ ὅτε ἐθεώρει
15 πολλὰς ψυχὰς εἰσερχομένας διὰ τῆς στενῆς πύλης, τότε
ἀνίστατο ἀπὸ τῆς γῆς καὶ ἐκαθέζετο ἐπὶ τοῦ θρόνου αὐτοῦ
ἐν εὐφροσύνῃ πολλῇ χαίρων καὶ ἀγαλλόμενος. ἠρώτησεν δὲ
ὁ Ἀβραὰμ τὸν ἀρχιστράτηγον· Κύριέ μου ἀρχιστράτηγε,
τίς ἐστιν οὗτος ὁ ἀνὴρ ὁ πανθαύμαστος, ὁ ἐν τοιαύτῃ δόξῃ
20 κοσμούμενος, καὶ ποτὲ μὲν κλαίει καὶ ὀδύρεται, ποτὲ δὲ
χαίρεται καὶ ἀγάλλεται; εἶπεν δὲ ὁ ἀσώματος· Οὗτός
ἐστιν ὁ πρωτόπλαστος Ἀδάμ, ὁ ἐν τοιαύτῃ δόξῃ, καὶ
βλέπει τὸν κόσμον, καθότι πάντες ἐξ αὐτοῦ ἐγένοντο· καὶ
ὅτε ἴδῃ ψυχὰς πολλὰς εἰσερχομένας διὰ τῆς στενῆς πύλης,
25 τότε ἀνίσταται καὶ κάθηται ἐπὶ τοῦ θρόνου αὐτοῦ χαίρων
καὶ ἀγαλλόμενος ἐν εὐφροσύνῃ, ὅτι αὕτη ἡ πύλη ἡ στενὴ
τῶν δικαίων ἐστὶ<ν>, ἡ ἀπάγουσα εἰς τὴν ζωήν, καὶ οἱ

texts are as follows: δύο ὁδοὺς, μία ὁδὸς πλατεῖα καὶ εὐρύχορος ἅμα τὰ τῆς πλατείας ὁδοῦ καὶ μία πύλη στενὴ καὶ κατὰ τῆς στενῆς ὁδοῦ. ἔξωθεν δὲ τῶν πυλαίων
τῶν ἐκεῖσαι τῶν δύο ἴδον κ.τ.λ. A; om B, see above; δύο ὁδούς· ἡ μία ὁδὸς στενὴ
καὶ τεθλοιμένοι καὶ ἡ ἑτέρα πλατεῖα καὶ εὐρύχορος ἔξοθεν τῶν β̄ πηλῶν εἶδεν CE;
D as CE, but with the words κατὰ τῆς στενῆς ὁδοῦ before ἔξωθεν. I have supplied the mention of 'the two gates' which is needed.
4 θρόνου]+κάτω B   5 δεσπότου] A; κυρίου ἡμῶν Ἰησοῦ Χριστοῦ CE; τῷ
δεσπ. χριστῷ D   ἴδον] εἶδεν B; ἴδεν CE   16 γῆς]+ἧς ἐκαθέζετο χρυ-
σῆς καὶ ἐκάθητο B   17 ἀγαλλόμ.] ἀγαλλιωμ. ACDE   19 ὁ ἐν] om ὁ
ACDE   τοιαύτῃ] τῇ ταύτῃ A; τῇ αὐτοῦ B; τῇ αὐτῇ CDE   19—23 δόξῃ
—κόσμον] δόξῃ ζῇ ἐπὶ τῶν κόσμων C   23 καθότι] καθὼς B; ὅτι CDE
25 ἀνίστ. καὶ] om BCDE   26, 27 αὕτη—ζωὴν καὶ] om B; om τῶν δικ. and
οἱ and ἔρχονται A   27 εἰς τ. ζωὴν] εἰς ζ. αἰώνιον CE

ABCDER εἰσερχόμενοι δι' αὐτῆς εἰς τὸν παράδεισον ἔρχονται· καὶ
διὰ τοῦτο χαίρει ὁ πρωτόπλαστος Ἀδάμ, διότι θεωρεῖ τὰς
ψυχὰς σωζομένας· καὶ ὅταν ἴδῃ ψυχὰς πολλὰς εἰσερχομένας διὰ τῆς πλατείας πύλης, τότε ἀνασπᾷ τὰς τρίχας
τῆς κεφαλῆς αὐτοῦ καὶ ῥίπτει ἑαυτὸν χαμαὶ κλαίων καὶ 5
ὀδυρόμενος πικρῶς· διότι ἡ πύλη ἡ πλατεῖα τῶν ἁμαρτωλῶν ἐστίν, ἡ ἀπάγουσα εἰς τὴν ἀπώλειαν καὶ εἰς τὴν κόλασιν τὴν αἰώνιον· καὶ διὰ τοῦτο ὁ πρωτόπλαστος Ἀδὰμ ἀπὸ
τοῦ θρόνου αὐτοῦ πίπτει κλαίων καὶ ὀδυρόμενος ἐπὶ τῇ
ἀπωλείᾳ τῶν ἁμαρτωλῶν, διότι πολλοί εἰσιν οἱ ἀπολλύ- 10
μενοι, ὀλίγοι δὲ οἱ σωζόμενοι· εἰς γὰρ τὰς ἑπτὰ χιλιάδας
μόλις εὑρίσκεται μία ψυχὴ σωζομένη δικαία καὶ ἀμό-
λυντος.

XII. ἔτι δὲ ἐμοὶ ταῦτα λαλοῦντος ἰδοὺ δύο ἄγγελοι
πύρινοι τῇ ὄψει καὶ ἀνηλεεῖς τῇ γνώμῃ καὶ ἀπότομοι τῷ 15
βλέμματι, καὶ ἤλαυνον μυριάδας ψυχὰς ἀνηλεῶς τύπτοντες
αὐτοὺς ἐν πυρίναις χαρζαναῖς· καὶ μίαν ψυχὴν ἐκράτει ὁ
ἄγγελος· καὶ διήγαγον πάσας τὰς ψυχὰς εἰς τὴν πλατεῖαν
πύλην πρὸς τὴν ἀπώλειαν· ἠκολουθήσαμεν οὖν καὶ ἡμεῖς
τοῖς ἀγγέλοις καὶ ἤλθομεν ἔσωθεν τῆς πύλης ἐκείνης τῆς 20
πλατείας· καὶ ἐν μέσῳ τῶν δύο πυλῶν ἵστατο θρόνος φο-
βερὸς ἐν εἴδει κρυστάλλου φοβεροῦ ἐξαστράπτων ὡς πῦρ.
καὶ ἐπ' αὐτῷ ἐκάθητο ἀνὴρ θαυμαστὸς ἡλιόρατος ὅμοιος
υἱῷ θεοῦ. ἔμπροσθεν δὲ αὐτοῦ ἵστατο τράπεζα κρυσταλ-
λοειδὴς ὅλος διὰ χρυσοῦ καὶ βύσσου· ἐπάνω δὲ τῆς τρα- 25

1 ἔρχονται] ἀνέρχονται CE   1, 2 καὶ—χαίρει] om CD   2 πρωτόπλ.] om B
4 ἀνασπᾷ] ἁρπάζει AB; τίλη D; ἀνασπάζῃ E   5—12 κεφαλῆς—σωζομένη]
κεφ. αὐτοῦ κ. τ. παρειὰς τοῦ πόγονος (αὐτ.) κλαίων κ. ὀδυρόμ. διότι αὕτη ἡ πύλη ἡ
πλατ. τῶν ἁμαρτ. ἐστιν ἡ ἀπολια (ἀπάγουσα εἰς τὴν κολ. D) εἰς γὰρ τὰς ἑπτὰ χιλ.
μία ψυχὴ σώζεται CDE   14 ἔτι δὲ—λαλοῦντος] A with ὑμῖν for ἐμοί: om
B; ἔτη δὲ (ἐμέ του C) λαλοῦντας CE; ἔτι δὲ αὐτοῦ λαλοῦντος D   14—18
ἰδοὺ—ἐκράτει ὁ ἄγγελος] (μυριάδαν and om αὐτοὺς) A; καὶ ἰδοὺ δύο ἄγγελοι μυρ.
ψυχ.—ἀλξάνες B; ἰδοὺ δύο ἀγγ. μυριάδαν ψυχ. ἀνηλεῶς—χαρξανες CE; ἰδοὺ δύο
ἀγγ. τύπτοντες ψυχάς· τότε κεινω μυρίων ἐν πυρινῶ θεάφη καὶ μίαν ψυχ. ἀνηλ.
ἐκράτουν εἰς χεῖρας αὐτῶν D   17 ὁ ἄγγελος] ἀνηλεως CE   19 οὖν καὶ]
om B   20, 21 καὶ ἤλθ.—πλατείας] om B   22 ἐν εἴδει—φοβεροῦ] om
CDE   23 ἡλιόρατος] ἡλοιόρατος A; ἡλιωρότατος B; ἡλιόρατος ἡλιόμορφος
CE; om D   24 υἱῷ] υἱὸς ACE: υἱὸν B   κρυσταλλοειδὴς] κρυσταλλινος
B; om CDE   25 διὰ χρυσοῦ] διὰ χρύσεως B; διὰ λίθων κ. μαργάρων D
25—p. 91, l. 4 ἐπάνω—προσώπου δὲ] om B

RECENSION A.

πέζης ἦν βιβλίον κείμενον, τὸ πάχος αὐτοῦ πηχέων ἕξ, τὸ
δὲ πλάτος αὐτοῦ πηχέων δέκα· ἐκ δεξιῶν δὲ αὐτῆς καὶ ἐξ
ἀριστερῶν ἵσταντο δύο ἄγγελοι κρατοῦντες χάρτην καὶ
μέλανα καὶ κάλαμον. πρὸ προσώπου δὲ τῆς τραπέζης
5 ἐκάθητο ἄγγελος φωτοφόρος, κρατῶν ἐν τῇ χειρὶ αὐτοῦ
ζυγόν· <ἐξ> ἀριστερῶν δὲ ἐκάθητο ἄγγελος πύρινος ὅλος
ἀνιλέως καὶ ἀπότομος ἐν τῇ χειρὶ αὐτοῦ κρατῶν σάλπιγγα
ἔνδον αὐτῆς κατέχων πῦρ παμφάγον δοκιμαστήριον τῶν
ἁμαρτωλῶν. καὶ ὁ μὲν ἀνὴρ ὁ θαυμάσιος ὁ καθήμενος ἐπὶ
10 τοῦ θρόνου, αὐτὸς ἔκρινεν καὶ ἀπεφήνατο τὰς ψυχάς· οἱ δὲ
δύο ἄγγελοι οἱ ἐκ δεξιῶν καὶ ἀριστερῶν ἀπεγράφοντο· ὁ
μὲν ἐκ δεξιῶν ἀπεγράφετο τὰς δικαιοσύνας, ὁ δὲ ἐξ ἀριστερῶν τὰς ἁμαρτίας· καὶ ὁ μὲν πρὸ προσώπου τῆς τραπέζης,
ὁ τὸν ζυγὸν κατέχων, ἐζυγίαζεν τὰς ψυχάς· καὶ ὁ πύρινος
15 ἄγγελος, ὁ τὸ πῦρ κατέχων, ἐδοκίμαζεν τὰς ψυχάς. καὶ
ἠρώτησεν Ἀβραὰμ τὸν ἀρχιστράτηγον Μιχαήλ· Τί ἐστιν
ταῦτα ἃ θεωροῦμεν ἡμεῖς; καὶ εἶπεν ὁ ἀρχιστράτηγος·
Ταῦτα ἅπερ βλέπεις, ὅσιε Ἀβραάμ, ἔστιν ἡ κρίσις καὶ
ἀνταπόδοσις. καὶ ἰδοὺ ὁ ἄγγελος ὁ κρατῶν τὴν ψυχὴν ἐν
20 τῇ χειρὶ αὐτοῦ, καὶ ἤνεγκεν αὐτὴν ἔμπροσθεν τοῦ κριτοῦ.
καὶ εἶπεν ὁ κριτὴς ἕνα τῶν ἀγγέλων τῶν καθυπουργούντων
αὐτῷ· Ἄνοιξόν μοι τὴν βίβλον ταύτην καὶ εὑρέ μοι τὰς
ἁμαρτίας τῆς ψυχῆς ταύτης. καὶ ἀνοίξας τὴν βίβλον
εὗρεν αὐτῆς ζυγίας τὰς ἁμαρτίας καὶ τὰς δικαιοσύνας ἐξ
25 ἴσου, καὶ οὔτε τοῖς βασανισταῖς ἐξέδωκεν αὐτὴν οὔτε τοῖς
σωζομένοις, ἀλλ' ἔστησεν αὐτὴν εἰς τὸ μέσον.

XIII. καὶ εἶπεν Ἀβραάμ· Κύριέ μου ἀρχιστράτηγε,
τίς ἐστιν οὗτος ὁ κριτὴς ὁ πανθαύμαστος; καὶ τίνες οἱ

1 ἕξ] τριάκοντα A; ὀκτὼ D   τὸ δὲ—δέκα] om A   2 δέκα] δώδεκα D
ἐξ] om ABCE ; (καὶ ἐξ εὐωνύμων ἴσταται(ι)) D   7 κρατῶν σάλπιγγα] κρατῶν
σάλπιγγος CE ; κατέχων σάλπιγγα (-ος A) AB   8 πῦρ παμφ.] om CDE
δοκιμαστ.] δοκιμαστικὸν B   9 ἁμαρτωλ.] ἁμαρτιῶν CDE   14 ἐζυγίαζεν]
ἐζυγησεν AB   πύρινος] πονηρὸς B   15 ἄγγελος] om CDE   πῦρ] πῶς CE
ἐδοκ. τὰς ψυχ.] ἐδοκ. διὰ πυρὸς τὰς ψ. τῶν ἀνθρώπων A   17 ταῦτα—
θεωρ.] ἢ τα τοιαῦτα θαιωρῶμεν CE   ἡμεῖς] om ACDE   18 ἅπερ βλέπεις]
ἀποβλέπεις B   19, 20 ἐν τῇ χειρὶ] εἰς τὴν χεῖρα A   20 κριτοῦ] κρίνοντος B
22, 23 καὶ εὑρέ—ἀνοίξας] om C   23, 24 ταύτης—εὗρεν αὐτῆς] om B   24 ζυ-
γίας] ζυγαδας A ; ζυγὸς δὲ B   25 ἐξέδωκεν] ἐξέδοτο BCDE   26 ἔστησεν]
ἴστησιν BCE

7 *

ABCDER ἄγγελοι οἱ ἀπογραφόμενοι; καὶ τίς ὁ ἄγγελος ὁ ἡλιόμορφος ὁ τὸν ζυγὸν κατέχων; καὶ τίς ὁ ἄγγελος ὁ πύρινος ὁ τὸ πῦρ κατέχων; εἶπεν δὲ ὁ ἀρχιστράτηγος· Θεωρεῖς, πανόσιε Ἀβραάμ, τὸν ἄνδρα τὸν φοβερὸν τὸν ἐπὶ τοῦ θρόνου καθήμενον; οὗτός ἐστιν υἱὸς Ἀδὰμ τοῦ πρωτο- 5 πλάστου, ὁ ἐπιλεγόμενος Ἀβελ, ὃν ἀπέκτεινε Κάϊν ὁ πονηρός· καὶ κάθηται ὧδε κρῖναι πᾶσαν τὴν κτίσιν καὶ ἐλέγχων δικαίους καὶ ἁμαρτωλούς· διότι εἶπεν ὁ θεός· Ἐγὼ οὐ κρίνω ὑμᾶς, ἀλλὰ πᾶς ἄνθρωπος ἐξ ἀνθρώπου κριθήσεται· τούτου χάριν αὐτῷ δέδωκεν κρίσιν, κρῖναι τὸν 10 κόσμον μέχρι τῆς μεγάλης καὶ ἐνδόξου αὐτοῦ παρουσίας· καὶ τότε, δίκαιε Ἀβραάμ, γίνεται τελεία κρίσις καὶ ἀνταπόδοσις, αἰωνία καὶ ἀμετάθετος, ἣν οὐδεὶς δύναται ἀνακρῖναι· πᾶς γὰρ ἄνθρωπος ἐκ τοῦ πρωτοπλάστου γεγέννηται, καὶ διὰ τοῦτο ἐνταῦθα πρῶτον ἐκ τοῦ υἱοῦ αὐτοῦ 15 κρίνονται· καὶ ἐν τῇ δευτέρᾳ παρουσίᾳ κριθήσονται ὑπὸ τῶν δώδεκα φυλῶν τοῦ Ἰσραήλ, καὶ πᾶσα πνοὴ καὶ πᾶσα κτίσις. τὸ δὲ τρίτον, ὑπὸ τοῦ δεσπότου θεοῦ τῶν ἁπάντων κριθήσονται καὶ τότε λοιπὸν τῆς κρίσεως ἐκείνης τὸ τέλος ἐγγύς, καὶ φοβερὰ ἡ ἀπόφασις, καὶ ὁ λύων οὐδείς· καὶ 20 λοιπὸν διὰ τριῶν βημάτων γίνεται ἡ κρίσις τοῦ κόσμου καὶ ἡ ἀνταπόδοσις· καὶ διὰ τοῦτο ἐπὶ ἑνὸς ἢ δύο μαρτύρων οὐκ ἀσφαλίζεται λόγος εἰς τέλος· ἀλλ' ἐπὶ τριῶν μαρτύρων σταθήσεται πᾶν ῥῆμα. οἱ δὲ δύο ἄγγελοι ὁ ἐκ δεξιῶν

1—3 καὶ τίς—ἀρχιστρ.] om CE   3 κατέχων] δοκημάζον A   4 φοβερόν] φωτοφόρον CE   7 πονηρὸς]+καὶ ἀδελφοκτόνος Β; πονηρότατος A; πονηρώτ. ὁ βροτοκτόνος E   κάθηται ὧδε] καθέζεται οὗτος B   8, 9 διότι—ὑμᾶς] διότι—θεός· ὅτι οὐκ ἐγὼ κρίνω τὸν κόσμον A; δι' αὐτοῦ εἶπεν ὁ θεὸς σὺ κρίνῃ λέγων ἡμᾶς B   10, 11 τούτου—κόσμον] A (but ἔδωκεν); τούτου γὰρ χάριν ἔδωκεν αὐτὰ ὁ θεὸς ὅτι ἔκρινεν αὐτά· καὶ αὐτὸς κρίνῃ τὸν κοσμον B; om κρίσιν —κόσμον CE   13, 14 ἣν—ἀνακρῖναι] ἣν ἄλλος οὐδεὶς δυνήσεται ἀνακρῖναι AD; ἣν—ἀντακρῖναι CE; ἣν—κρῖναι τῶν ἀνῶν Β   14—16 πᾶς—κρίνονται] πᾶς γὰρ ὁ ἐκ…ἐνταῦθα πρὸς τὸν ἐκ τοῦ υἱοῦ κρίνονται Β; πᾶς—ἐκ τοῦ τουούτου ἀνοῦ κρίνεται A; πᾶς—ἐκ τοῦ υἱοῦ τοῦ πρωτοπλ. κρίνονται CE; διὰ τοῦτο καὶ ὁ υἱὸς αὐτοῦ κρίνει πρῶτον D   16—18 καὶ ἐν—κτίσις] καὶ ἐπὶ τὴν δ. π. ὑπὸ τῶν ἀποστόλων κριθήσονται αἱ δωδ. φυλαὶ τοῦ Ἰσ. καὶ πάσης πνοῆς καὶ πάσης ἀνοῖς B; καὶ ἐν τῇ δ. π. ὑπὸ τῶν ιβ ἀποστ. κ.τ.λ. CE; καὶ ἐν—ὑπὸ τῶν ιβ' ἀποστ. κριθήσεται πᾶσα ἡ οἰκουμένη D   18 δεσπότου θεοῦ τῶν ἁπάντων] δεσπ. καὶ κριτοῦ CE; δεσπ. θεοῦ καὶ σρος D   20 ἐγγὺς] ὀργῆς CE   καὶ φοβερά—οὐδείς] om B   22 τοῦτο]+καὶ νῦν A   23, 24 λόγος—σταθ.] om CE   23 εἰς τέλος] om A

RECENSION A. 93

καὶ ὁ ἐξ ἀριστερῶν, οὗτοί εἰσιν οἱ ἀπογραφόμενοι τὰς ABCDER
ἁμαρτίας καὶ τὰς δικαιοσύνας· ὁ μὲν ἐκ δεξιῶν ἀπογρά-
φεται τὰς δικαιοσύνας, ὁ δὲ ἐξ ἀριστερῶν τὰς ἁμαρτίας.
ὁ δὲ ἡλιόμορφος ἄγγελος, ὁ τὸν ζυγὸν κατέχων ἐν τῇ χειρὶ
5 αὐτοῦ, οὗτός ἐστιν ὁ Δοκιὴλ ὁ ἀρχάγγελος ὁ δίκαιος ζυγοστάτης, καὶ ζυγιάζει τὰς δικαιοσύνας καὶ τὰς ἁμαρτίας ἐν
δικαιοσύνῃ θεοῦ· ὁ δὲ πύρινος καὶ ἀνιλέως ἄγγελος, ὁ κατέχων ἐν τῇ χειρὶ αὐτοῦ τὸ πῦρ, οὗτός ἐστιν Πυρουὴλ ὁ
ἀρχάγγελος ὁ ἐπὶ τοῦ πυρὸς ἔχων τὴν ἐξουσίαν, καὶ δοκι-
10 μάζει τὰ τῶν ἀνθρώπων ἔργα διὰ πυρός· καὶ εἴ τινος τὸ
ἔργον κατακαύσει τὸ πῦρ, εὐθὺς λαμβάνει αὐτὸν ὁ ἄγγελος
τῆς κρίσεως καὶ ἀποφέρει αὐτὸν εἰς τὸν τόπον τῶν ἁμαρτωλῶν, πικρότατον κολαστήριον. εἴ τινος δὲ τὸ ἔργον τὸ
πῦρ δοκιμάσει καὶ μὴ ἅψεται αὐτοῦ, οὗτος δικαιοῦται, καὶ
15 λαμβάνει αὐτὸν ὁ τῆς δικαιοσύνης ἄγγελος καὶ ἀναφέρει
αὐτὸν εἰς τὸ σώζεσθαι ἐν τῷ κλήρῳ τῶν δικαίων· καὶ
οὕτως, δικαιότατε Ἀβραάμ, τὰ πάντα ἐν πᾶσιν ἐν πυρὶ
καὶ ζυγῷ δοκιμάζονται.

XIV. εἶπεν δὲ Ἀβραὰμ πρὸς τὸν ἀρχιστράτηγον·
20 Κύριέ μου ἀρχιστράτηγε, τὴν ψυχὴν ἣν κατεῖχεν ὁ ἄγγελος ἐν τῇ χειρὶ αὐτοῦ, πῶς κατεδικάσθη εἰς τὸ μέσον;
εἶπεν δὲ ὁ ἀρχιστράτηγος· Ἄκουσον, δίκαιε Ἀβραάμ·
διότι εὗρεν ὁ κριτὴς τὰς ἁμαρτίας αὐτῆς καὶ τὰς δικαιοσύνας ἐξ ἴσου, καὶ οὔτε εἰς κρίσιν ἐξέδοτο αὐτὴν οὔτε εἰς
25 τὸ σώζεσθαι, ἕως οὗ ἔλθῃ ὁ κριτὴς τῶν ἁπάντων. εἶπεν δὲ
Ἀβραὰμ <πρὸς> τὸν ἀρχιστράτηγον Καὶ τί ἔτι λείπεται
τῇ ψυχῇ εἰς τὸ σώζεσθαι; καὶ εἶπεν ὁ ἀρχιστράτηγος ὅτι
Ἐὰν κτήσηται μίαν δικαιοσύνην ὑπεράνω τῶν ἁμαρτιῶν
ἔρχεται εἰς τὸ σώζεσθαι. εἶπεν δὲ Ἀβραὰμ πρὸς τὸν

5 ὁ Δοκιὴλ] (ὁδοκιὴλ) A; δίκαιος ἄγγελος BCDE   6 ζυγιάζει] ζυγήζει
A; στυγίζει B; ζυγῇ CE; ζυγοστατῶν D   τὰς δικ.—θεοῦ] τὰς ἁμαρτ. τῶν
ἀνων καὶ τὰς δικ. τοῦ θεοῦ B   7—18 ὁ δὲ πύρινος—δοκιμάζονται] om CDE
7 καὶ ἀνιλ. ἀγγ.] ἀγγ. κ. ἀπότομος A   8, 9 Πυρουὴλ—πυρός] Πυρουὴλ ὁ
ἀγγ. ὁ ἐπὶ τὸ πῦρ A; πῦρ ὁ κλῶν ὁ ἀρχάγγ. ὁ ἐπὶ τοῦ πυρὸς B   10 διὰ
πυρός] διὰ παντὸς A   12, 13 εἰς τὸν τόπον—κολαστήριον] A (but ποτήριον
for κολαστ.); εἰς τὰ πικρότατα τῶν ἁμαρτιῶν κολαστ. B   15 ἀναφέρει]
ἀποφέρει B   24 ἐξ ἴσου] ζυγάδας A; ζυγᾶς ἐπίσης E; ζυγᾶς C   διὰ
τούτων οὗτος ἐν τῇ κρίσει ἐξέδ. αὐτὴν B   25 ἕως οὗ] ἕως ἂν CE   26 ἔτι]
ἐστι BC   27 τῇ ψυχῇ] ἡ ψυχὴ ACD; τὴν ψυχὴν B

ABCDER ἀρχιστράτηγον· Δεῦρο Μιχαὴλ ἀρχιστράτηγε, ποιήσωμεν
εὐχὴν ὑπὲρ τῆς ψυχῆς ταύτης, καὶ ἴδωμεν εἰ ἐπακούσεται
ἡμῶν ὁ θεός. καὶ εἶπεν ὁ ἀρχιστράτηγος· Ἀμὴν γένοιτο.
καὶ ἐποίησαν δέησιν καὶ εὐχὴν ὑπὲρ τῆς ψυχῆς· καὶ εἰσήκουσεν αὐτοὺς ὁ θεὸς καὶ ἀναστάντες ἀπὸ τῆς προσευχῆς 5
οὐκ εἶδον τὴν ψυχὴν ἱσταμένην ἐκεῖσε. καὶ εἶπεν Ἀβραὰμ
πρὸς τὸν ἄγγελον· Ποῦ ἐστὶν ἡ ψυχὴ ἣν ἐκράτεις εἰς τὸ
μέσον; καὶ εἶπεν ὁ ἄγγελος· Σέσωται διὰ τῆς εὐχῆς σου
τῆς δικαίας, καὶ ἰδοὺ ἔλαβεν αὐτὴν ἄγγελος φωτοφόρος
καὶ ἀνήνεγκεν αὐτὴν ἐν τῷ παραδείσῳ. εἶπεν δὲ Ἀβραάμ· 10
Δοξάζω τὸ ὄνομα τοῦ θεοῦ τοῦ ὑψίστου καὶ τὸ ἔλεος αὐτοῦ
τὸ ἀμέτρητον. εἶπεν δὲ Ἀβραὰμ πρὸς τὸν ἀρχιστράτηγον·
Δέομαί σου, ἀρχάγγελε, εἰσάκουσον τῆς δεήσεώς μου, καὶ
παρακαλέσωμεν ἔτι τὸν κύριον καὶ προσπέσωμεν τοῖς
οἰκτιρμοῖς αὐτοῦ καὶ δεηθῶμεν αὐτοῦ τοῦ ἐλέους ὑπὲρ τῶν 15
ψυχῶν τῶν ἁμαρτωλῶν οὕσπερ ἐγώ ποτε κακοφρονήσας
κατηρασάμην καὶ ἀπώλεσα, οὕσπερ κατέπιεν ἡ γῆ καὶ οὓς
διεμερίσαντο τὰ θηρία, καὶ οὕσπερ κατέφαγεν τὸ πῦρ διὰ
τοὺς ἐμοὺς λόγους· νῦν ἔγνωκα ἐγὼ ὅτι ἥμαρτον ἐνώπιον
κυρίου τοῦ θεοῦ ἡμῶν· δεῦρο, Μιχαὴλ ἀρχιστράτηγε τῶν 20
ἄνω δυνάμεων, δεῦρο παρακαλέσωμεν τὸν θεὸν μετὰ δακρύων, ὅπως ἀφήσει μοι τὸ ἁμάρτημα καὶ αὐτοὺς συγχω-
ρήσει μοι. καὶ εἰσήκουσεν αὐτὸν ὁ ἀρχιστράτηγος καὶ
ἐποίησαν δέησιν ἐνώπιον τοῦ θεοῦ· ἐπὶ πολλὴν δὲ ὥραν
παρακαλούντων αὐτῶν, ἦλθεν φωνὴ ἐκ τοῦ οὐρανοῦ λέ- 25
γουσα· Ἀβραάμ, Ἀβραάμ, εἰσήκουσα τῆς φωνῆς σου καὶ
τῆς δεήσεώς σου καὶ ἀφίημί σοι τὴν ἁμαρτίαν, καὶ οὕσπερ
σὺ νομίζεις ὅτι ἀπώλεσα, ἐγὼ αὐτοὺς ἀνεκαλεσάμην καὶ
εἰς ζωὴν αὐτοὺς ἤγαγον δι᾽ ἄκραν ἀγαθότητα· διότι πρὸς

4—6 καὶ εἰσήκ.—ψυχήν] om A   7, 8 ἣν—μέσον] om ABCD   8 σέσωται]
ἰδοὺ B   9, 10 καὶ ἰδοὺ—παραδ.] om CDE   10—12 εἶπεν—ἀμέτρητον]
om BCDE   14 κύριον] + ἡμῶν ἰησοῦν χριστόν C   16 κακοφρ.] καταφρ.
BDE   16—23 οὕσπερ—συγχωρ. μοι] AB; CDE shorten variously
26 Ἀβραὰμ (sec.)] om ABDE   26, 27 εἰσήκουσα—δεήσ. σου] εἰσηκουσε σε κ̅ς̅
A; εἰσηκούσθη ἡ δ. σου B   27 οὕσπερ ἐκατηράσω καὶ ἀπώλεσα αὐτοὺς δὲ πάλιν
διὰ δεήσεώς σου ἐγὼ E   28 ἀπώλεσα] ἀπώλεσας A   ἀνεκαλ.] ἐνηγκα-
λισάμην καὶ—ἤγαγον· διότι πρόσκαιρον αὐτοῖς κρίσιν ἀνταπέδωκας· ἐγὼ δὲ—ἀπώλεσα—γῆς, ζῶντας ἐν τῷ θανάτῳ οὐκ ἀποδώσω D   29 δι᾽ ἄκρ. ἀγαθ.] om
CDE   29—p. 95, 1 διότι—ἀνταπ.] om A; διότι—ἀποδώσω] καὶ εἰ μὲν διὰ
τὸν πρόσκαιρον κρίσιν αὐτοὺς ἀνταπέδωκας, ἐγὼ δὲ οὐ κολάσω (sc. οὐκ ὀλέσω?) B

καιρὸν εἰς κρίσιν αὐτοὺς ἀνταπέδωκα· ἐγὼ δὲ οὕσπερ ABCDER ἀπολέσω ἐπὶ τῆς γῆς ζῶντας, ἐν τῷ θανάτῳ οὐκ ἀποδώσω.

XV. εἶπεν δὲ καὶ τὸν ἀρχιστράτηγον ἡ φωνὴ τοῦ 5 κυρίου· Μιχαὴλ, Μιχαὴλ, ὁ ἐμὸς λειτουργὸς, ἀπόστρεψον τὸν Ἀβραὰμ εἰς τὸν οἶκον αὐτοῦ, ὅτι ἰδοὺ ἤγγικεν τὸ τέλος αὐτοῦ καὶ τὸ μέτρον τῆς ζωῆς αὐτοῦ τελειοῦται, ὅπως ποιήσει διάταξιν περὶ πάντων καὶ εἶθ᾽ οὕτως παράλαβε αὐτὸν καὶ ἀνάγαγε πρός με. διαστρέψας δὲ ὁ ἀρχι-10 στράτηγος τὸ ἅρμα καὶ τὴν νεφέλην, ἤγαγεν τὸν Ἀβραὰμ εἰς τὸν οἶκον αὐτοῦ· καὶ ἀπελθὼν ἐν τῷ τρικλίνῳ αὐτοῦ, ἐκάθισεν ἐπὶ τῆς κλίνης αὐτοῦ· ἦλθεν δὲ Σάρρα ἡ γυνὴ αὐτοῦ καὶ περιεπλάκη τοῖς ποσὶν τοῦ ἀσωμάτου καὶ ἱκετεύουσα ἔλεγεν· Εὐχαριστῶ σοι, κύριέ μου, ὅτι ἤνεγκας τὸν 15 κύριόν μου Ἀβραάμ· ἰδοὺ γὰρ ἐνομίζομεν ἀναληφθῆναι ἀφ᾽ ἡμῶν. ἦλθεν δὲ καὶ Ἰσαὰκ ὁ υἱὸς αὐτοῦ, καὶ περιεπλάκη ἐπὶ τὸν τράχηλον αὐτοῦ· ὁμοίως δὲ καὶ πάντες οἱ δοῦλοι καὶ αἱ δουλίδες αὐτοῦ περιεκύκλωσαν κύκλῳ τὸν Ἀβραὰμ καὶ περιεπλάκησαν αὐτὸν δοξάζοντες τὸν θεόν. εἶπεν δὲ 20 ὁ ἀσώματος πρὸς αὐτόν· Ἄκουσον, δίκαιε Ἀβραάμ· ἰδοὺ ἡ γυνή σου Σάρρα, ἰδοὺ καὶ ὁ ἠγαπημένος σου υἱὸς Ἰσαὰκ, ἰδοὺ καὶ πάντες οἱ παῖδες καὶ παιδίσκαι σου κυκλῷ σου· ποίησον διάταξιν περὶ πάντων ὧν ἔχεις· ὅτι ἤγγικεν ἡ ἡμέρα ἐν ᾗ μέλλεις ἐκ τοῦ σώματος ἐκδημεῖν καὶ ἔτι ἅπαξ 25 πρὸς τὸν κύριον ἔρχεσθαι. εἶπεν δὲ Ἀβραάμ· Ὁ κύριος εἶπεν, ἢ σὺ ἀφ᾽ ἑαυτοῦ λέγεις ταῦτα; ὁ δὲ ἀρχιστράτηγος εἶπεν· Ἄκουσον δίκαιε Ἀβραάμ· ὁ δεσπότης ἐκέλευσεν καὶ ἐγώ σοι λέγω. εἶπεν δὲ Ἀβραάμ· Οὐ μή σοι ἀκολουθήσω. ἀκούσας δὲ ὁ ἀρχιστράτηγος τὸν λόγον τοῦτον, εὐθέως 30 ἐξῆλθεν ἐκ προσώπου τοῦ Ἀβραὰμ καὶ ἀνῆλθεν εἰς τοὺς

2 ἀπολέσω] ἀποδώσω A   2, 3 ἀποδώσω] ἀπετίσωμαι A   6, 7 ὅτι ἰδοὺ —τελειοῦται] ὅτι καὶ τὸ μετρ.—ἐτελειοῦτο B; ὅτι ἰδοὺ ἠγγ. τὸ τέλ. τῆς ϛ. αὐτοῦ CE   8 πάντων] περὶ τοῦ οἴκου αὐτοῦ (+καὶ τὰ ὑπάρχοντα αὐτοῦ B) καὶ πάντα ὅσα βούλεται AB   9, 10 διαστρέψας—νεφέλην] ADE (om τὸ ἅρμα καὶ A); διμερέψας B; om C   14 κύριέ μου] κύριε ὁ θς μου B   15 ἀναληφθῆναι] ἀναληφθέντα αὐτὸν A   21 ἰδού—Ἰσαὰκ] om B   23 ὧν ἔχεις] ὃ ἐὰν βούλῃ A; ὅσα βουλέσαι B   24 ἔτι ἅπαξ] om BCDE   27 ἄκουσον] om B   δίκαιε] om C   ὁ δεσπότης] ἅπερ ὁ δ. AB   27, 28 καὶ—λέγω] κἀγὼ ὑπήκω B   30 ἐξῆλθεν—Ἀβρ.] om CE

96   THE TESTAMENT OF ABRAHAM.

ABCDER οὐρανοὺς καὶ ἔστη ἐνώπιον τοῦ θεοῦ τοῦ ὑψίστου καὶ
εἶπεν· Κύριε παντοκράτορ, ἰδοὺ εἰσήκουσα τοῦ φίλου σου
Ἀβραὰμ πάντα ὅσα εἶπεν πρός σε καὶ τὴν αἴτησιν αὐτοῦ
ἐπλήρωσα, καὶ ἔδειξα αὐτῷ τὴν δυναστείαν σου καὶ
πᾶσαν τὴν ὑπ' οὐρανὸν γῆν τε καὶ θάλασσαν, κρίσιν καὶ 5
ἀνταπόδοσιν διὰ νεφέλης καὶ ἁρμάτων ἔδειξα αὐτῷ, καὶ
πάλιν λέγει ὅτι Οὐκ ἀκολουθῶ σοι. καὶ ὁ ὕψιστος ἔφη
πρὸς τὸν ἄγγελον· Εἰ καὶ πάλιν οὕτως λέγει ὁ φίλος μου
Ἀβραὰμ ὅτι Οὐκ ἀκολουθῶ σοι; ὁ δὲ ἀρχάγγελος εἶπεν·
Κύριε παντοκράτορ, οὕτως λέγει· καὶ ἐγὼ φείδομαι τοῦ 10
ἅψασθαι αὐτοῦ, ὅτι ἐξ ἀρχῆς φίλος σου τυγχάνει καὶ
πάντα τὰ ἀρεστὰ ἐνώπιόν σου ἐποίησεν· καὶ οὐκ ἔστιν
ἄνθρωπος ὅμοιος αὐτοῦ ἐπὶ τῆς γῆς, οὐ κἂν Ἰὼβ ὁ θαυμάσιος ἄνθρωπος· καὶ διὰ τοῦτο φείδομαι τοῦ ἅψασθαι αὐτοῦ·
κέλευσον οὖν, ἀθάνατε βασιλεῦ, τί ῥῆμα γενήσεται.   15

XVI.   τότε ὁ ὕψιστος λέγει· Κάλεσόν μοι ὧδε τὸν
θάνατον τὸν κεκλημένον τὸ ἀναίσχυντον πρόσωπον καὶ
ἀνέλεον βλέμμα. καὶ ἀπελθὼν Μιχαὴλ ὁ ἀσώματος εἶπεν
τῷ θανάτῳ· Δεῦρο, καλεῖ σε ὁ δεσπότης τῆς κτίσεως, ὁ
ἀθάνατος βασιλεύς. ἀκούσας δὲ ὁ θάνατος ἔφριξεν καὶ 20
ἐτρόμαξεν δειλίᾳ πολλῇ συνεχόμενος, καὶ ἐλθὼν μετὰ
φόβου πολλοῦ ἔστη ἔμπροσθεν τοῦ ἀοράτου πατρός, φρίτ-
των στένων καὶ τρέμων, ἀπεκδεχόμενος τὴν κέλευσιν τοῦ
δεσπότου. λέγει οὖν ὁ ἀόρατος θεὸς πρὸς τὸν θάνατον·
Δεῦρο, τὸ πικρὸν καὶ ἄγριον τοῦ κόσμου ὄνομα, κρύψον 25

1 τοῦ θεοῦ τοῦ ὑψίστου] om τοῦ θεοῦ B; om τοῦ ὑψ. C   2, 3 ἰδοὺ
—πρός σε] om CE   4 ἐπλήρωσα] ἐπλήρωσας B   5 γῆν—θάλασσαν]
γῆς τε καὶ θαλάσσης A; γῆν θάλασσαν B; γῆν τε καὶ θαλάσσης CE   7 and
9 ἀκολουθῶ] -ήσω E   9—12 εἶπεν—πάντα] καὶ εἶπεν ἐκπροσώπου κῦ τοῦ
θῦ ἡμῶν ὅτι ἐξ ἀρχῆς φ. σ. καὶ πάντα A; καὶ ὁ ἄγγελος ἔφη οὕτω λέγει ὁ φ.
σου Ἀ. καὶ ἔτι φείδομαι τοῦ ἅψασθαι αὐτόν· ἐπεὶ κ.τ.λ. B   11 ὅτι ἐξ ἀρχῆς]
ἐπεὶ δὲ ὑπάρχει φίλος σου τυγχάνει B; ἐπὶ ἀρχήν—ἐστιν CE   12 ἐποίησεν]
πράτων CE   13, 14 οὐ—θαυμάσιος ἄνθρωπος] om CE   13 οὐ—'Ἰὼβ] κἂν Ἰὼβ
B; οὐ κἂν Ἰακὼβ A   15 κέλευσον] καὶ βλέψον CE   16 μοι ὧδε] ἡμῖν
ἐδῶ B   17 τὸν κεκλ.] om BCE   18 ἀνέλεον βλέμμα] ἀνελεεῖ τὸ βλεμματι
A; τὸν θάν. τὸν ἀναισχύντην καὶ ἀνελεεῖ καὶ ἀνείδη B   19 τῆς κτίσ.] om CE
21—23 καὶ ἐλθὼν—ἀπεκδεχ.] om A   22 ἀοράτου πατρός] δεσπ. θῦ B   24 ἀόρατος θῦ] om θῦ B; ὁ ἀσώματος CE   πρὸς] om AB   25 τὸ πικρὸν—ὄνομα]
δεῦρο τοῦ κόσμ. ἀγρ. ὄν. B; τὸ πικρ. ποτ. κ. ἀγροιον ομα. CE (= ἄγριον ὄνομα)
25—p. 97, 2 κρύψον—ἀποβαλοῦ] κρύψαι σου τὴν πικρ. καὶ πάσας σου τὰς παρολας κ.
τὰς πικρ. πασ. κ.τ.λ. A;   κρυψον σου τ. πικρ. καὶ πᾶσαν σου τὴν σαπρίαν ἀποβ. CE

RECENSION A. 97

σου τὴν ἀγριότητα, σκέπασόν σου τὴν σαπρίαν, καὶ τὴν ABCDER
πικρίαν σου ἀπό σου ἀποβαλοῦ, καὶ περιβαλοῦ τὴν ὡραιότητά σου καὶ πᾶσαν τὴν δόξαν σου, καὶ κάτελθε εἰς τὸν
φίλον μου τὸν Ἀβραὰμ καὶ λάβε αὐτὸν καὶ ἄγαγε αὐτὸν
5 πρός με· ἀλλὰ καὶ νῦν λέγω σοι ὅτι μὴ ἐκφοβήσῃς αὐτὸν
ἀλλὰ μετὰ κολακίας τοῦτον παράλαβε, ὅτι φίλος μου
γνήσιος ὑπάρχει. ταῦτα ἀκούσας ὁ θάνατος ἐξῆλθεν ἀπὸ
προσώπου τοῦ ὑψίστου καὶ περιεβάλετο στολὴν λαμπρο-
τάτην καὶ ἐποίησεν ὄψιν ἡλιόμορφον καὶ γέγονεν εὐπρεπὴς
10 καὶ ὡραῖος ὑπὲρ τοὺς υἱοὺς τῶν ἀνθρώπων, ἀρχαγγέλου
μορφὴν περικείμενος, τὰς παρειὰς αὐτοῦ πυρὶ ἀστράπτων,
καὶ ἀπῆλθεν πρὸς τὸν Ἀβραάμ. ὁ δὲ δίκαιος Ἀβραὰμ
ἐξῆλθεν ἐκ τοῦ τρικλίνου αὐτοῦ καὶ ἐκάθητο ὑποκάτω τῶν
δένδρων τῶν Μαμβρινῶν, τὴν σιαγόνα αὐτοῦ τῇ χειρὶ
15 κατέχων καὶ ἐκδεχόμενος τὴν ἔλευσιν τοῦ ἀρχαγγέλου
Μιχαήλ. καὶ ἰδοὺ ὀσμὴ εὐωδίας ἤρχετο πρὸς αὐτὸν, καὶ
φωτὸς ἀπαύγασμα· περιστραφεὶς δὲ Ἀβραὰμ εἶδεν τὸν
θάνατον ἐρχόμενον πρὸς αὐτὸν ἐν πολλῇ δόξῃ καὶ ὡραιό-
τητι· καὶ ἀναστὰς Ἀβραὰμ ὑπήντησεν αὐτῷ, νομίζων
20 εἶναι τὸν ἀρχιστράτηγον τοῦ θεοῦ· καὶ ἰδὼν αὐτὸν ὁ θάνατος προσεκύνησεν αὐτὸν λέγων· Χαίροις, τίμιε Ἀβραάμ,
δικαία ψυχή, φίλε γνήσιε τοῦ θεοῦ τοῦ ὑψίστου, καὶ τῶν
ἁγίων ἀγγέλων ὁμόσκηνε. εἶπεν δὲ Ἀβραὰμ πρὸς τὸν
θάνατον· Χαίροις ἡλιόρατε, ἡλιόμορφε, συλλήπτωρ ἐν-
25 δοξότατε, φωτοφόρε, ἀνὴρ θαυμάσιε, πόθεν ἥκει ἡ σὴ
ἐνδοξότης πρὸς ἡμᾶς, καὶ τίς εἶ σὺ, καὶ πόθεν ἐλήλυθας;
λέγει οὖν ὁ θάνατος· Ἀβραὰμ δικαιότατε, ἰδοὺ λέγω σοι
τὴν ἀλήθειαν· ἐγὼ εἰμὶ τὸ πικρὸν τοῦ θανάτου ποτήριον.

2, 3 τὴν ὡραι.—καὶ κάτελθε] (ὅλην τὴν ἐνδοξότητα) CDE; τὴν ὡρ. σου τὴν
εὐπρεπεστάτην καὶ κατ. B   3 εἰς] πρὸς AD   4 ἄγαγε] ἄγεις B; φέρεις
CE   αὐτὸν] τὴν ψυχὴν αὐτοῦ καὶ ἔλθῃς ἐνθάδε A   5 ἀλλὰ–ἐκφοβ.
αὐτὸν] om B   6 τοῦτον] ταύτην B   7 ὑπάρχει] ἐστιν ACE
11 περικείμ.] περιβαλλόμενος A; προκειμ. CE   τὰς παρ.—ἀστράπτων]
τὰς παρίας αὐτοῦ πῦρ ἀπαυγάζων A; ταῖς παρειαῖς αὐτ. περιαστρ. B; om CE
14 μαμβρ.] μαυριν. ACE; μελλιβρινων B   15 ἔλευσιν] κέλευσιν A   16—
18 κ. φ. ἀπαύγ.—πρὸς αὐτὸν] om CE   19 ὑπήντησεν αὐτῷ] ὑπήντησεν αὐτὸν
AE; ὑπηντήθη αὐτῷ B   20 εἶναι—θεοῦ] ἕνα τῶν ἀρχιστ. ὑπάρχων τοῦ θῦ B
22 τοῦ θεοῦ τοῦ ὑψίστου] om τοῦ θῦ E; τοῦ δεσπότου B   23 ἁγίων] om A
24 συλλήπτωρ] om B; θεομοσυλληπτωρ A   25 πόθεν—ἡ σὴ] πόθεν ἔοικας ἡ
οὐ A; πόθεν η καινὴ σὴ B; πόθεν αἴηκεν ἡ ἐν σοι CE   26 ἐνδοξ.] ὑπερένδοξε A

J.   7

ABCDER λέγει αὐτῷ Ἀβραάμ· Οὐχί, ἀλλὰ σὺ εἶ ἡ εὐπρέπεια τοῦ κόσμου, σὺ εἶ ἡ δόξα καὶ τὸ κάλλος τῶν ἀγγέλων καὶ τῶν ἀνθρώπων, σὺ εἶ πάσης μορφῆς εὐμορφότερος, καὶ λέγεις ὅτι Ἐγώ εἰμὶ τὸ πικρὸν τοῦ θανάτου ποτήριον καὶ οὐ λέγεις μᾶλλον ὅτι Ἐγώ εἰμὶ παντὸς ἀγαθοῦ εὐμορφότερος; εἶπεν 5 δὲ ὁ θάνατος· Ἐγὼ γὰρ λέγω σοι τὴν ἀλήθειαν· ὅπερ ὠνόμασέν με ὁ θεός, ἐκεῖνο καὶ λέγω σοι. εἶπεν δὲ Ἀβραάμ· Εἰς τί ἐλήλυθας ὧδε; εἶπεν δὲ ὁ θάνατος· Διὰ τὴν σὴν ἁγίαν ψυχὴν παραγέγονα. λέγει οὖν Ἀβραάμ· Οἶδα τί λέγεις, ἀλλ' οὐ μή σε ἀκολουθήσω. ὁ δὲ θάνατος 10 ἐν σιωπῇ γενόμενος οὐκ ἀπεκρίθη αὐτῷ λόγον.

XVII. ἀνέστη δὲ Ἀβραὰμ καὶ ἦλθεν εἰς τὸν οἶκον αὐτοῦ· ἠκολούθει δὲ καὶ ὁ θάνατος ἕως ἐκεῖ· ἀνέβη δὲ Ἀβραὰμ εἰς τὸ τρίκλινον αὐτοῦ· ἀνέβη δὲ καὶ ὁ θάνατος μετ' αὐτοῦ· ἀνέπεσεν δὲ Ἀβραὰμ ἐπὶ τῆς κλίνης αὐτοῦ· 15 ἦλθεν δὲ καὶ ὁ θάνατος καὶ ἐκαθέσθη παρὰ τοὺς πόδας αὐτοῦ. εἶπεν δὲ Ἀβραάμ· Ἄπελθε, ἄπελθε ἀπ' ἐμοῦ, ὅτι θέλω ἀναπαύεσθαι ἐν τῇ κλίνῃ μου. λέγει ὁ θάνατος· Οὐκ ἀναχωρῶ ἕως οὗ λάβω τὸ πνεῦμά σου ἀπό σου. λέγει αὐτῷ Ἀβραάμ· Κατὰ τοῦ θεοῦ τοῦ ἀθανάτου σοι 20 λέγω ἵνα μοι εἴπῃς τὸ ἀληθές· σὺ εἶ ὁ θάνατος; λέγει αὐτῷ ὁ θάνατος· Ἐγώ εἰμι ὁ θάνατος· ἐγώ εἰμι ὁ τὸν κόσμον λυμαίνων. εἶπεν δὲ Ἀβραάμ· Δέομαί σου, ἐπειδὴ σὺ εἶ ὁ θάνατος, ἀνάγγειλόν μοι, καὶ πρὸς πάντας οὕτως ἀπέρχῃ ἐν εὐμορφίᾳ καὶ δόξῃ καὶ ὡραιότητι τοιαύτῃ; καὶ 25 ὁ θάνατος εἶπεν· Οὐχί, κύριέ μου Ἀβραάμ· αἱ γὰρ δικαιοσύναι σου καὶ τὸ ἄμετρον πέλαγος τῆς φιλοξενίας σου καὶ τὸ μέγεθος τῆς ἀγάπης σου τῆς πρὸς θεὸν ἐγένετο

1, 2 τοῦ κόσμου—ἀγγ. καὶ] om CE; om τῶν ἀγγ. καὶ B   5 ἀγαθοῦ] παν ανου A   6 ὅπερ] ὁποῖον ὄνομα ὠνόμασεν A   8, 9 διὰ—ψυχήν] διὰ τῆς δικαίας σου ψυχῆς AB   12—17 ἀνέστη—πόδας αὐτοῦ] A; various clauses are omitted by each of the others   21 ἵνα—ἀληθές] εἰπέ ἡμῖν τὸ ἀλ. A; ἵνα μὴ εἴπῃς (εἰ) BCE   22 ἐγὼ—θάνατος] om ACDE   22, 23 ὁ—λυμαίνων] τοῦ κόσμου ὁ λυμεών B   25 καὶ ὡραι.] om B   27—p. 99, 5 τὸ ἄμετρον—ἀνίλεῳ] om πέλαγος; has ἄγων τὸν στέφανον for ἐγέν. στεφ.; τοῖς δὲ οὕτοις (οὕτως) ἀπέρχομαι ἐν πολλῇ...ἀγριότητα...ἀνηλαίῳ ἀπέρχομαι τοῖς ἁμαρτ. τοὺς μὴ πράξαντας ἔλαιον A; στέφανος ἐπὶ τὴν κεφ. σου κ. ἐν δόξῃ κ. εὐπρεπεία κ. ἡσυχ. κ. ἀγαλλιάσει κ. ἀκολακία προσερχ....σαπρια κ. ἀγρ. τῷ βλέμματι κ. μεγίστη πικρία κ. ἀνηλεῶς B; τὸ μέτρον τῆς φιλοξ. σου ἐγεν. ἡ μορφή μου· τοῖς δὲ ἀμ. ἐν ἀγριότητι κ. πικρίᾳ πολλῇ CE

RECENSION A.

στέφανος ἐπὶ τῆς ἐμῆς κεφαλῆς, καὶ ἐν ὡραιότητι καὶ ἐν ABCDER
ἡσυχίᾳ πολλῇ καὶ κολακίᾳ προσέρχομαι τοῖς δικαίοις·
τοῖς δὲ ἁμαρτωλοῖς προσέρχομαι ἐν πολλῇ σαπρίᾳ καὶ
ἀγριότητι καὶ μεγίστῃ πικρίᾳ καὶ ἀγρίῳ τῷ βλέμματι καὶ
5 ἀνίλεῳ. εἶπεν δὲ Ἀβραάμ· Δέομαί σου, ἐπάκουσόν μου
καὶ δεῖξόν μοι τὴν ἀγριότητά σου καὶ πᾶσαν τὴν σαπρίαν
καὶ πικρίαν. καὶ εἶπεν ὁ θάνατος· Οὐ μὴ δυνηθῇς θεάσασθαι τὴν ἐμὴν ἀγριότητα, δικαιότατε Ἀβραάμ. εἶπεν δὲ
Ἀβραάμ· Ναὶ, δυνήσομαι θεάσασθαί σου πᾶσαν τὴν
10 ἀγριότητα ἕνεκεν τοῦ ὀνόματος τοῦ θεοῦ τοῦ ζῶντος, ὅτι
ἡ δύναμις τοῦ θεοῦ μου τοῦ ἐπουρανίου μετ᾽ ἐμοῦ ἐστίν.
τότε ὁ θάνατος ἀπεδύσατο πᾶσαν αὐτοῦ τὴν ὡραιότητα
καὶ τὸ κάλλος, καὶ πᾶσαν τὴν δόξαν καὶ τὴν ἡλιόμορφον
μορφὴν ἣν περιέκειτο, καὶ περιεβάλετο στολὴν τυραννικήν,
15 καὶ ἐποίησεν ὄψιν ζοφερὰν καὶ παντοίων θηρίων ἀγριω-
τέραν καὶ πάσης ἀκαθαρσίας ἀκαθαρσιωτέραν· καὶ ἐπέδει-
ξεν τῷ Ἀβραὰμ κεφαλὰς δρακόντων πυρίνους ἑπτά, καὶ
πρόσωπα δεκατέσσαρα, πυρὸς φλογεστάτου καὶ πολλῆς
ἀγριότητος, καὶ πρόσωπον σκοτοειδὲς καὶ πρόσωπον ἐχίδ-
20 νης ζοφωδέστατον καὶ πρόσωπον κρημνοῦ φρικωδεστάτου
καὶ πρόσωπον ἀσπίδος ἀγριώτερον καὶ πρόσωπον λέοντος
φοβεροῦ καὶ πρόσωπον κεραστοῦ καὶ βασιλίσκου· ἔδειξεν
δὲ καὶ πρόσωπον ῥομφαίας πυρίνης καὶ πρόσωπον ξιφη-
φόρον καὶ πρόσωπον ἀστραπῆς φοβερῶς ἐξαστράπτον καὶ
25 ἦχος βροντῆς φοβερᾶς· ἔδειξεν δὲ καὶ ἕτερον πρόσωπον
θαλάσσης ἀγρίας κυματιζούσης καὶ ποταμὸν ἄγριον κο-
χλάζοντα καὶ δράκοντα τρικέφαλον φοβερὸν καὶ ποτήριον
μεμεστωμένον φαρμάκων, καὶ ἁπλῶς εἰπεῖν ἔδειξεν αὐτῷ
πολλὴν ἀγριότητα καὶ πικρίαν ἀβάστακτον καὶ πᾶσαν

6 δεῖξον] δίδαξον AB   8—10 Ἀβρ. εἶπεν—ἀγριότητα om B   10, 11 τοῦ ζῶντος—θεοῦ μου] om C; om τοῦ ζῶντος E; om μου B   12 ἀπεδύσατο] ἀπεκδ. A; om B   13 ἡλιόμ.] om BCDE   14 ἦν] om B   περιέκειτο] περιεκέκτητο A   15 ζοφ.] φοβερὰν B   παντ. θηρ.] παντὸς θηρίου A; πάντων θηρ. τὴν ἀγριότητα B   16 καὶ πασ. ἀκαθ.] om CE   ἀκαθαρσιωτέραν] om B   ἐπέδειξεν] ὑπέδ. AB   17 τῷ] τὸν codd   πυρίνους] om. CE   18 πυρὸς φλογεστάτου] πυρὸς φλογέστερον A; πυρὸς ἀγριώτερον C; πυρὸς καὶ πολλὴν ἀγρ. E   18, 19 καὶ πολλ. ἀγρ.] om B   19—28 The text mainly from A. The variations are innumerable, chiefly in the matter of omissions.

7—2

ABCDER νόσον θανατηφόρον ὡς τῆς ὀσμῆς τοῦ θανάτου. καὶ ἐκ τῆς πολλῆς πικρίας καὶ ἀγριότητος ἐτελεύτησαν παῖδες καὶ παιδίσκαι τὸν ἀριθμὸν ὡσεὶ χιλιάδες ἑπτά· καὶ ὁ δίκαιος Ἀβραὰμ ἦλθεν εἰς ὀλιγωρίαν θανάτου ὥστε ἐκλείπειν τὸ πνεῦμα αὐτοῦ.

XVIII. καὶ ταῦτα οὕτως ἰδὼν ὁ πανίερος Ἀβραὰμ εἶπεν πρὸς τὸν θάνατον· Δέομαί σου, πανώλεθρε θάνατε, κρύψον σου τὴν ἀγριότητα καὶ περιβαλοῦ τὴν ὡραιότητα καὶ μορφὴν ἣν εἶχες τὸ πρότερον. εὐθέως δὲ ὁ θάνατος ἔκρυψεν τὴν ἀγριότητα αὐτοῦ καὶ περιεβάλετο τὴν ὡραιότητα αὐτοῦ ἣν εἶχεν τὸ πρότερον. εἶπεν δὲ Ἀβραὰμ πρὸς τὸν θάνατον· Τί τοῦτο ἐποίησας, ὅτι ἀπέκτεινας πάντας τοὺς παῖδας καὶ παιδίσκας μου; εἰ ὁ θεὸς ἕνεκεν τούτου σε σήμερον ἀπέστειλεν ὧδε; καὶ ὁ θάνατος εἶπεν· Οὐχί, κύριέ μου Ἀβραάμ, οὐκ ἔστιν καθὼς σὺ λέγεις· ἀλλὰ διά σε ἀπεστάλην ἕως ὧδε. εἶπεν δὲ Ἀβραὰμ πρὸς τὸν θάνατον· Καὶ πῶς οὗτοι τεθνήκασιν; οὐ κἂν ὁ κύριος εἶπεν; εἶπεν δὲ ὁ θάνατος· Πίστευσον, Ἀβραὰμ δικαιότατε, ὅτι καὶ τοῦτο θαυμαστόν ἐστιν, ὅτι κἂν καὶ σὺ μετ' αὐτῶν οὐχ ἡρπάγης· ἀλλ' ὅμως λέγω σοι τὴν ἀλήθειαν· καὶ γὰρ εἰ μὴ ἦν ἡ δεξιὰ χεὶρ τοῦ θεοῦ μετά σου ἐν τῇ ὥρᾳ ἐκείνῃ, καὶ σὺ τοῦ βίου τούτου ἀπαλλάξαι εἶχες. ὁ δὲ δίκαιος Ἀβραὰμ εἶπεν· Νῦν ἔγνωκα ἐγὼ ὅτι εἰς ὀλιγωρίαν θανάτου ἦλθον, ὥστε ἐκλείπειν τὸ πνεῦμά μου· ἀλλὰ δέομαί σου, πανώλεθρε θάνατε, ἐπειδὴ καὶ οἱ παῖδες ἀώρως τεθνή- κασιν, δεῦρο δεηθῶμεν κυρίῳ τῷ θεῷ ἡμῶν ὅπως ἐπακούσῃ ἡμῶν καὶ ἀναστήσῃ τοὺς ἀώρως τεθνήξαντας διὰ τῆς σῆς ἀγριότητος. καὶ εἶπεν ὁ θάνατος· Ἀμὴν γένοιτο. ἀναστὰς οὖν ὁ Ἀβραὰμ ἔπεσεν ἐπὶ πρόσωπον τῆς γῆς προσευχό- μενος καὶ ὁ θάνατος μετ' αὐτοῦ, καὶ ἀπέστειλεν ὁ θεὸς πνεῦμα ζωῆς ἐπὶ τοὺς τελευτήσαντας, καὶ ἀνεζωοποιήθη- σαν. τότε οὖν ὁ δίκαιος Ἀβραὰμ ἔδωκεν δόξαν τῷ θεῷ.

XIX. καὶ ἀνελθὼν ἐν τῷ τρικλίνῳ αὐτοῦ, ἀνέπεσεν· ἐλθὼν δὲ καὶ ὁ θάνατος ἔστη ἔμπροσθεν αὐτοῦ. εἶπεν δὲ

1 θανατηφ. ὡς τῆς ὀσμῆς τοῦ θαν.] θανατηφ. ἀώρως θνήσκοντα ἀλλ' ὑπερέ- βαινεν ἐκ πολλῆς B ὡς—θανάτου] om CE 3 τὸν ἀριθμ.—χιλιάδες] om A 17 οὐ—εἶπεν] ἢ εἰς τοῦτο κ̅ς̅ ἀπέστειλέ σε σήμερον τοῦ θανατῶσαι αὐτούς; καὶ πῶς τούτους ἀπέκτεινας θανάτῳ, εἰ οὐκ εἶπε σοι κ̅ς̅ D

Ἀβραὰμ πρὸς αὐτόν· Ἔξελθε ἀπ' ἐμοῦ ὅτι θέλω ἀνα- ABCDER
παύεσθαι ὅτι ἐν ὀλιγωρίᾳ περίκειται τὸ πνεῦμά μου. καὶ
ὁ θάνατος εἶπεν· Οὐκ ἀναχωρῶ ἀπό σου ἕως οὗ λάβω τὴν
ψυχήν σου. καὶ ὁ Ἀβραὰμ αὐστηρῷ τῷ προσώπῳ καὶ
5 ὀργίλῳ τῷ βλέμματι εἶπεν πρὸς τὸν θάνατον· Τίς ὁ προσ-
τάξας σοι ταῦτα λέγειν; σὺ ἀφ' ἑαυτοῦ λέγεις ταῦτα τὰ
ῥήματα καυχώμενος, καὶ οὐ μή σε ἀκολουθήσω, ἕως οὗ ὁ
ἀρχιστράτηγος Μιχαὴλ ἔλθῃ πρός με καὶ ἀπέλθω μετ'
αὐτοῦ· ἀλλὰ καὶ τοῦτο λέγω σοι, εἰ μὲν θέλεις ἵνα ἀκο-
10 λουθήσω σοι, δίδαξόν με πάσας σου τὰς μεταμορφώσεις,
τὰς ἑπτὰ κεφαλὰς τῶν δρακόντων τὰς πυρίνας, καὶ τί τὸ
πρόσωπον τοῦ κρημνοῦ, καὶ τίς ἡ ῥομφαία ἡ ἀπότομος,
καὶ τίς ὁ ποταμὸς ὁ μεγάλα κοχλάζων, καὶ τίς ἡ βεβορ-
βορωμένη θάλασσα ἡ ἀγρίως κυματίζουσα· δίδαξόν με καὶ
15 περὶ τῆς βροντῆς τῆς ἀνυποφόρου καὶ τῆς φοβερᾶς ἀστραπῆς καὶ τί τὸ ποτήριον τὸ δυσῶδες τὸ φάρμακα μεμεστω-
μένον· δίδαξόν με περὶ πάντων. καὶ ὁ θάνατος εἶπεν·
Ἄκουσον, δίκαιε Ἀβραάμ, τοὺς ἑπτὰ αἰῶνας ἐγὼ λυμαίνω
τὸν κόσμον καὶ πάντας εἰς ᾅδην κατάγω, βασιλεῖς καὶ
20 ἄρχοντας, πλουσίους καὶ πένητας, δούλους καὶ ἐλευθέρους
εἰς πυθμένα ᾅδου παραπέμπω· καὶ διὰ τοῦτο ἔδειξά σοι
τὰς ἑπτὰ κεφαλὰς τῶν δρακόντων· τὸ δὲ πρόσωπον τοῦ
πυρὸς ἔδειξά σοι, διότι πολλοὶ ὑπὸ πυρὸς κεκαυμένοι
τελευτῶσιν καὶ διὰ προσώπου πυρὸς τὸν θάνατον βλέ-
25 πουσιν· τὸ δὲ πρόσωπον τοῦ κρημνοῦ ἔδειξά σοι διότι
πολλοὶ τῶν ἀνθρώπων ἀπὸ ὕψους δένδρων ἢ κρημνῶν
φοβερῶν κατερχόμενοι, καὶ ἀνύπαρκτοι γινόμενοι, τελευτῶσιν, καὶ εἰς τύπον κρημνοῦ φοβεροῦ θεωροῦσιν τὸν
θάνατον· τὸ δὲ πρόσωπον τῆς ῥομφαίας ἔδειξά σοι, διότι
30 πολλοὶ ἐν πολέμοις ὑπὸ ῥομφαίας ἀναιροῦνται, καὶ θεωροῦσιν ἐν ῥομφαίᾳ τὸν θάνατον· τὸ δὲ πρόσωπον τοῦ
μεγάλου ποταμοῦ τοῦ κοχλάζοντος ἔδειξά σοι, διότι πολ-

2 περίκειται] πεπίρακται B (? τετάρακται)   4, 5 αὐστηρῷ—βλέμμ.] στερρῷ
τῷ βλεμμ. κ. ὀργ. τῷ προσ. A   7—17 ἕως οὗ—θάνατος εἶπεν] om CE
20 δούλ. κ. ἐλ.] γέροντας καὶ νέους D   21 εἰς πυθμ. ᾅδου παραπ.]; om ACDE
22, 23 τοῦ πυρὸς] πικρῶς B   23 διότι πολλοὶ—παραλόγως (§ xix. fin)] om
CE (which read ἔδειξά σοι διὰ τὴν πολλήν σου ἄδιαν τῆς διατάξεως); om D
23, 24 πυρὸς κεκαυμ.—διὰ] om B   27 κατερχ.—γινόμ.] om B

102   THE TESTAMENT OF ABRAHAM.

ABCDER λοὶ ὑπὸ ἐμβάσεως ὑδάτων πολλῶν ἁρπαζόμενοι καὶ ὑπὸ
μεγίστων ποταμῶν ἐπαιρόμενοι ἀποπνίγονται καὶ τελευτῶσιν καὶ ἀώρως τὸν θάνατον βλέπουσιν· τὸ δὲ πρόσωπον
τῆς θαλάσσης τῆς ἀγρίας κυματιζούσης ἔδειξά σοι, διότι
πολλοὶ ἐν θαλάσσῃ κλυδωνίῳ μεγάλῳ περιπεσόντες ναυά- 5
γιοι γεγονότες ὑποβρύχιοι γίνονται θαλάσσιον θάνατον
βλέποντες· τὴν δὲ βροντὴν τὴν ἀνυπόφορον καὶ τὴν φοβερὰν ἀστραπὴν ἔδειξά σοι διότι πολλοὶ τῶν ἀνθρώπων
ἐν ὥρᾳ θυμοῦ τυχόντες βροντῆς ἀνυποφόρου καὶ ἀστραπῆς
φοβερᾶς ἐλθούσης ἐν ἁρπαγῇ ἀνθρώπων γίνονται καὶ 10
οὕτως τὸν θάνατον βλέπουσιν· ἔδειξά σοι καὶ θηρία
ἰόβολα, ἀσπίδας καὶ βασιλίσκους καὶ παρδάλεις καὶ λέ-
οντας καὶ σκύμνους καὶ ἄρκους καὶ ἐχίδνας καὶ ἁπλῶς
εἰπεῖν παντὸς θηρίου πρόσωπον ἔδειξά σοι, δικαιότατε,
διότι πολλοὶ τῶν ἀνθρώπων ὑπὸ θηρίων ἀναιροῦνται, ἕτεροι 15
δὲ ὑπὸ ὄφεων ἰοβόλων <δρακόντων καὶ ἀσπίδων καὶ
κεραστῶν καὶ βασιλίσκων> καὶ ἐχίδνης ἀποφυσούμενοι
ἐκλείπουσιν· ἔδειξά σοι δὲ καὶ ποτήρια δηλητήρια φάρμακα μεμεστωμένα διότι πολλοὶ τῶν ἀνθρώπων ὑπὸ ἑτέρων ἀνθρώπων φάρμακα ποτισθέντες παρ' εὐθὺς ἀπαλ- 20
λάσσονται παραλόγως.

XX. εἶπεν δὲ Ἀβραάμ· Δέομαί σου, ἔστιν καὶ παρά-
λογος θάνατος; ἀνάγγειλόν μοι. λέγει ὁ θάνατος· Ἀμὴν
ἀμὴν, λέγω σοι ἐν ἀληθείᾳ θεοῦ, ὅτι ἑβδομήκοντα δύο εἰσὶν
θάνατοι· καὶ εἷς μὲν θάνατος ὑπάρχει ὁ δίκαιος ὁ ἔχων 25
ὅρον· καὶ πολλοὶ τῶν ἀνθρώπων παρὰ μίαν ὥραν εἰς
θάνατον ἔρχονται παραδιδόμενοι τῷ τάφῳ· ἰδοὺ γὰρ ἀνήγ-
γειλά σοι πάντα ὅσα ᾔτησω· ἄρτι λέγω σοι, δικαιότατε
Ἀβραὰμ, ἄφησαι πᾶσαν βουλὴν καὶ κατάλιπε τοῦ ἐρωτᾶν

1 ὑπὸ ἐμβάσεως] ὑπὸ δάσεως A; ὑπὸ ἐμμάσεως B   3 ἀώρως] ἀέρος A;
ἀοράτως B   6 ὑποβρύχιοι] ὑποβρύχιον A; om B   7 τὴν δὲ βρ. κ.τ.λ.]
B; τῆς thrice A   8—10 This passage is corrupt. A has: διότι—ἀνῶν ἐν ὥρᾳ
θυμοῦ δρακόντων—βασιλίσκων (v. l. 16) καὶ σπαρδάλις καὶ λεοντας. B has εδειξα
σοι εν ω θυμον δρακ. κ. ασπ. και τυχοντες (? read θανάτου for θυμοῦ)   11 οὕτως]
οὗτοι B   18 ἐκλείπουσιν] a blank space of two lines occurs here in A
22, 23 δέομαι—ὁ θάνατος] καὶ τί ἐστιν ὁ ἄωρος θανατος· ἀμὴν λέγω σοι ἰδοὺ ἀνάγ-
γηλαν σοι πάντα ἀρτίως γάρ σοι λέγω δικ. Ἀβρ. (l. 28) C; δέομαί σου θάνατε
ἀνάγγειλόν μοι· καὶ τί ἐστιν ἄορος θανατος εἰς τὴν παραλογίαν· ἀμὴν λέγω σοι
ἐν ἀληθείᾳ τοῦ θῦ ὅτι εὐδομήκοντα δύο θάνατοι εἰσὶν καὶ ἰδοὺ κ.τ.λ. (as C) E

RECENSION A. 103

τι ἅπαξ· καὶ δεῦρο ἀκολούθει μοι καθὼς ὁ θεὸς καὶ κριτὴς ABCDER
τῶν ἁπάντων προσέταξέν μοι. εἶπεν δὲ Ἀβραὰμ πρὸς
τὸν θάνατον· Ἄπελθε ἀπ' ἐμοῦ ἔτι μικρὸν, ἵνα ἀναπαύ-
σωμαι ἐν τῇ κλίνῃ μου, ὅτι ἀθυμία πολλή μοι ἐστίν· ἀφ'
5 οὗ γὰρ ἐθεασάμην σε τοῖς ὀφθαλμοῖς μου, ἡ ἰσχύς μου
ἐξέλιπεν, πάντα δὲ τὰ μέλη τῆς σαρκός μου δίκην μολύ-
βδου βάρος μοι φαίνονται, καὶ τὸ πνεῦμά μου ἐπὶ πολὺ
ταλανίζεται. μεταστῆθι ἐν ὀλίγοις· εἶπον γὰρ, οὐχ ὑπο-
φέρω θεωρεῖν σου τὸ εἶδος. ἦλθεν δὲ Ἰσαὰκ ὁ υἱὸς αὐτοῦ
10 καὶ ἔπεσεν ἐπὶ τὸ στῆθος αὐτοῦ κλαίων· ἦλθεν δὲ καὶ ἡ
γυνὴ αὐτοῦ Σάρρα καὶ περιεπλάκη τοῖς ποσὶν αὐτοῦ ὀδυ-
ρομένη πικρῶς. ἤλθοσαν καὶ πάντες οἱ δοῦλοι αὐτοῦ καὶ
αἱ δοῦλαι καὶ περιεκύκλουν τὴν κλίνην αὐτοῦ ὀδυρόμενοι
σφόδρα. ὁ δὲ Ἀβραὰμ ἦλθεν εἰς ὀλιγωρίαν θανάτου·
15 καὶ εἶπεν ὁ θάνατος πρὸς τὸν Ἀβραάμ· Δεῦρο ἄσπασαι
τὴν δεξιάν μου· καὶ ἔλθῃ σοι ἱλαρότης καὶ ζωὴ καὶ δύναμις. πεπλάνηκεν γὰρ τὸν Ἀβραὰμ ὁ θάνατος· καὶ ἠσπάσατο τὴν χεῖρα αὐτοῦ, καὶ εὐθέως ἐκολλᾶτο ἡ ψυχὴ αὐτοῦ
ἐν τῇ χειρὶ τοῦ θανάτου· καὶ εὐθέως παρέστη Μιχαὴλ ὁ
20 ἀρχάγγελος μετὰ πλήθους ἀγγέλων, καὶ ἦραν τὴν τιμίαν
αὐτοῦ ψυχὴν ἐν ταῖς χερσὶν αὐτῶν ἐν σινδόνι θεοϋφάντῳ·
καὶ μυρίσμασι θεοπνεύστοις καὶ ἀρώμασιν ἐκήδευσαν
τὸ σῶμα τοῦ δικαίου Ἀβραὰμ ἕως τρίτης ἡμέρας τῆς
τελειώσεως αὐτοῦ, καὶ ἔθαψαν αὐτὸν ἐν τῇ γῇ τῆς ἐπαγ-
25 γελίας, ἐν τῇ δρυῒ τῇ Μαμβρῇ, τήν τε τιμίαν αὐτοῦ ψυχὴν
ὠψίκευον οἱ ἄγγελοι καὶ ἀνήρχοντο εἰς τὸν οὐρανὸν ψάλ-
λοντες τὸν τρισάγιον ὕμνον τῷ δεσπότῃ τῶν ὅλων θεῷ, καὶ
ἔστησαν αὐτὴν εἰς προσκύνησιν τοῦ θεοῦ καὶ πατρός· καὶ
δὴ πολλῆς ἀνυμνήσεως καὶ δοξολογίας γενομένης πρὸς
30 κύριον, προσκυνήσαντος δὲ τοῦ Ἀβραάμ, ἦλθεν ἡ ἄχραντος
φωνὴ τοῦ θεοῦ καὶ πατρὸς λέγουσα οὕτως· Ἄρατε οὖν τὸν

9 εἶδος] + ὡσεὶ θρόμβη αἵματος A   10 ἔπεσεν] πεσὼν A   10, 11 κλαίων—
Σ. καὶ] περιεπλάκη τοῖς ποσὶν τοῦ Ἀ. ὀδυρόμενος A   14 σφόδρα] + καὶ ἐπέταξεν
ἐλευθερωθῆναι αὐτοὺς πάντας D   18 ἐκολλεῖτο A; κεκόληκεν B; κολυται C;
κεκολληται E   24 ἐν τῇ γῇ τῆς ἐπ.] om BCDE   29 ἀνυμνήσεως] δεήσεως
B; ὑμνήσεως CE   29—31 γενομένης—ἄρατε οὖν] γενομένης πρὸς κν̄, ὑπάγουν
τὴν τιμίαν αὐτοῦ ψ. εἰς τ. II. B   30 προσκ. δὲ τοῦ Ἀ.] CE; om ABD   31 τοῦ
—πατρὸς] om BCDE

8

ABCDER φίλον μου τὸν Ἀβραὰμ εἰς τὸν παράδεισον, ἔνθα εἰσὶν αἱ σκηναὶ τῶν δικαίων μου καὶ μοναὶ τῶν ἁγίων μου Ἰσαὰκ καὶ Ἰακὼβ ἐν τῷ κόλπῳ αὐτοῦ, ἔνθα οὐκ ἔστιν πόνος, οὐ λύπη, οὐ στεναγμός, ἀλλ' εἰρήνη καὶ ἀγαλλίασις καὶ ζωὴ ἀτελεύτητος. [μεθ' οὗ καὶ ἡμεῖς, ἀδελφοί μου ἀγαπητοὶ, 5 τοῦ πατριάρχου Ἀβραὰμ τὴν φιλοξενίαν μιμησώμεθα καὶ τὴν ἐνάρετον αὐτοῦ κτησώμεθα πολιτείαν, ὅπως ἀξιωθῶμεν τῆς αἰωνίου ζωῆς, δοξάζοντες τὸν πατέρα καὶ τὸν υἱὸν καὶ τὸ ἅγιον πνεῦμα· αὐτῷ ἡ δόξα καὶ τὸ κράτος εἰς τοὺς αἰῶνας. Ἀμήν.] 10

2, 3 μου καὶ μοναὶ—κόλπῳ αὐτοῦ] om BCDE (παραδ. ἔνθα εἰσελεύσονται αἱ ψ. τῶν δικ. ἔνθα οὐκ B) 5 οὗ] ὧν CE 6 μιμησώμεθα] μιμίσασθε CE ; ζηλώσωμεν A 6, 7 καὶ—πολιτ.] om B ; κ. τὴν ἀγάπην κτισώμεθα CE 8, 9 δοξάζ.—πνεῦμα] ἅμα σὺν τῷ ἀνάρχῳ αὐτοῦ π̅ρ̅ι̅ καὶ τῷ ὁμοουσίῳ καὶ ζωοποιῷ αὐτοῦ π̅ν̅ι̅ πάντοτε B 9, 10 αὐτῷ—ἀμήν] νῦν καὶ ἀεὶ κ. εἰς τ. αἰ. τῶν αἰ. ἀμὴν ABE

B.

ΔΙΑΘΗΚΗ ΤΟΥ ΠΑΤΡΙΑΡΧΟΥ ΑΒΡΑΑΜ.

[Τῇ κυριακῇ πρὸ τῆς χριστοῦ γεννήσεως τῶν ἁγίων πατέρων. Εὐλόγησον δέσποτα.]

I. Ἐγένετο ἡνίκα ἤγγισαν αἱ ἡμέραι τοῦ θανάτου ABC τοῦ Ἀβραάμ, εἶπεν κύριος πρὸς Μιχαήλ· Ἀνάστηθι καὶ πορεύθητι πρὸς Ἀβραὰμ τὸν δοῦλόν μου, καὶ εἰπὲ αὐτῷ ὅπως ἐξελεύσῃ τοῦ βίου, ὅτι ἰδοὺ ἐπληρώθησαν αἱ ἡμέραι 5 τῆς προσκαίρου ζωῆς σου· ὅπως διοικήσῃ τὰ τοῦ οἴκου αὐτοῦ πρὶν ἀποθανεῖν.

II. καὶ ἐπορεύθη Μιχαὴλ καὶ ἦλθεν πρὸς Ἀβραάμ, καὶ εὗρεν αὐτὸν καθιζόμενον ἔμπροσθεν τῶν βοῶν αὐτοῦ εἰς ἀροτριασμόν· ὑπῆρχεν δὲ γηραλέος πάνυ τῇ ἰδέᾳ· εἶχεν 10 δὲ ἐνηγκαλισμένον τὸν υἱὸν αὐτοῦ. ἰδὼν οὖν Ἀβραὰμ τὸν ἀρχάγγελον Μιχαήλ, ἀναστὰς ἐκ τῆς γῆς ἠσπάσατο αὐτόν,

A=Par. Gr. 1613. B=Par. Suppl. Grec 162. C=Cod. Vind. Theol. Gr. cxxvi.

Tit. Διήγησις περὶ τῆς διαθήκης καὶ περὶ τοῦ θανάτου τοῦ ἐν ἁγίοις π̄ρ̄ς ἡμῶν Ἀ. τοῦ π̄ρ̄ιάρχου καὶ δικαίου καὶ φιλοξένου. Δέσπ. εὐλ. B; Λόγος περὶ τῆς θανῆς τοῦ Ἀ. ὅτε ἀπέστειλεν κ̄ς̄ ὁ θ̄ς̄ τὸν ἄγγελον αὐτοῦ καὶ ἧρεν αὐτὸν σωματικῶς εἰς τὰ ἐπουράνια C

1, 2 ἐγένετο—Μιχαήλ] Ἡνίκα ἐπληροῦντο αἱ ἡμ. τῆς ὅλης βιωτῆς τοῦ παντευλογήτου κ. δικαίου π̄ρ̄ς ἡμῶν Ἀ. τοῦ πατριάρχου, εἶπεν κ̄ς̄ πρὸς τὸν μέγαν ἀρχιστράτηγον Μιχ. B; ἐγένετο ἡνίκα ἐφθησεν ἡ θανὴ τοῦ Ἀ., ἀπέστειλεν κ̄ς̄ θ̄ς̄ Μιχ. τὸν ἀρχιστράτηγον κ. εἶπεν αὐτῷ C   8, 9 ἔμπροσθεν—ἀροτρ.] ἔμπρ. τῶν ἀροτριωτῶν ἐν τῷ ἀγρῷ αὐτοῦ C   9, 10 εἶχεν—αὐτοῦ] om AC   11 ἀναστὰς—γῆς] om AB

106   THE TESTAMENT OF ABRAHAM.

ABC μὴ εἰδὼς τίς ἐστιν, καὶ εἶπεν πρὸς αὐτόν· Σῶσόν σε ὁ θεός· ἄναστα καλῶς πορευόμενος τὴν ὁδόν σου. καὶ ἀπεκρίθη αὐτῷ Μιχαήλ· Φιλάνθρωπος εἶ σύ, καλὲ πάτερ. καὶ ἀπεκρίθη Ἀβραὰμ καὶ εἶπεν αὐτῷ· Ἐλθέ, ἔγγισόν μοι, ἀδελφέ, καὶ καθέζου ὀλίγην ὥραν ἵνα προστάξω ἐνεχθῆναι 5 ζῶον, ἵνα ἀπέλθωμεν ἐν τῷ οἴκῳ μου καὶ ἀναπαύῃς μετ' ἐμοῦ, ὅτι πρὸς ἑσπέρᾳ ἐστὶν, καὶ τῷ πρωῒ ἀναστὰς πορεύου ὅπου ἂν βούλῃ, μήπως συναντήσῃ σοι θηρίον πονηρὸν καὶ καταικίσῃ σε. ἠρώτησεν δὲ Μιχαὴλ τὸν Ἀβραὰμ λέγων· Εἰπέ μοι τὸ ὄνομά σου, πρὶν εἰσελθεῖν 10 ἐν τῷ οἴκῳ σου, μὴ ἐπιβαρὴς γένωμαί σοι. καὶ ἀπεκρίθη Ἀβραὰμ καὶ εἶπεν· Οἱ γονεῖς μου ὠνόμασάν με Ἀβρὰμ, καὶ ὁ κύριος ἐπωνόμασέν με Ἀβραὰμ, λέγων· Ἀνάστηθι καὶ πορεύου ἐκ τοῦ οἴκου σου καὶ ἐκ τῆς συγγενείας σου, καὶ δεῦρο εἰς γῆν ἣν ἄν σοι δείξω· καὶ ἀπελθόντος μου εἰς 15 τὴν γῆν ἣν ὑπέδειξέ μοι ὁ κύριος, εἴρηκέν μοι· Οὐκέτι κληθήσεται τὸ ὄνομά σου Ἀβράμ, ἀλλ' ἔσται τὸ ὄνομά σου Ἀβραάμ. ἀπεκρίθη Μιχαὴλ καὶ εἶπεν αὐτῷ· Συγχώρησόν μοι, πάτερ μου, ἄνθρωπε τοῦ θεοῦ μεμελετημένε, ὅτι ξένος εἰμὶ, καὶ ἤκουσα περί σου ὅτε ἀπῆλθες σταδίους 20 τεσσαράκοντα καὶ ἤνεγκας μόσχον, καὶ ἔθυσας αὐτὸν, ξενιζόμενος ἀγγέλους ἐν τῷ οἴκῳ σου, ἵνα ἀναπαυθῶσιν. ταῦτα ἀμφότεροι λαλήσαντες, ἀναστάντες ἐν τῷ οἴκῳ ἐπορεύοντο. ἐκάλεσεν δὲ Ἀβραὰμ ἕνα τῶν παίδων αὐτοῦ καὶ εἶπεν αὐτῷ· Πορεύθητι, ἄγαγέ μοι κτῆνος ὅπως καθίσῃ ἐπ' 25

4, 5 κ. εἶπεν—καθέζου] εἶπεν· εὐλογημένος εἶ· καὶ σὺ καλὲ πέρ κ. ὁ Ἀ. αὐθης πρὸς αὐτὸν φιλάνθρωπος ἐλθὲ ἀδελφὲ ἔγγιστα μου κ. κάθησον Β   4—11 κ. εἶπεν—ἀπεκρίθη] κ. καθίσαντες ὁμοῦ ἠρώτησεν Ἀ. τὸν ἄγγελον λέγων· ἄνθρωπε πορευόμενος τὴν ὁδὸν πόθεν ἔρχει κ. ποῦ ἀπέρχει· ἀπεκρίθη αὐτῷ Μ. στρατιώτης εἰμὶ κ. πορευομ. τ. ὁδ. ἔμαθον περὶ τῆς φιλανθρωπίας σου κ. ἦλθον πρὸς σὲ τοῦ ἰδεῖν τίς εἶ σύ· κ. εἶπεν C   5, 6 ἵνα—ζῶον] ὅπως φθάσῃ ἄλογον ζῶον Α; ὅπως παρακελεύσομαι τοῦ ἀχθῆναι ζῶα C   7—9 ὅτι—καταικ. σε] νῦν δὲ ἐὰν πορεύει πρὸς ἑσπέραν ἐστίν κ. ἴσως πορευόμενος τῇ νυκτὶ ταραχθῇς διὰ τηνὸς νυκτερινοῦ φαντάσματος Β   9 καταικίσῃ] κατηχήσῃ Α; ταραχθεὶς C   12, 13 οἱ γονεῖς—λέγων] Ἀβρὰμ μὲν ἤκουον τὸ πρότερον ὁ δὲ κς ἐκάλεσέν με τὸ δεύτερον κ. εἶπεν μοι Β   18, 19 Συγχώρ.—μεμελετημ.] ξενίζομαί σε ἄνθρωπε τοῦ θῦ ὑπερεπενούμεναι Β; συγχωρ. μοι πάτερ ὅτι ἐπιξενοῦμαι ἄνθρωπε τοῦ θῦ καὶ μέμνημαι C   21 ἔθυσας αὐτὸν] ἔθηκας αὐτῷ μόσχους Α; om B   21, 22 ξενιζόμ. ἀγγ.] ξενιζομένους Α; om B   22, 23 ταῦτα—λαλήσ.] om AC   23— p. 31, 3 ἐν τῷ οἴκῳ—οἴκῳ σου] ἐπορεύθησαν· ἐκάλεσεν—εἶπεν· πορεύθητι ἀγαγεῖν

RECENSION B. 107

αὐτὸν ὁ ξένος, ὅτι ἐκοπιάθη ἐκ τῆς ὁδοιπορίας. καὶ εἶπεν ABC
Μιχαήλ· Μὴ σκύλλε τὸ παιδάριον, ἀλλὰ ἀπέλθωμεν μετεωριζόμενοι
ἕως οὗ φθάσωμεν ἐν τῷ οἴκῳ σου, διότι ἠγάπησά σου τὴν ὁμιλίαν.

5 III. καὶ ἀναστάντες ἐπορεύοντο· καὶ ὡς ἤγγισαν τῇ πόλει, ὡς ἀπὸ σταδίων τριῶν, εὗρον δένδρον μέγα ἔχον κλάδους τριακοσίους, ὅμοιον ἐρηκινοῦ· καὶ ἤκουον φωνὴν ἐκ τῶν κλάδων αὐτοῦ ᾀδομένην· Ἅγιος ὅτι τὴν πρόφασιν ἤνεγκας περὶ ὧν ἀπεστάλης· καὶ ἤκουσεν Ἀβραὰμ τῆς
10 φωνῆς, καὶ ἔκρυψεν τὸ μυστήριον ἐν τῇ καρδίᾳ αὐτοῦ, λέγων ἐν ἑαυτῷ· Ἆρα τί ἐστιν τὸ μυστήριον ὅπερ ἀκήκοα; ὡς δὲ ἦλθεν ἐν τῷ οἴκῳ, λέγει Ἀβραὰμ τοῖς παισὶν αὐτοῦ· Ἀναστάντες ἐξέλθατε εἰς τὰ πρόβατα, καὶ ἐνέγκατε τρία θρέμματα καὶ σφάξατε ταχέως καὶ ὑπηρετήσατε ἵνα φά-
15 γωμεν καὶ πίωμεν· ὅτι εὐφρασία ἐστὶν ὡς ἡ ἡμέρα αὕτη. καὶ ἤνεγκαν οἱ παῖδες τὰ θρέμματα, καὶ ἐκάλεσεν Ἀβραὰμ τὸν υἱὸν αὐτοῦ τὸν Ἰσαὰκ καὶ εἶπεν αὐτῷ· Τέκνον Ἰσαάκ, ἀνάστηθι καὶ βάλε ὕδωρ ἐπὶ τῆς λεκάνης, ἵνα νίψωμεν τοὺς πόδας τοῦ ξένου τούτου. καὶ ἤνεγκεν ὡς προσετάχθη·
20 καὶ εἶπεν Ἀβραάμ· Κατανόησιν ἔχω ὅπερ καὶ γενήσεται, ὅτι ἐν τῷ τρυβλίῳ τούτῳ οὐ μὴ νίψω ἔτι τοὺς πόδας

—μὴ σύλε τὸ π. ἀλλὰ περιπατήσωμεν—σου Α; ἐν—ἐπορεύοντο—ἕνα ἐκ τῶν παιδαρίων—κτῆνος καὶ γενέσθωσαν ἐδέσματα ὅπως συνεσθιασθῶμεν μετὰ τοῦ ξένου ὅτι ἐκτὸς ὁδοπορίας ἐστίν· ἀποκριθεὶς δὲ ὁ ἀρχάγγ. Μ. εἶπεν πρὸς αὐτόν· μισκυλε τὸ π. —οἴκω σου Β; ἐπορ. καθήμενοι τοῖς ἵπποις· ὅτε δὲ ἦλθον ἐν τῷ οἴκω ἐκάλ. Ἀ. ἕνα τῶν οἰκοπαίδων αὐτοῦ κ. εἶπ. αὐτῷ· πορεύου κ.—κτῆνος· κ. καθήσας ἐν αὐτῷ πορεύθητι ἐπὶ τὰ πρόβατα κ. κόμισόν μοι τρία θρέμματα· ὅπως θύσαντες εὐφρανθῶμεν μετὰ τοῦ ξένου ὅτι ἐκάμαμεν ἐκ τῆς ὁδοιπ. ἀπεκρ. δὲ Μ. μηκέτι τὸ π. ἀλλὰ περιπατήσωμεν ἀμφότεροι μετεωρ. ἕως φθ. εἰς τὸ ποίμνιον κ. πάλιν στραφῶμεν C
3, 4 διότι—ὁμιλίαν] om AB   5, 6 καὶ ὡς—τριῶν] κ. πορεβόμενοι ὡς ἀπὸ σταδ. δύο ἐγγίσαντες τῇ πόλει Β; καὶ ὡς ἤγγ. ἀπὸ σταδ. δύο τῆς ποίμνης C
6, 7 ἔχον—ἐρηκινοῦ] τριακ. κλαδ. ἔχοντα Β; ὅμοιον τρεκίνου C   7 ἐρηκινοῦ] ἐρηκινόν Α   8 ᾀδομένην] λέγουσαν AC; ἀδωμένην B   8, 9 ἅγιος—ἀπεστ.] ὅτι προφανῆ—ἀπέστειλας Α; ἁγία ἡ πρόφασις περὶ οὗ ἀπεστάλης Β   10 φωνῆς]+ἧς ἤχησεν ἐν αὐτῷ C   11 ἀκήκοα]+ἦλθον δὲ κ. παῖδες δύο κ. ἐκόμισαν ἐκ τοῦ ποιμνίου θρέμματα τρία κ. ἔσφαξαν ταχέως κ. ἐξυπηρέτησαν τῇ τραπέζῃ C
13, 14 ἀναστάντες—ταχέως καὶ] om C   15 εὐφρασία—αὕτη] εὐφρ. σήμερον γίνεται A(C); εὐφρόσυνος ἐστιν ὡσὶ ἡμ. αὕτη Β   16 καὶ—θρέμ.] om C
19, 20 καὶ ἤνεγκεν—Ἀβρ.] κ. ἤν. Ἀ. ἐν τῇ καρδίᾳ αὐτοῦ λέγων Α; κ. ποίησας ὡς προσετ. κ. εἶπεν Ἀ. Β; κ. ἤν. κ. εἶπεν Ἀ. νίψον τέκνον τοὺς πόδας τοῦ ξένου· ὅτι C
20 κατανόησιν—γενήσεται] γενήσεται Α; ὑπολαμβάνω ἐν τῇ ψυχῇ μου C

8*

ABC ἀνθρώπου ξενιζομένου πρὸς ἡμᾶς. ἀκούσας δὲ Ἰσαὰκ τοῦ πατρὸς αὐτοῦ λαλοῦντος ταῦτα, ἐδάκρυσεν, καὶ λέγει πρὸς αὐτόν· Πάτερ μου, τί ἐστιν τοῦτο ὅτι εἶπας Ἔσχατόν μου ἐστὶν νίψαι πόδας ἀνθρώπου ξένου; καὶ ἰδὼν Ἀβραὰμ τὸν υἱὸν αὐτοῦ κλαίοντα, ἔκλαυσεν καὶ αὐτὸς σφόδρα· καὶ Μιχαὴλ ἰδὼν αὐτοὺς κλαίοντας, ἔκλαυσεν· καὶ αὐτός· καὶ ἔπεσαν τὰ δάκρυα Μιχαὴλ ἐπὶ τῆς λεκάνης, καὶ ἐγένετο λίθος πολύτιμος.

IV. ὡς δὲ ἤκουσεν ἡ Σάρρα τοῦ κλαυθμοῦ αὐτῶν ἔσω οὖσα ἐν τῇ οἰκίᾳ αὐτῆς, ἐξελθοῦσα εἶπεν τῷ Ἀβραάμ· Κύριε, τί ἐστιν ὅτι οὕτως κλαίετε; καὶ ἀπεκρίθη Ἀβραὰμ καὶ εἶπεν αὐτῇ· Οὐδὲν κακόν ἐστιν· εἴσελθε ἐν τῇ οἰκίᾳ σου, καὶ ἐργάζου τὰ ἴδιά σου, μὴ ἐπιβαρεῖς γενώμεθα τῷ ἀνθρώπῳ. καὶ ἀνεχώρησεν ἡ Σάρρα, ὅτι ἔμελλεν ἑτοιμάζειν τὸν δεῖπνον. καὶ ἤγγισεν ὁ ἥλιος τοῦ δῦναι· καὶ ἐξῆλθεν Μιχαὴλ ἔξω τοῦ οἴκου, καὶ ἀνελήφθη εἰς τοὺς οὐρανοὺς προσκυνῆσαι ἐνώπιον τοῦ θεοῦ· τοῦ γὰρ ἡλίου δύνοντος πάντες προσκυνοῦσιν ἄγγελοι τὸν θεόν· πρῶτος δέ ἐστιν ὁ αὐτὸς Μιχαὴλ τῶν ἀγγέλων. καὶ προσεκύνησαν πάντες καὶ ἀπῆλθον, ἕκαστος εἰς τὸν τόπον αὐτοῦ. ἀποκριθεὶς δὲ Μιχαὴλ ἐνώπιον τοῦ θεοῦ εἶπεν· Κύριε, κέλευσόν με ἐρωτηθῆναι ἐνώπιον τῆς ἁγίας δόξης σου. καὶ λέγει κύριος πρὸς Μιχαήλ· Ἀνάγγειλον ὅπερ βούλῃ. ἀποκριθεὶς δὲ ὁ ἀρχάγγελος εἶπε· Κύριε, σύ με ἀπέστειλας πρὸς Ἀβραάμ, εἰπεῖν αὐτῷ· Ὑποχώρησον ἐκ τοῦ σώματός σου, καὶ ἔξελθε ἐκ τοῦ κόσμου· καλεῖ σε ὁ κύριος· κἀγὼ

2 ταῦτα—καὶ λέγει] τὰ δάκρυα ταῦτα εἰσήνεγκεν λέγων Α; ταῦτα δάκρυα εἰσήνεγκεν C   10—12 εἶπεν τῷ Ἀ.—αὐτῇ] om B   11 κύριε] om C   τί —κλαίετε] τίς οὕτως οὗ κλέετε Α   13, 14 ἐπιβαρεῖς—ἀνθρώπῳ] προξενισθῶμεν τὸ παρόντι ξένῳ λύπην Β; ἐπιβ. γένη. τῷ ξένῳ ἀνθ. τούτῳ C   14—16 ἀνεχώρ. —ἐξῆλθεν] ἀνεχύρ.—ὅτε δὲ ἔμελλον—δεῖπνον, ἤγγισεν—εἰς τὸ δύνειν κ. ἐξῆλθεν C; ἀναχωρήσασα ἡ Σ. μέλοντος τοῦ δ. ἑτοιμάζεσθαι τοῦ ἡλίου δύνοντος ἐξελθὼν Β 16, 17 τοὺς οὐρ.] τὸν οὐρανόν Β   18—20 προσκυνῆσαι—τόπον αὐτοῦ] καὶ προσεκύνησεν τὸν θν̄ κ. οὕτως οἱ λιποὶ ἄγγελοι· τύπος γὰρ ἦν προσκυνεῖν δύνοντος τοῦ ἡλ. πάντας τοὺς ἀγγ. ἐνωπ. τ. θῡ πρῶτον ὁ ἀρχάγγ. Μ. κ. οὕτως οἱ λιποὶ ἀγγ. ὑποχωρησάντων δὲ τῶν ἀγγ. εἰς τ. ἰδίους τόπους κ. τοῦ Μ. ἡσταμένου ἐνόπιον τοῦ θεοῦ Β   22 ἐρωτηθῆναι] ἐρωτῶ σε Α; λαλῆσαι C   τῆς ἁγ. δοξ. σου] σου, κύριε Α   22—24 καὶ λέγει—ἀρχάγγ. εἶπε] om A; κ. λέγει ὁ κς̄ λέγε, Μ., ὃ βούλει C   26—p. 109, 2 κἀγὼ—ὑποδεχόμενος] κ. ἀπελθὼν οὐδ' ἐν λόγῳ ἔφρηξα αὐτόν, διὰ τὸ γινώσκειν αὐτὸν φίλον σου καθαρὸν κ. ἀψευδέστατον

οὐ τολμῶ, κύριε, ἐμφανισθῆναι αὐτῷ, ὅτι φίλος σου ἐστὶν ABC
καὶ δίκαιος ἄνθρωπος, ξένους ὑποδεχόμενος· ἀλλὰ παρακαλῶ σε, κύριε, κέλευσον τὴν μνήμην τοῦ θανάτου τοῦ
Ἀβραὰμ εἰς τὴν καρδίαν αὐτοῦ εἰσελθεῖν, καὶ μὴ αὐτῷ
5 ἐγὼ εἴπω· μεγάλη γὰρ συντομία τοῦτό ἐστιν, εἰπεῖν ὅτι
Τὸν κόσμον ἔξελθε, μάλιστα δὲ καὶ ἀπὸ τοῦ ἰδίου σώματος· σὺ γὰρ ἐξ ἀρχῆς ἐποίησας αὐτὸν ἐλεεῖν ψυχὰς
πάντων ἀνθρώπων. τότε κύριος πρὸς Μιχαὴλ εἶπεν·
Ἀνάστηθι καὶ πορεύου πρὸς Ἀβραάμ, καὶ ξενίζου πρὸς
10 αὐτόν· καὶ ὅτι ἂν ἴδῃς ἐσθίοντα, φάγε καὶ σύ, καὶ ὅπου ἂν
κοιμηθῇ, κοίμησαι καὶ σὺ ἐκεῖ· ἐγὼ γὰρ ῥίψω τὴν μνήμην
τοῦ θανάτου τοῦ Ἀβραὰμ εἰς τὴν καρδίαν Ἰσαὰκ τοῦ υἱοῦ
αὐτοῦ κατ' ὄναρ.

V. τότε Μιχαὴλ ἀπῆλθεν εἰς τὸν οἶκον Ἀβραὰμ
15 ἐν τῇ ἑσπέρᾳ ἐκείνῃ, καὶ εὗρεν αὐτοὺς ἑτοιμάζοντας τὸν
δεῖπνον· καὶ ἔφαγον καὶ ἔπιον καὶ εὐφράνθησαν. καὶ εἶπεν
Ἀβραὰμ τῷ υἱῷ αὐτοῦ Ἰσαάκ· Ἀνάστηθι, τέκνον, στρῶσον τὴν κλίνην τοῦ ἀνθρώπου ἵνα ἀναπαύῃ, καὶ θὲς τὸν
λύχνον ἐπὶ τὴν λυχνίαν. καὶ ἐποίησεν Ἰσαὰκ καθὰ συνέ-
20 ταξεν ὁ πατὴρ αὐτοῦ. καὶ εἶπεν Ἰσαὰκ τῷ πατρὶ αὐτοῦ·
Πάτερ, ἔρχομαι κἀγὼ ἔγγιστα ὑμῶν κοιμηθῆναι. καὶ ἀπεκρίθη Ἀβραὰμ πρὸς αὐτόν· Οὐχί, τέκνον μου, μήποτε
ἐπιβαρεῖς γενώμεθα τῷ ἀνθρώπῳ τούτῳ, ἀλλὰ ἄπελθε ἐν
τῷ ταμείῳ σου καὶ ἀναπαύου. μὴ θέλων δὲ Ἰσαὰκ παρα-
25 κοῦσαι <τὸ> τοῦ πατρὸς αὐτοῦ πρόσταγμα, ἀπελθὼν ἀνεπαύσατο ἐν τῷ ταμείῳ αὐτοῦ.

VI. καὶ ἐγένετο περὶ ὥραν ἑβδόμην τῆς νυκτός,
ἐξυπνισθεὶς ὁ Ἰσαὰκ ἦλθεν εἰς τὴν θύραν τοῦ οἴκου τοῦ
πατρὸς αὐτοῦ κράζων καὶ λέγων· Πάτερ, ἄνοιξον, ἵνα σε
30 ἀπολαύσω πρίν σε ἀροῦσιν ἀπ' ἐμοῦ. ἀνέστη δὲ Ἀβραὰμ
καὶ ἤνοιξεν, καὶ εἰσῆλθεν Ἰσαὰκ καὶ ἐκρεμάσθη ἐπὶ τοῦ

εἶναι κ. δίκαιον ἄνον κ. ξενοδόχον ἐμπερεχαρῆ κ. ἀονείδησον Β 1 ἐμφανισθῆναι] ἐκφάναι λόγον C 4 καρδίαν]+τοῦ υἱοῦ Β 5, 6 μεγάλη—
ἔξελθε] μεγάλως γὰρ λυπηθήσεται ἐὰν ἄφνω ἀκούσῃ ἀπ' ἐμοῦ ὅτι μέλλει ἀπὸ τοῦ
κόσμου ἐξέρχεσθαι Β; μεγάλη γὰρ συντομὴ αὐτοῦ ἐστὶν τὸ εἰπεῖν—ἐξέρχει μάλιστα
κ. ἐκ τοῦ σώματος C 18, 19 καὶ θές—λυχνίαν] καὶ τὴν λυχνίαν κ. τὸν λ. Α; κ.
ἄψον λύχνον Β 21 ἔρχομαι] om Α ἔρχομαι—κοιμηθῆναι] ἃς κοιμηθῶ
μετά σου Β 24, 25 μὴ θέλων—πρόσταγμα] om AC 30 ἀπολαύσω] + κ. καταφιλήσω κ. χορτάσω τὴν σὴν ὡραιότητα C

ABC τραχήλου τοῦ πατρὸς αὐτοῦ κλαίων, καὶ θρηνῶν κατεφίλει αὐτόν· ἔκλαυσεν δὲ Ἀβραὰμ σὺν τῷ υἱῷ αὐτοῦ· εἶδεν δὲ αὐτοὺς ὁ Μιχαὴλ κλαίοντας καὶ ἔκλαυσεν καὶ αὐτός. καὶ ἀκούσασα ἡ Σάρρα τὸν κλαυθμὸν ἐκ τοῦ κοιτῶνος αὐτῆς ἔκραξε λέγουσα· Κύριέ μου Ἀβραάμ, τί ἐστιν ὁ κλαυθ- 5 μός; μή σοι εἶπεν ὁ ξένος περὶ τοῦ ἀδελφιδοῦ σου Λὼτ ὅτι ἀπέθανεν; ἢ ἄλλο τι συνέβη εἰς ἡμᾶς; ἀποκριθεὶς δὲ Μιχαὴλ εἶπε πρὸς τὴν Σάρραν· Οὐχὶ, Σάρρα, οὐκ ἤνεγκα φάσιν περὶ Λώτ· ἀλλὰ περὶ πάσης φιλανθρωπίας ὑμῶν ἔγνων ὅτι διαφέρετε πάντων ἀνθρώπων τῶν ἐπὶ τῆς γῆς, 10 καὶ ἐμνήσθη ὑμῶν ὁ θεός. τότε λέγει Σάρρα τῷ Ἀβραάμ· Πῶς ἐτόλμησας κλαῦσαι εἰσελθόντος τοῦ ἀνθρώπου τοῦ θεοῦ ἐν σοί; καὶ πῶς ἐδάκρυσάν σου οἱ ὀφθαλμοὶ τῶν ζευμάτων τοῦ φωτός; ὅτι σήμερον εὐφροσύνη γίνεται. λέγει οὖν πρὸς αὐτὴν Ἀβραάμ· Πόθεν γινώσκεις ὅτι ἄν- 15 θρωπος τοῦ θεοῦ ἐστίν; ἀποκριθεὶς δὲ ἡ Σάρρα εἶπεν· Ὅτι παραφέρω καὶ λέγω ὅτι οὗτός ἐστιν τῶν τριῶν ἀνδρῶν εἷς, τῶν ἐν τῇ δρυὶ τῇ Μαμβρῇ ἐπιξενισθέντων ἡμῖν, ὅτε ἀπῆλθεν ἓν τῶν παιδίων καὶ ἤνεγκε μόσχον καὶ ἔθυσας· καὶ εἶπές μοι, Ἀνάστα, ποίησον ἵνα φάγωμεν 20 μετὰ τῶν ἀνθρώπων τούτων εἰς τὸν οἶκον ἡμῶν. καὶ ἀπεκρίθη Ἀβραὰμ καὶ εἶπεν· Καλῶς ἐνόησας, ὦ γύναι· ὅτι κἀγὼ ὅτε τοὺς πόδας αὐτοῦ ἔπλυνα, ἔγνων ἐν τῇ καρδίᾳ μου ὅτι οὗτοί εἰσιν οἱ πόδες οὓς ἔπλυνα ἐν τῇ δρυὶ τῇ Μαμβρῇ, καὶ καθὼς ἠρξάμην ἐρωτᾶν τὴν πορείαν, εἶπέ 25

1 κλαίων] om B   1, 2 κ. θρηνῶν κατεφίλει αὐτόν] κ. λέγων καταφιλῶν αὐτ. A; κ. καταφιλῶν αὐτ. κ. τοῖς δάκρυσι πλύνων τὸ στῆθος αὐτοῦ C   4 ἐκ τοῦ κοιτ. αὐτῆς] ἐκ τῆς κλίνης αὐτ. A; ἔσω οὖσα ἐν τῇ σκηνῇ C   5, 6 τί ἐστιν—ἀδελφιδοῦ] τί ἔχετε ὅτι οὕτως κλέετε ὀψὲ Α. ἄρτι· μὴ φθέγξω ὦ ἄνε τω κω μου Ἀ. μὴ περὶ τοῦ ἀδελφοῦ A; τί ἐστιν...—ἀνεψιοῦ B; τί ἔχετε—κλαίετε. ὅρα μή τινα φάσιν ἤνεγκεν ὁ ξ. τῷ κυρίῳ μου Ἀ.—ἀδελφιδοῦ C   7 συνέβη]+λυπηρὸν B 8, 9 οὐκ—περὶ] οὐκ ἐλάλησά τι διὰ Λὼτ B   9—11 ἀλλὰ—θεός] ἀλλὰ πάσας φιλανίας ἡμῶν ἔγνω—θεὸς A; ἀλλ' ἔγνων ὅτι ἐμνήσθη—θεός, κ. γέγωνεν σωτηρία πᾶσοις φύλοις των ἐπὶ γῆς B   13 ἐν σοί] ἐφ' ἡμᾶς B; πρὸς ἡμᾶς C   13—16 καὶ πῶς—θεοῦ ἐστίν] om A   14 ζευμάτων] κοιμάτων B   17 ὅτι παραφέρω] πιστεῦσον παρα ρω A; προσφέρω B   19 ἀπῆλθεν ἓν τῶν παιδίων] ἀπ. ἓν τ. παιδων A; σὺ ἐνεγκὼν ἐν τῷ παιδίῳ B; ἀπῆλθες εἰς τὸ πεδίον C   ἤνεγκεν] ἤνεγκας BC   22 ἐνόησας ὦ γύναι] om B; ἀδελφή, ἐνόησας C   22—p. 111, 4 καλῶς—ὧδε] καλλως εἶπας ὅτι κ. τὸν Λὼτ ἐρρυσώμεθα ἀπὸ Σοδόμων ὅτε ἐγνωρίσαμεν τὸ μυστήριον B   25—p. 111, 2 καὶ καθὼς—μυστ.] οἱ κ. ἀπελθόντες κ. ρυσάμενοι τὸν ἀδ. τὸν ἡμέτερον ἀπὸ τῶν Σ., τὸν Λὼτ A

μοι ὅτι ὑπάγω τηρῆσαι τὸν ἀδελφὸν Λὼτ ἀπὸ Σοδόμων· ABC
καὶ τότε ἐγνώρισα τὸ μυστήριον.

VII. ὁ δὲ Ἀβραὰμ εἶπεν πρὸς Μιχαήλ· Εἰπέ μοι,
ἄνθρωπε τοῦ θεοῦ, καὶ φανέρωσόν μοι τί ἦλθες ὧδε. καὶ
5 εἶπεν Μιχαήλ· Ὁ υἱός σου Ἰσαὰκ δηλώσει σοι. καὶ
λέγει Ἀβραὰμ τῷ υἱῷ αὐτοῦ· Υἱέ μου ἀγαπητέ, εἰπέ μοι
τί εἶδες κατ' ὄναρ σήμερον καὶ ἐθροήθης· ἀνάγγειλόν μοι.
καὶ ἀπεκρίθη Ἰσαὰκ τῷ πατρὶ αὐτοῦ· Εἶδον κατ' ὄναρ
†ἐμαυτὸν† τὸν ἥλιον καὶ τὴν σελήνην· καὶ στέφανος ἐπὶ τῆς
10 κεφαλῆς μου ἐγένετο· καὶ ἦν ἀνὴρ παμμεγεθὴς λίαν λάμ-
πων ἐκ τοῦ οὐρανοῦ, ὡς φῶς καλούμενον πατὴρ τοῦ φωτός·
καὶ ἔλαβεν τὸν ἥλιον ἐκ τῆς κεφαλῆς μου· καὶ λοιπὸν
ἀφῆκεν τὰς ἀκτῖνας ἐν μέσῳ μου· καὶ ἔκλαυσα ἐγὼ καὶ
εἶπον· Παρακαλῶ σε, κύριέ μου, μὴ ἐπάρῃς τὴν δόξαν τῆς
15 κεφαλῆς μου καὶ τὸ φῶς τοῦ οἴκου μου καὶ πᾶσαν τὴν
δόξαν τὴν ἐμήν. ἐπένθησε δὲ ὁ ἥλιος καὶ ἡ σελήνη καὶ οἱ
ἀστέρες λέγοντες· Μὴ ἐπάρῃς τὴν δόξαν τῆς δυνάμεως
ἡμῶν. καὶ ἀποκριθεὶς ὁ φωτεινὸς ἐκεῖνος ἀνὴρ εἰπέ μοι·
Μὴ κλαύσῃς ὅτι ἔλαβον τὸ φῶς τοῦ οἴκου σου· ἀνελήφθη
20 γὰρ ἀπὸ καμάτων εἰς ἀνάπαυσιν, καὶ ἀπὸ ταπεινώσεως εἰς
ὕψος, αἴρουσιν αὐτὸν ἀπὸ στενοχωρίας εἰς εὐρυχωρίαν,
αἴρουσιν αὐτὸν ἀπὸ σκότους εἰς φῶς. ἐγὼ δὲ εἶπον αὐτῷ·
Παρακαλῶ σε, κύριε, λάβε καὶ τὰς ἀκτῖνας μετ' αὐτοῦ.
ὁ δὲ εἶπέν μοι· Δώδεκα ὧραι τῆς ἡμέρας εἰσίν, καὶ τότε
25 ὅλας τὰς ἀκτῖνας λαμβάνω. ταῦτα λέγοντος τοῦ φωτεινοῦ
ἀνδρός, εἶδον τὸν ἥλιον τοῦ οἴκου μου ἀναβαίνοντα εἰς τὸν
οὐρανόν, τὸ δὲ στέφος ἐκεῖνον πλεῖον οὐκ εἶδον· ἦν δὲ ὁ
ἥλιος ἐκεῖνος ὅμοιός σου τοῦ πατρός μου. καὶ εἶπεν Μιχαὴλ τῷ Ἀβραάμ· Ἀλήθειαν εἴρηκεν ὁ υἱός σου Ἰσαάκ·

7 κ. ἐθροήθης· ἀνάγγ. μοι] om AB   9 ἐμαυτὸν] ἑαυτὸν μου B ; +ὡς C
10 ἐγένετο]+κ. ἀφῆκεν τὰς ἀκτῖνας A   11 καλούμ.] om B; καὶ καλουμ. C
τοῦ] om C   12, 13 κ. λοιπὸν—μέσῳ μου] om A   12—15 κ. λοιπὸν—κεφ.
μου] om B by homœot.   18 φωτ. ἐκ. ἀνήρ] φωτήρ. ἐκ. ὁ παμμεγεθεὶς C
19 ἔλαβον] ἄβλαβον C   20 καμάτων] καύματος AC   ἀνάπαυσιν] ἀπόλαυσιν B
21, 22 ἀπὸ στενοχ.—αἴρ. αὐτὸν] om B; ἀπὸ στεν. εἰς εὐρήχωρον δοξαν· αἴρ. αὐτ C
24, 25 δώδεκα—λαμβάνω] οὐ λαμβάνω ταύτας ἕως ἂν πληρωθῶσιν αἱ δωδ. ὧρ. τ.
ἡμ. τ. τότε ὁρᾷς τὰς ἀκτῖνας λάμπειν C   27 στέφος—εἶδον] σῶμα αὐτοῦ
μένοντα ἐπὶ τῆς γῆς B; σῶμα αὐτοῦ μένει ἐπὶ τ. γῆς ἕως ἂν (p. 112, 2) A
29—p. 112, 1 ἀλήθειαν—οὐρανοὺς] νῦν ἤκουσας τὸ ἀληθὲς κ. τάξον περὶ τοῦ οἴκου
σου· ἰδοὺ γὰρ ἀπέσταλμαι παρὰ κῡ τοῦ θῦ λαβεῖν τὴν ψυχὴν σου C

112   THE TESTAMENT OF ABRAHAM.

ABC σὺ γὰρ εἶ· καὶ ἀναλαμβανέσαι εἰς τοὺς οὐρανούς, τὸ δὲ σῶμά σου μένει ἐπὶ τῆς γῆς ἕως ἂν πληρωθῶσιν ἑπτακισχίλιοι αἰῶνες· τότε γὰρ ἐγερθήσεται πᾶσα σάρξ. νῦν οὖν, Ἀβραάμ, διάθες τὰ τοῦ οἴκου σου, καὶ περὶ τῶν τέκνων σου, τελείως γὰρ ἤκουσας τὴν οἰκονομίαν σου. 5 καὶ ἀποκριθεὶς Ἀβραὰμ εἶπεν πρὸς Μιχαήλ· Παρακαλῶ σε, κύριε, ἐὰν ἐξέρχωμαι ἐκ τοῦ σώματός μου, σωματικῶς ἤθελον ἀναληφθῆναι, ἵνα θεάσομαι τὰ κτίσματα ἃ ἐκτίσατο κύριος ὁ θεός μου ἐν οὐρανῷ καὶ ἐπὶ γῆς. καὶ ἀπεκρίθη Μιχαὴλ καὶ εἶπεν· Τοῦτο οὐκ ἔστιν ἐμὸν ποίημα· 10 ἀλλὰ ἀπελθὼν ἐγὼ ἀπαγγελῶ τῷ κυρίῳ περὶ τούτου, καὶ ἐὰν κελεύωμαι, ὑποδείξω σοι ταῦτα πάντα.

VIII. καὶ ἀνῆλθεν Μιχαὴλ ἐν τοῖς οὐρανοῖς καὶ ἐλάλησεν ἐνώπιον κυρίου περὶ Ἀβραάμ· καὶ ἀπεκρίθη κύριος πρὸς Μιχαήλ· Ἀπελθε καὶ ἀναλαβοῦ ἐν σώματι 15 τὸν Ἀβραὰμ καὶ ὑποδεῖξον αὐτῷ πάντα, καὶ ὃ ἐὰν εἴπῃ σοι ποίησον ὡς αὐτῷ ὄντι φίλῳ μου. ἐξελθὼν οὖν ὁ Μιχαὴλ ἀνέλαβεν τὸν Ἀβραὰμ ἐπὶ νεφέλης ἐν σώματι, καὶ ἀνήνεγκεν αὐτὸν ἐπὶ τὸν Ὠκεανὸν ποταμόν· καὶ ἀτενίσας Ἀβραὰμ εἶδεν δύο πύλας, μίαν μὲν μικράν, τὴν δὲ 20 ἑτέραν μεγάλην· καὶ ἀνάμεσον τῶν δύο πυλῶν ἐκάθητο ἀνὴρ ἐπὶ θρόνου δόξης μεγάλης· καὶ πλῆθος ἀγγέλων κύκλῳ αὐτοῦ· καὶ ἦν κλαίων, καὶ πάλιν γελῶν, καὶ ὁ κλαυθμὸς ὑπερέβαινεν τὸ γέλος αὐτοῦ ἑπταπλασίονα. καὶ εἶπεν Ἀβραὰμ πρὸς τὸν Μιχαήλ· Τίς ἐστιν οὗτος ὁ 25 καθήμενος ἀνάμεσον τῶν δύο πυλῶν μετὰ δόξης πολλῆς· ποτὲ μὲν γελᾷ, ποτὲ μὲν κλαίει, καὶ ὁ κλαυθμὸς ὑπερβαίνει τὸ γέλος ἑπταπλασίως; καὶ εἶπεν Μιχαὴλ πρὸς Ἀβραάμ· Οὐκ ἔγνως αὐτὸν τίς ἐστιν; καὶ εἶπεν· Οὐχί, κύριε. καὶ εἶπεν Μιχαὴλ πρὸς Ἀβραάμ· Θεωρεῖς τὰς δύο 30

2, 3 ἑπτακ. αἰῶνες] τὰ ἔτη C   5 τελείως—οἰκονομ. σου] πεπληροφορῆσαι γὰρ τὴν κεφαλήν σου B   7 ἐὰν—σώματός μου] ἐπειδὴ παρέρχωμαι τοῦδε τοῦ κοσμου B; ναί, ἐξέρχομαι ἐκ τοῦ σώμ. ἀλλὰ C   σωματικῶς] ἐν σώματι B 8 ἤθελον] θέλω B; ἤλπιζον C   10 κ. εἶπεν] + πάτερ μου B   11 κυρίῳ] πατρὶ A; πατρὶ τῷ ἐν τοῖς οὐρανοῖς C   15 ἀναλ. ἐν σώμ.] λαβὲ σωματικῶς A; ἀνάλαβε σωματικῶς C   19 ὠκεανὸν] αἰκιανὸν AC; ὀκεανὸν B   20, 21 μίαν—μεγάλην] μι. μικρ. κ. ἑτ. μεγ. A; ἀφ' ὧν μία στενὴ κ. ἡ ἑτέρα εὐρήχορος B 23 κύκλῳ] + τοῦ θρόνου C   24 ἑπταπλασ.] om BC   26 πολλῆς] + κ. πλῆθος ἀγγέλων κύκλῳ αὐτοῦ C

πύλας ταύτας, τὴν μικρὰν καὶ τὴν μεγάλην; αὗταί εἰσιν ABC
αἱ ἀπάγουσαι εἰς τὴν ζωὴν καὶ εἰς τὴν ἀπώλειαν. ὁ ἀνὴρ
δὲ οὗτος ὁ καθήμενος ἐν μέσῳ αὐτῶν, οὗτός ἐστιν ὁ Ἀδάμ,
ὁ πρῶτος ἄνθρωπος ὃν ἔπλασεν ὁ κύριος· καὶ ἔθηκεν αὐτὸν
5 εἰς τὸν τόπον τοῦτον θεωρῆσαι πᾶσαν ψυχὴν ἐξερχομένην
ἐκ τοῦ σώματος, ἐπειδὴ ἐξ αὐτοῦ εἰσὶν πάντες. ὅταν οὖν
θεωρῇς αὐτὸν κλαίοντα, γνῶθι ὅτι ἐθεάσατο ψυχὰς πολλὰς
ἀπαγομένας εἰς τὴν ἀπώλειαν· ὅταν δὲ ἴδῃς αὐτὸν γελῶντα,
ἐθεάσατο ψυχὰς ὀλίγας ἀπαγομένας εἰς τὴν ζωήν. θεωρεῖς
10 αὐτὸν πῶς ὑπερβαίνει ὁ κλαυθμὸς τὸ γέλος; ἐπεὶ θεωρεῖ
τὸ περισσότερον τοῦ κόσμου ἀπαγομένους διὰ τῆς πλατείας εἰς τὴν ἀπώλειαν, διὰ τοῦτο ὑπερβαίνει ὁ κλαυθμὸς
τὸ γέλος ἑπταπλασίως.

IX. καὶ εἶπεν Ἀβραάμ· Καὶ ὁ μὴ δυνάμενος εἰσελθεῖν
15 διὰ τῆς στενῆς πύλης, οὐ δύναται εἰσελθεῖν εἰς τὴν ζωήν;
τότε ἔκλαυσεν Ἀβραάμ, λέγων· Οὐαί μοι, τί ποιήσω ἐγώ;
ὅτι εἰμὶ ἄνθρωπος εὐρὺς τῷ σώματι, καὶ πῶς δυνήσομαι
εἰσελθεῖν εἰς τὴν στενὴν πύλην, εἰς ἣν οὐ δύναται ἐλθεῖν
παιδίον πέντε καὶ δέκα ἐτῶν; καὶ ἀποκριθεὶς Μιχαὴλ
20 εἶπεν πρὸς Ἀβραάμ· Σὺ μὴ φοβοῦ, πάτερ, μηδὲ λυποῦ,
ἀκωλύτως γὰρ εἰσερχέσαι δι' αὐτῆς, καὶ πάντες οἱ συνό-
μοιοί σου. καὶ ἑστῶτος τοῦ Ἀβραὰμ καὶ θαυμάζοντος,
ἰδοὺ ἄγγελος κυρίου ἐλαύνων ἐξ μυριάδας ψυχὰς ἁμαρτωλῶν εἰς τὴν ἀπώλειαν· καὶ λέγει Ἀβραὰμ πρὸς Μιχαήλ·
25 Οὗτοι πάντες εἰς τὴν ἀπώλειαν ἀπέρχονται; καὶ λέγει
αὐτῷ Μιχαήλ· Ναί, ἀλλὰ ἀπέλθωμεν καὶ ἀναζητήσωμεν
ἐν ταῖς ψυχαῖς ταύταις, εἰ ἔστιν ἐξ αὐτῶν κἂν μία δικαία.
ἀπελθόντων δὲ αὐτῶν, εὗρον ἄγγελον κατέχοντα ἐν τῇ
χειρὶ αὐτοῦ μίαν ψυχὴν γυναικὸς ἐξ αὐτῶν τῶν ἐξ μυριά-

5 ἐξερχομένην] ἐξελουμένην A   14, 15 εἰσελθεῖν—οὐ δύναται] om B
16 τότε ἔκλ. Ἀ. λέγων] om B   16—19 οὐαί μοι—ἐτῶν] οἴμοι οἴμοι τί λοιπὸν
ποιήσω κἀγώ· πῶς δυνηθῶ ἐν σώματι εἰσελθεῖν ἐν τῇ τοιαύτῃ στενῇ πύλῃ ἣν οὐδὲ
δεκάπεντε ἐνιαυτοῦ παιδίων δύναται εἰσελθῆναι B   17 εὐρὺς τῷ σώμ.] βαρὺς
τῷ σώμ. μέγας C   δυνήσομαι] δυνάμενος A   18, 19 εἰς ἣν—ἐτῶν] εἰ μὴ
παιδία δυετῶν C   20 σὺ—λυποῦ] om AC   21 ἀκωλύτως γὰρ εἰσερχέσαι]
ὁ ἀκατάλυτος εἰσέρχεται A; σὺ ὁλοστὸς εἰσέρχει C   23 ἐξ] om B   ἁμαρτω-
λῶν] + κ. ἀπήγαγεν C   24, 25 καὶ λέγει Ἀ.—ἀπέρχονται] om C   28, 29 ἄγγελον—χειρὶ αὐτοῦ] om B   29—p. 114, 4 μίαν ψυχὴν—ἀπώλειαν] μίαν—
ἰσοζυγούσας μετὰ τῆς ἁμαρτίας αὐτῆς πασας· κ. οὐκ ἦσαν ἐν αὐχθω οὐδὲ ἀνά-

J.   8

ABC δων, ὅτι εὗρεν τὰς ἁμαρτίας ἰσοζυγούσας μετὰ τὰ ἔργα
αὐτῆς ἅπαντα, καὶ οὐκ ἦσαν ἐν μόχθῳ οὐδὲ ἐν ἀναπαύσει,
ἀλλ' ἐν τόπῳ μεσότητος. τὰς δὲ ψυχὰς ἐκείνας ἦρεν εἰς
τὴν ἀπώλειαν. καὶ εἶπεν Ἀβραὰμ πρὸς Μιχαήλ· Κύριε,
οὗτός ἐστιν ὁ ἄγγελος ὁ ἐκφέρων τὰς ψυχὰς ἐκ τοῦ σώ- 5
ματος, ἢ οὔ; ἀπεκρίθη Μιχαὴλ καὶ εἶπεν· Οὗτός ἐστιν ὁ
θάνατος, καὶ ἀπάγει αὐτὰς εἰς τὸν τόπον τοῦ κριτηρίου,
ἵνα ὁ κριτὴς κρίνῃ αὐτάς.

X. καὶ λέγει Ἀβραάμ· Κύριέ μου, παρακαλῶ σε ἵνα
ἀναγάγῃς με εἰς τὸν τόπον τοῦ κριτηρίου ὅπως κἀγὼ 10
θεάσωμαι αὐτὰς πῶς κρίνονται. τότε Μιχαὴλ ἔλαβεν
τὸν Ἀβραὰμ ἐπὶ νεφέλης, καὶ ἤγαγεν αὐτὸν εἰς τὸν παρά-
δεισον· καὶ ὡς ἔφθασεν εἰς τὸν τόπον ὅπου ἦν ὁ κριτής,
ἦλθεν ὁ ἄγγελος καὶ ἔδωκεν τὴν ψυχὴν ἐκείνην εἰς τὸν
κριτήν· ἔλεγεν δὲ ἡ ψυχή· Ἐλέησόν με, κύριε. καὶ εἶπεν 15
ὁ κριτής· Πῶς ἐλεήσω σε, ὅτι σὺ οὐκ ἠλέησας τὴν θυγα-
τέρα σου ἥνπερ εἶχες, τὸν καρπὸν τῆς κοιλίας σου; διὰ τί
ἐφόνευσας αὐτήν; καὶ ἀπεκρίθη· Οὐχί, κύριε· φόνος ἐξ
ἐμοῦ οὐ γέγονεν, ἀλλ' αὐτὴ ἡ θυγάτηρ μου κατεψεύσατό
μου. ὁ δὲ κριτὴς ἐκέλευσεν ἐλθεῖν τὸν τὰ ὑπομνήματα 20
γράφοντα. καὶ ἰδοὺ χερουβὶμ βαστάζοντα βιβλία δύο,
καὶ ἦν μετ' αὐτῶν ἀνὴρ παμμεγεθὴς σφόδρα· καὶ εἶχεν
ἐπὶ τὴν κεφαλὴν αὐτοῦ τρεῖς στεφάνους, καὶ ὁ εἷς στέφανος
ὑψηλότερος ὑπῆρχεν τῶν ἑτέρων δύο στεφάνων· οἱ δὲ
στέφανοι ἐκαλοῦντο στέφανοι μαρτυρίας. καὶ εἶχεν ὁ ἀνὴρ 25
ἐν τῇ χειρὶ αὐτοῦ κάλαμον χρυσοῦν· καὶ λέγει ὁ κριτὴς
πρὸς αὐτόν· Σύστησον τὴν ἁμαρτίαν τῆς ψυχῆς ταύτης.

παυσιν ἡλέστω κατὰ σώματος· τας—ἐκείνας εἴρηνται εἰς τὴν ἀπόλειαν A; ἀπ' αὐτὰς
τὰς μυριάδας μίαν ψ. γυναικὸς ἡσυνέχου τὴν διαγωγὴν· ἐπαὶ ται τῶν καλῶν αὐτοῖς
ἔργων κ. τῶν ἐναντίων κ. οὕτη ἐπ' ἀπολεία οὐχ ὑπῆρχεν οὔτε μὴν ἐπ' ἀναπαύσεως
ἀλλ' ἐν μέσῳ τούτων B; μίαν ψ. δικαίαν ἐξ—μυριάδων γυναικὸς σῶμα εὗρεν γὰρ
—ἰσοζυγ. μετὰ τὰ ἔργα αὐτῆς ἅπαντα· καὶ οὐκ ἦσαν ἐν μόχθῳ οὐδὲ ἐν ἀναπαύσει
ἀλλ'—ἀπώλειαν C   6 οὔ] σὺ A   7 κριτηρίου]+μου A   11, 12 ἔλαβεν—νεφέλης] λαβὼν—νεφ. B; ἐποίησεν τὴν νεφέλην ἀναλαβεῖν τὸν Ἀ. C
12, 13 εἰς τ. παράδ.—τόπον] om C   15 κύριε]+ὅτι οὐχ ἥμαρτον C
18 αὐτὴν] om AC   18—21 φόνος—κατεψεύσ. μου] ψευδέται ἡ θυγάτηρ μου
B   21 βαστάζοντα] om A; κατάξοντα C   23 τρεῖς στεφάνους] τρία A
24 ἑτέρων δύο] τεσσάρων A; ἑτέρων C   25 στέφ. μαρτυρίας] στέφ. μαρτύρων
A; μαρτυρία C

καὶ ἀναπτύξας ὁ ἀνὴρ ἐκεῖνος μίαν τῶν βιβλίων τῶν ABC
ὄντων ἐκ τῶν χερουβὶμ ἀνεζήτησεν τὴν ἁμαρτίαν τῆς
ψυχῆς τῆς γυναικὸς, καὶ εὗρεν. καὶ εἶπεν ὁ κριτής· Ὢ
ταλαίπωρε ψυχή, πῶς λέγεις ὅτι φόνον οὐκ ἐποίησας;
5 οὐχὶ σὺ ἀπελθοῦσα μετὰ τὴν τελευτὴν τοῦ ἀνδρός σου,
ἐμοίχευσας τὸν ἄνδρα τῆς θυγατρός σου, καὶ ἀπέκτεινας
αὐτήν; ἤλεγχε δὲ καὶ τὰς ἄλλας ἁμαρτίας αὐτῆς, καὶ εἴ
τι ἔπραξεν ἐκ νεότητος αὐτῆς. ταῦτα ἀκούσασα ἡ γυνὴ
ἐβόησεν λέγουσα· Οἴμοι, οἴμοι, ὅτι πάσας τὰς ἁμαρτίας
10 μου ἃς ἐποίησα ἐν τῷ κόσμῳ ἐληθάργησα· ἐνταῦθα δὲ οὐκ
ἐληθαργήθησαν. τότε ἦραν καὶ αὐτὴν καὶ παρέδωκαν τοῖς
βασανισταῖς.

XI. καὶ εἶπεν Ἀβραὰμ πρὸς Μιχαήλ· Κύριε, τίς
ἐστιν οὗτος ὁ κριτής, καὶ τίς ἐστιν ὁ ἄλλος, ὁ ἐλέγχων τὰς
15 ἁμαρτίας; καὶ λέγει Μιχαὴλ πρὸς Ἀβραάμ· Θεωρεῖς τὸν
κριτήν; οὗτός ἐστιν ὁ Ἄβελ, ὁ ἐν πρώτοις μαρτυρήσας·
καὶ ἤνεγκεν αὐτὸν ὧδε ὁ θεὸς κρίνειν· καὶ ὁ ἀποδεικνύ-
μενος οὗτός ἐστιν ὁ διδάσκαλος τοῦ οὐρανοῦ καὶ τῆς γῆς
καὶ γραμματεὺς τῆς δικαιοσύνης Ἐνώχ· ἀπέστειλεν γὰρ
20 κύριος αὐτοὺς ἐνταῦθα, ἵνα ἀπογράφωσιν τὰς ἁμαρτίας καὶ
τὰς δικαιοσύνας ἑκάστου. καὶ λέγει ὁ Ἀβραάμ· Καὶ πῶς
δύναται Ἐνὼχ βαστάσαι τὸ βάρος τῶν ψυχῶν, μὴ ἰδὼν
θάνατον; ἢ πῶς δύναται δοῦναι πασῶν τῶν ψυχῶν ἀπόφασιν; καὶ εἶπεν Μιχαήλ· Ἐὰν δώσῃ ἀπόφασιν περὶ

4 φόνον οὐκ ἐποίησας] ὁ φώνος διά σου οὐ γέγονεν B ; φόνος ἐξ ἐμοῦ οὐ γέγονεν
C   7, 8 καὶ εἴ τι—νεότ. αὐτῆς] om B   8 γυνὴ] om B ; ψυχὴ C
10 ἃς—κόσμῳ] om A   κόσμῳ]+κατὰ πρόσωπόν μου βλέπω καὶ τί ποιήσω ἡ
τάλαινα ὅτι ἐνταῦθα μετάνοια οὐκ ἔστιν B   10, 11 ἐνταῦθα—ἐληθαργ.] om B
11 ἦραν αὐτήν]+οἱ ὑπηρέται τῆς ὀργῆς C   14, 15 καὶ τίς—ἁμαρτ.] om C
14 ἐλέγχων] κατέχων B   17 ἤνεγκεν] προσέταξεν B ; ἔταξεν C   17—19 ὁ
ἀποδεικν. οὗτος—Ἐνώχ] ὁ ἕτερος ὁ προσκομίζων τὰς ἁμαρτίας κ. ἐλέγχων τὰς ἀγα-
θὰς κ. πονηρὰς πράξεις ἐστὶν ἔνωχ ὁ μαρτὺς τῆς ἐσχάτης ἡμέρας B   19 γραμ-
ματεὺς] γραφεὺς A   19—21 Ἐνὼχ—δικαιοσύνας] om A (which reads γραφεὺς τῆς δικ. κ. τῶν ἁμαρτιῶν ἑκάστου)   ἀπέστειλεν—ἑκάστου] κ. προσετάγειν
παρὰ κυ ἐν τῷ κόσμω διάγειν κ. ἀπογράφεσθαι πράξεις κ. λογισμοὺς ἑνὸς ἑκάστου
ἀνθρώπου B   22 βαστάσαι τὸ βάρος τῶν ψ.] βλέπειν κ. προσκομίζειν
ἑνὸς ἑκάστου τὰς ἁμαρτίας B. τὰς δικαιοσύνας B ; βαστᾶσαι τὸ μέρος τῶν ψ. C
24 ἀπόφασιν] ἀπολογίαν A ; ἀποφάσεις ἢ κ. σώζειν τοὺς ἐξομολογουμένους B
24—p. 116, 10 ἐὰν—κόλασιν] ταῦτα κ. αὐτὸς ὁ Ε. πρὸς κν ἐλάλησεν ἵνα μὴ πρὸς
τοὺς ἀνους ἐπιβαρὴς γύνεται ἀλλ᾿ ὁ κς οὐκ ἤκουσεν αὐτοῦ ἀλλ᾿ ἐκέλευσεν αὐτὸν
οὕτως ποιεῖν B

8—2

ABC αὐτῶν, οὐ συγχωρεῖται· ἀλλ' οὐ τὰ τοῦ Ἐνὼχ αὐτοῦ ἀποφαίνεται, ἀλλ' ὁ κύριός ἐστιν ὁ ἀποφαινόμενος, καὶ τούτου οὐκ ἔστιν εἰ μὴ μόνον τὸ γράψαι. ἐπειδὴ ηὔξατο Ἐνὼχ πρὸς κύριον λέγων· Οὐ θέλω, κύριε, ἀποδοῦναι τῶν ψυχῶν ἀπόφασιν, ὅπως μὴ τινὸς ἐπιβαρὴς γένωμαι· καὶ εἶπεν 5 κύριος πρὸς Ἐνώχ· Ἐγὼ κελεύσω σε ἵνα γράφῃς τὰς ἁμαρτίας ψυχῆς ἐξιλεουμένης, καὶ εἰσελεύσεται εἰς τὴν ζωήν· καὶ ἡ ψυχὴ ἐὰν μὴ ἐξιλεωθῇ καὶ μετανοήσῃ, εὑρήσεις τὰς ἁμαρτίας αὐτῆς γεγραμμένας, καὶ βληθήσεται εἰς τὴν κόλασιν. 10

XII. καὶ μετὰ τὸ θεωρῆσαι Ἀβραὰμ τὸν τόπον τοῦ κριτηρίου, κατήγαγεν αὐτὸν ἡ νεφέλη ἐν τῷ στερεώματι κάτω. καὶ κατανοήσας Ἀβραὰμ ἐπὶ τὴν γῆν, εἶδεν ἄνθρωπον μοιχεύοντα γυναῖκα ὕπανδρον. καὶ στραφεὶς λέγει Ἀβραὰμ πρὸς Μιχαήλ· Θεωρεῖς τὴν ἁμαρτίαν ταύ- 15 την; ἀλλά, κύριε, πέμψον πῦρ ἐξ οὐρανοῦ, ἵνα καταφάγῃ αὐτούς. καὶ εὐθὺς κατῆλθεν πῦρ καὶ κατέφαγεν αὐτούς· διότι εἶπεν κύριος τῷ Μιχαὴλ ὅτι "Οσα αἰτήσεταί σε ὁ Ἀβραὰμ ποιῆσαι αὐτῷ, ποίησον. καὶ πάλιν ἀναβλέψας Ἀβραάμ, εἶδεν ἄλλους ἀνθρώπους καταλαλοῦντας ἑταί- 20 ρους, καὶ εἶπεν· Ἀνοιχθήτω ἡ γῆ καὶ καταπιέτω αὐτούς. καὶ ἐν τῷ εἰπεῖν αὐτῷ, κατέπιεν αὐτοὺς ἡ γῆ ζῶντας. καὶ πάλιν ἀνήγαγεν αὐτὸν ἡ νεφέλη ἐν ἑτέρῳ τόπῳ· καὶ εἶδεν Ἀβραάμ τινας ἀπερχομένους εἰς ἔρημον τόπον τοῦ ποιῆσαι φόνον. καὶ εἶπεν πρὸς Μιχαήλ· Θεωρεῖς τὴν ἁμαρτίαν 25 ταύτην; ἀλλ' ἐλθέτωσαν θηρία ἐκ τῆς ἐρήμου καὶ διαμερίσονται αὐτούς. καὶ αὐτῇ τῇ ὥρᾳ ἐξῆλθον θηρία ἐκ τῆς ἐρήμου καὶ κατέφαγον αὐτούς. τότε ἐλάλησεν κύριος ὁ θεὸς πρὸς τὸν Μιχαὴλ λέγων· Ἀπόστρεψον τὸν Ἀβραὰμ εἰς τὸν οἶκον αὐτοῦ καὶ μὴ ἀφήσεις αὐτὸν κυκλῶσαι πᾶσαν 30 τὴν κτίσιν ἣν ἐποίησα, ὅτι οὐ σπλαγχνίζεται ἐπὶ τοὺς ἁμαρτωλούς, ἀλλ' ἐγὼ σπλαγχνίζομαι ἐπὶ τοὺς ἁμαρτωλοὺς ὥστε ἐπιστρέφουσιν καὶ ζήσωσιν καὶ μετανοήσωσιν ἐκ

6 ἐγὼ κελεύσω σε] ἐγέρθητί μοι σημειῶν πρὸς σὲ C   8 μὴ ἐξιλεωθῇ καὶ] om A   9 βληθήσεται] -ονται A; κληθήσεται C   26, 27 διαμερίσονται αὐτούς] διαφάγωσιν αὐτοὺς A; καταφαγέτωσαν αὐτοὺς ὅτι τοιοῦτον ἀνόμημα ὅρμησαν ποιῆσαι B   33—p. 117, 1 ὥστε—σωθήσονται] ὡς τὸ ἐπιστρέψαι κ. ζήσωσιν—σωθήσ. A; om B; ὥστε ἐπιστρέψωσιν κ. μετανοήσωσιν—σωθήσ. C

τῶν ἁμαρτιῶν αὐτῶν, καὶ σωθήσονται. καὶ κατὰ τὴν ΑΒ(
ἐνάτην ὥραν ὑπέστρεψεν Μιχαὴλ τὸν Ἀβραὰμ εἰς τὸν
οἶκον αὐτοῦ. Σάρρα δὲ ἡ γυνὴ αὐτοῦ, μὴ θεωρήσασα τὸν
Ἀβραὰμ τί γέγονεν, κατεπόθη τῇ λύπῃ καὶ παρέδωκε τὴν
5 ψυχήν· καὶ μετὰ τὸ ὑποστρέψαι τὸν Ἀβραάμ, εὗρεν
αὐτὴν νεκράν, καὶ ἔθαψεν αὐτήν.

XIII. ὅτε δὲ ἤγγισαν αἱ ἡμέραι τοῦ θανάτου τοῦ
Ἀβραάμ, εἶπεν κύριος ὁ θεὸς πρὸς Μιχαήλ· Οὐ μὴ τολ-
μήσῃ θάνατος ἐγγίσαι τοῦ ἐξενεγκεῖν τὴν ψυχὴν τοῦ
10 δούλου μου, ὅτι φίλος μου ἐστίν· ἀλλὰ ἄπελθε καὶ κόσ-
μησον τὸν θάνατον ἐν πολλῇ ὡραιότητι, καὶ οὕτως ἀπό-
στειλον αὐτὸν πρὸς Ἀβραὰμ ὅπως θεάσηται αὐτὸν τοῖς
ὀφθαλμοῖς αὐτοῦ. καὶ ὁ Μιχαὴλ εὐθὺς καθὼς προσ-
ετάχθη ἐκόσμησεν τὸν θάνατον ἐν πολλῇ ὡραιότητι, καὶ
15 οὕτως ἀπέστειλεν αὐτὸν πρὸς Ἀβραάμ, ὅπως θεάσηται
αὐτόν. καὶ ἐκάθισεν πλησίον τοῦ Ἀβραάμ· ἰδὼν δὲ ὁ
Ἀβραὰμ τὸν θάνατον πλησίον αὐτοῦ καθήμενον ἐφοβήθη
φόβον μέγαν. καὶ εἶπεν ὁ θάνατος πρὸς Ἀβραάμ· Χαίροις,
ἁγία ψυχή· χαῖρε, φίλος κυρίου τοῦ θεοῦ· χαῖρε, τὸ παρα-
20 μύθιον τοῦ ξενισμοῦ τῶν ὁδοιπόρων. καὶ εἶπεν Ἀβραάμ·
Καλῶς ἐλήλυθας, δοῦλε θεοῦ ὑψίστου· παρακαλῶ σε, εἰπέ
μοι τίς εἶ σύ, καὶ εἰσελθὼν ἐν τῷ οἴκῳ μετάλαβε βρώσεως
καὶ πόσεως, καὶ ἀπόστηθι ἀπ' ἐμοῦ· ἀφ' οὗ γὰρ ἐθεασάμην σε καθήμενον ἔγγιστά μου, ἐταράχθη ἡ ψυχή μου.
25 πάντως γὰρ οὐκ εἰμὶ ἄξιος μετά σου πλησιάζειν, σὺ γὰρ
εἶ ὑψηλὸν πνεῦμα, ἐγὼ δὲ σὰρξ καὶ αἷμα, καὶ διὰ τοῦτο
οὐ δύναμαι βαστάσαι τὴν δόξαν σου. θεωρῶ γὰρ τὴν
ὡραιότητά σου, ὅτι οὐκ ἔστιν ἐκ τοῦ κόσμου τούτου. καὶ ΑΒ
εἶπεν ὁ θάνατος πρὸς Ἀβραάμ· Λέγω σοι, ἐν ὅλῳ τῷ
30 κτίσματι ὃ ἔκτισεν ὁ θεός, οὐχ εὑρέθη ὅμοιός σου· καὶ

1, 2 καὶ—ὥραν] κ. ταύτην τὴν ὥραν Α; ἐν ἐκείνῃ τῇ ἡμέρᾳ· καὶ C   3—
6 Σάρρα δὲ—ἔθαψεν αὐτήν] κ. οὕτως ἀπέθανεν ἡ γυνὴ αὐτοῦ—αὐτὴν ὁ Ἀβρ. Α;
κ. πρῶτον τέθνηκεν ἡ γυνὴ αὐτοῦ κ. ἔθ. αὐτήν Β   7—9 τοῦ Ἀβρ.—ἐγγί-
σαι] om Β   12, 13 τοῖς ὀφθ. αὐτοῦ] ἔμπροσθεν αὐτοῦ πρὸς θάνατον Α; om Β
16 καὶ ἐκάθ.—Ἀβρ.] om AC   καὶ] om Β   18—21 καὶ εἶπεν ὁ θάν.—ὑψί-
στου] om AB   22, 23 σὺ—πόσεως] om AB   27, 28 θεωρῶ—κόσμου τούτου]
om B   28—p. 118, 26 τούτου—ψυχὴν τοῦ Ἀ.] om C, a leaf of which is lost
here   30 κτίσματι ὃ] κτισμ. ἦν Α; κόσμῳ ὃ Β

AB αὐτὸς γὰρ ὁ θεὸς ζητήσας οὐχ εὗρεν τοιοῦτον ἐπὶ πάσης τῆς γῆς. καὶ εἶπεν Ἀβραὰμ πρὸς τὸν θάνατον· Πῶς ἐτόλμησας ψεύσασθαι; ὅτι ὁρῶ τὴν ὡραιότητά σου ὅτι οὐκ ἔστιν ἐκ τοῦ κόσμου τούτου. καὶ εἶπεν ὁ θάνατος πρὸς Ἀβραάμ· Μὴ νομίσῃς, Ἀβραάμ, ὅτι ἡ ὡραιότης 5 αὕτη ἐμή ἐστιν, ἢ καὶ οὕτως πορεύομαι εἰς πάντα ἄνθρωπον· οὐχί, ἀλλ' ἐάν τις δίκαιος ὡς σύ, οὕτως λαμβάνω στεφάνους καὶ ἀπέρχομαι πρὸς αὐτόν· ἐὰν δὲ ἁμαρτωλός ἐστιν, ἀπέρχομαι ἐν μεγάλῃ σαπρότητι καὶ ἐκ τῆς ἁμαρτίας αὐτῶν ποιῶ στέφανον τῇ κεφαλῇ μου, καὶ ταράσσω 10 αὐτοὺς ἐν μεγάλῳ φόβῳ, ἵνα ἐκθαμβῆται. λέγει οὖν Ἀβραὰμ πρὸς αὐτόν· Καὶ πόθεν ἔστιν ἡ ὡραιότης αὕτη; καὶ λέγει ὁ θάνατος· Οὐκ ἐστὶν ἄλλος σαπρότερός μου. λέγει αὐτῷ ὁ Ἀβραάμ· Καὶ μὴ σὺ εἶ ὁ λεγόμενος θάνατος; ἀπεκρίθη αὐτῷ καὶ εἶπεν· Ἐγώ εἰμι τὸ πικρὸν ὄνομα· 15 ἐγώ εἰμι κλαυθμός....

A XIV. εἶπεν δὲ Ἀβραὰμ πρὸς τὸν θάνατον· Δεῖξον ἡμῖν τὴν σαπρότητά σου. καὶ ἐφανέρωσεν ὁ θάνατος τὴν σαπρότητα αὐτοῦ· καὶ εἶχεν δύο κεφαλάς· ἡ μία εἶχεν πρόσωπον δράκοντος, καὶ δι' αὐτοῦ τινὲς ὑπὸ ἀσπίδων 20 τελευτῶσιν ἄφνω· ἡ δὲ ἑτέρα κεφαλὴ ὁμοία ῥομφαίας· διὰ τοῦτο τινὲς ἐν ῥομφαίᾳ τελευτῶσιν ὡς ἐπὶ τόξοις. ἐν ἐκείνῃ τῇ ἡμέρᾳ ἐτελεύτησαν οἱ παῖδες τοῦ Ἀβραὰμ διὰ τὸν φόβον τοῦ θανάτου· οὓς ἰδὼν Ἀβραὰμ ηὔξατο πρὸς κύριον, καὶ ἀνέστησεν αὐτούς. ἐπέστρεψεν δὲ ὁ θεὸς καὶ 25
AC ἐξέτεινεν τὴν ψυχὴν τοῦ Ἀβραὰμ ὡς ἐν ὀνείροις, καὶ ὁ ἀρχιστράτηγος Μιχαὴλ ἦρεν αὐτὴν εἰς τοὺς οὐρανούς.

5 μὴ νομίσῃς, Ἀβρ.] om A   7—11 οὐχί—ἐκθαμβῆται] om B   9 τῆς] τὰς A   11—16 λέγει οὖν—κλαυθμὸς] om A   16 κλαυθμός] with this word B breaks off   19 σαπρότητα αὐτοῦ] + ἐφανέρωσεν δὲ αὐτοὺς A   21 ῥομφαίας] -α A   22 τόξοις] -ος A   26—p. 119, 5 ὀνείροις—ἀμήν] ὀνείροις· καὶ ἰδοὺ ἅρμα κυρίου τοῦ θεοῦ ἦρεν τὴν τιμίαν αὐτοῦ ψυχὴν εἰς τοὺς οὐρανοὺς, καὶ ἄγγελοι προάγοντες καὶ ἀκολουθοῦντες μετὰ λαμπάδων καὶ θυμιατῶν, δοξάζοντες καὶ εὐλογοῦντες τὸν θεὸν τὸν ὕψιστον. ἔδραμεν δὲ Ἰσαὰκ ὁ υἱὸς αὐτοῦ, καὶ ἔπεσεν εἰς τὸ πρόσωπον αὐτοῦ καὶ ἔκλαυσεν καὶ κατεφίλησεν αὐτόν, ὁμοίως καὶ οἱ οἰκοπαῖδες ἅπαντες· καὶ βαστάζοντες αὐτὸν τὸ τιμιώτατον ἐκεῖνο λείψανον ἀπήγαγον· καὶ ἔθαψεν αὐτὸ Ἰσαὰκ οἰκειοχείρως πλησίον τῆς μητρὸς αὐτοῦ Σάρρας. καὶ ὑπέστρεψαν δοξάζοντες καὶ ὑμνοῦντες τὸν θεὸν ἡμῶν· ὅτι αὐτῷ ὑπάρχει ἡ δόξα, ἡ τιμή, καὶ ἡ μεγαλοσύνη εἰς τοὺς αἰῶνας τῶν αἰώνων. ἀμήν. C   26, 27 κ. ὁ ἀρχιστρ. Μ.] ὁ ἀρχ. Μ. καὶ A.

ἔθαψεν δὲ Ἰσαὰκ τὸν πατέρα αὐτοῦ πλησίον τῆς μητρὸς AC
αὐτοῦ τῆς Σάρρας, δοξάζων καὶ αἰνῶν τὸν θεόν· ὅτι αὐτῷ
πρέπει δόξα, τιμὴ καὶ προσκύνησις, τοῦ πατρὸς καὶ τοῦ
υἱοῦ καὶ τοῦ ἁγίου πνεύματος νῦν καὶ ἀεὶ καὶ εἰς τοὺς
5 αἰῶνας τῶν αἰώνων. Ἀμήν.

NOTES ON THE TEXT.

A I. p. 77, l. 2. 995 *years*. This completely fabulous age together with most of the first 10½ lines I regard as belonging to the mediaeval redactor. Nothing of it appears in B.

A II. p. 78, l. 14. μετὰ τοὺς υἱοὺς Μασὲκ κ. ἑτέροις παισίν. The MSS are responsible for the defective grammar. The true reading, which no MS supports, is here τοῦ υἱοῦ Μασέκ (i.e. Eliezer), from Gen. xv. 2. Notice that B introduces Isaac in his father's arms, a pleasing and possibly original feature.

Michael, in B II. p. 106, l. 18, says that he has heard of Abraham's hospitality of old and has come to test it, which points to the main moral of this part of the book, viz. φιλοξενία. Incidentally it may be remarked that in much of this literature, special virtues are inculcated in special books. Thus each of the Testaments of the XII. Patriarchs emphasises a special vice or virtue, Reuben speaks περὶ πορνείας, Issachar περὶ ἁπλότητος, Joseph περὶ σωφροσύνης and so forth. The Testament of Job again lays stress on ἐλεημοσύνη as well as on ὑπομονή, and the Book of Aseneth on μετάνοια.

A p. 79, l. 7. Michael's unwillingness to ride probably points to a belief that he would as an angel burn up or otherwise destroy any beast which he mounted. Celestial horses and chariots are of frequent occurrence in Jewish literature (2 Kings ii., Zech. i. vi., Rev. vi.).

B III. p. 107, l. 8. The phrase in B ἤκουον—ᾀδομένην sounds to me more original than that in A. I rather doubt whether either of the clauses which follow Ἅγιος ἅγιος ἅγιος stood as they do now in the original book, but am inclined to suspect that A's Ἅγιος—θεός is right at any rate.

ibid., l. 20. The motive for Abraham's tears in B seems original, and A simply omits it.

A IV. p. 81, l. 22. πνεῦμα παμφάγον. Cf. Tobit xii. 19, πάσας τὰς ἡμέρας ὠπτανόμην ὑμῖν, καὶ οὐκ ἔφαγον οὐδὲ ἔπιον, ἀλλὰ ὅρασιν ὑμεῖς ἐθεωρεῖτε. This 'docetic' view is of course not identical with that in the Testament, which is very peculiar. The idea that angels could not eat is well seen in various patristic comments on the visit of the three angels to Abraham.

I will quote a few lines from Macarius Magnes, *Apocritica* IV. 27, τὴν δὲ βρῶσιν καὶ πόσιν οὐχ ὁμοίως τῷ Ἀβραὰμ λάβοντες ἀνήλωσαν, ἀλλὰ πυρὸς δίκην τὴν παρατεθεῖσαν αὐτοῖς δαπανήσαντες... and again, λαβόντες τὸ σιτίον ὡς ἄνθρω-

NOTES ON THE TEXT. 121

ποι παρα τῷ 'Αβραάμ, ὡς "Αγγελοι τοῦτο φαγόντες ἀνήλωσαν,...ἀσωμάτῳ θίξει τὴν τροφὴν ἀναλώσαντες.

B IV. p. 108, l. 17. τοῦ γὰρ ἡλίου δύνοντος πάντες προσκυνοῦσιν ἄγγελοι τὸν θεόν.
It has already been remarked in the introduction (p. 44) that this is one of the purple patches taken by the redactor of B from the Apocalypse of Paul (§ 7, p. 38). διὰ ταῦτα πάντα εὐλογεῖτε τὸν θεὸν ἀκαταπαύστως, ἔτι δὲ μᾶλλον δύνοντος τοῦ ἡλίου· ἐν αὐτῇ γὰρ τῇ ὥρᾳ πάντες οἱ ἄγγελοι ἔρχονται πρὸς τὸν θεὸν προσκυνῆσαι αὐτῷ.
Several other passages of Apocalyptic writings bear on this topic. Compare, first, Apocalypse of Moses § 7, p. 4, ἤγγισεν δὲ ἡ ὥρα τῶν ἀγγέλων τῶν φυλασσόντων τὴν μητέρα ὑμῶν τοῦ ἀναβῆναι καὶ προσκυνῆσαι τὸν κύριον: and again p. 9, περὶ ὥραν (ἐνάτην), ὅταν ἀνῆλθον οἱ ἄγγελοι τοῦ θεοῦ τοῦ προσκυνῆσαι, and also the Protevangelium xiii. 1.

The principal source of our information on this point is the fragmentary Testament of Adam (ed. Renan, *Journ. Asiat.* 1853, 427—471) of which the most interesting relic is an account of the hours of the day and night in respect of the prayers offered at each hour by different orders of beings. Besides the Syriac and Arabic fragments published by M. Renan a certain amount of material in Greek is available, of which I will here give a brief account.

(*a*) A passage in Cedrenus (ed. Paris, p. 9) which contains a *résumé* of the hours of the day. This was known to M. Renan.

(*b*) A fuller *résumé* of the hours of both day and night, preserved under the name of 'Απολλώνιος μαθηματικὸς in Cod. Par. Gr. 2419, f. 247 *b*. Parts of this were quoted by Gibert Gaulmyn in his notes to Psellus *de daemonum operatione* (col. 846, 853 of Migne's Cedrenus, vol. II.). I copied the whole, save the corrupt Hebrew names[1], from the MS in 1890, and the document is plainly a Greek version of the νυχθήμερον of the Testament of Adam.

The Coptic Apostolic Constitutions (ed. Tattam p. 86) contain a little of such matter, in their directions to pray at midnight: but there seems to be nothing in the Greek.

None of these documents, however, agree exactly with the account in the Apocalypse of Paul. In the Adamic documents several hours are assigned to the adoration of God by Angels: at the 6th hour of the day Cedrenus gives ἀγγέλων παράστασις καὶ διάκρισις πάσης κτίσεως: in Apollonius we have ὥρα ἕκτη ἐν ᾗ δυσωποῦσιν τὰ χερουβὶμ τὸν θεὸν ὑπὲρ ἀνθρώπων. But there is no special adoration at sunset.

p. 109, l. 7. σὺ γὰρ—ἀνθρώπων. This clause points to the originality of the story of Abraham's interceding for sinners, which B later on mutilates.

B VI. p. 110, l. 9. The explanation of Michael to Sarah is unintelligible to me.

ibid., l. 13. ζευμάτων. Hesychius s.v. has ζεῦμα(ν) τὴν πηγὴν Φρύγες.

---
[1] Each hour has a Hebrew name in the MS, so ill written as to defy my best efforts at deciphering it.

This gives a satisfactory sense: the eyes might well be called 'fountains of light.' But how the word got into this text is a problem.

A VI. p. 83, l. 12. The resuscitation of the slaughtered calf bears some resemblance to the Mohammedan legend of the victims sacrificed by Abraham (Gen. xv.), viz. that they were all pounded up in a mortar by Abraham, and then revived by God in order to furnish Abraham with a proof of the resurrection (v. Sale's Koran, Sur. ii. note).

A VII. On the vision of Isaac it may be further noted that the double form in which Abraham appears,—the sun representing his soul and the rays his body,—may very well be a reminiscence of the twofold appearance of Moses in the Assumption of Moses, as described by Clem. Alex., Origen, and Evodius.

B VII. p. 111, l. 11. ὡς φῶς καλούμενον πατὴρ τοῦ φωτός (and Ar.). Cf. James i. 17. I cannot help thinking that this phrase is technically used to denote some atmospheric phenomenon such as the 'Aurora borealis': but up to the present moment I have not been successful in my search for an instance of it. It corresponds to the ὑπὲρ ἑπτὰ ἡλίους ἀστράπτοντα of A, and may be merely a periphrasis for the sun.

A VII. p. 85, ll. 4, 5, 11. ἀλλ' ὅπερ κελεύει ποίησον. I take this to be the true reading of a rather puzzling clause. It seems to be a defiance of Michael, 'Do what thou art commanded.'

A IX. p. 87, l. 3. ἔτι ἐν τούτῳ τῷ σώματι ὢν θέλω ἰδεῖν πᾶσαν τὴν οἰκουμένην καὶ τὰ ποιήματα πάντα.

It is important to notice the stress laid on the point that the visit is to be paid while Abraham is yet in the body. This recurs in l. 9, ἐν τῇ ζωῇ μου πρὸ τοῦ ἀποθανεῖν με. Abraham knows that in the ordinary course he would visit all the world after death: what he wishes is to be allowed to anticipate this by a short time. The belief that every soul made a kind of tour of the universe after death is found prominently in four documents which I have seen, namely, 4 Esdras, the Pistis Sophia, the Apocalypse of Zephaniah, and a spurious Homily of Macarius. Of these the last three are Egyptian in origin. The reference to the Pistis Sophia is the only one which need be given here. The other passages will be found on pp. 123, 127.

Pistis Sophia, Lat. Transl. p. 179, posthac ueniunt παραλήμπτορες ἐριναῖοι ut ducant ψυχὴν illam e σώματι et posthac παραλήμπτορες ἐριναῖοι tres dies circumeunt cum ψυχῇ illa in τόποις omnibus, monstrantes ei αἰῶνας omnes κόσμου. pp. 237, 240, 242, ducent eius ψυχὴν e σώματι ut tres dies festinent cum ea docentes eam creaturas κόσμου.

As to the visit being made in the body, the idea may be paralleled from the Book of Enoch: in that, all the visions of the first part of the book are seen by Enoch in the body. Later parallels are S. Paul's εἴτε ἐν σώματι, εἴτε χωρὶς τοῦ σώματος (2 Cor. xii. 3), possibly the Apocalypse of Zephaniah, certainly that of Paul, founded on the words just quoted, that of the Virgin, and the passage in the Syriac *Obsequies of the Virgin* where the apostles are taken on a cloud and conducted over heaven and hell.

ibid., ll. 12, 14. νεφέλη φωτός, ἅρμα χερουβικόν. The cloud of light is a common method of conveyance in the Apocryphal Acts of the Apostles, e.g. *Acta Andr. et Matth.* § 21, *Petr. et Andr.* (Tischdf. *Apoc. Apocr.* p. 162), *Martyrium Simonis Sahidicum* ed. Guidi[1], *Dormitio Mariae* p. 101.

The chariot of the Cherubim is of less frequent occurrence. It is usually as in the O. T. the chariot of God. The θρόνος χερουβίμ occurs in *Dorm. Mariae*, p. 107, and something similar in *Apoc. Mosis* pp. 18, 20, as well as in *Apoc. Mariae* (MS), where, as here, the Virgin is being conducted by Michael to heaven and hell.

A XI. p. 88, l. 29. *The Two ways and Two gates.* Attention should be called to the very confused image. It is not clear why a soul whose character was sufficiently decided to allow of its being brought in by one of the two gates should then have to undergo a judgment. Perhaps it is only meant that doubtful or wicked souls were judged.

p. 89, l. 3. *Adam at the gate.* The *Jalkut Chadasch*, quoted by Eisenmenger, *Entdecktes Judenthum* II. 320, says that Adam sits at the gate of Paradise, encompassed by many souls of the righteous who have eschewed the road of Hell and walked in the path of Paradise.

Christians uniformly believed Adam to be with the other patriarchs in Hades until our Lord's coming, and he is prominent in the *Descensus ad Inferos* (*Acta Pilati*, pt. II.). I have already given (p. 30) an extract from a mediaeval vision which I believe to be derived from our book.

A XII. p. 90, l. 14. ἐμοί...ἡμεῖς. The employment of the first person is almost continuous in the corresponding Ar. and quite absent in B. It is no doubt original. Similar interchange of person is found in *Apoc. Mosis* § 34, *Protev. Jac.* xix., *Acta Thomae* § 1, *Acta Matthaei* § 24, and *Enoch*.

ibid. ἄγγελοι ἀπότομοι. To collect all the instances of chastising angels which occur in Apocalyptic literature is clearly out of the question. It may be broadly said that the later the book the more we hear of them; for the later visions show more interest in descriptions of torment. A particularly close parallel to one passage is to be found in the Apocalypse of Zephaniah, Frag. *c*, tr. by Stern *Zeitschr. f. Ägypt. Sprache*, 1886, p. 120, '(I saw) a soul which 5000 angels were driving and guarding: they brought it to the East and thence to the West and smote it and gave it... blows of the scourge continually.' Again, frag. *a* speaks of angels 'in whose hands were fiery scourges.' These are they who take the souls of godless men from their bodies. 'Three days do they fly with them about the heaven before they take them and cast them into their eternal torments.' Compare again Hippolytus, περὶ τοῦ παντός, ed. Lagarde, p. 69, οἱ δὲ ἄδικοι εἰς ἀριστερὰ ἕλκονται ὑπὸ ἀγγέλων κολαστῶν οὐκέτι ἑκουσίως πορευόμενοι ἀλλὰ μετὰ βίας ὡς δέσμιοι ἑλκόμενοι. Instances may very easily be multiplied: they are particularly frequent in the Apocalypse of Paul.

In the New Testament the idea of destroying angels occasionally occurs.

---

[1] *Rendiconti della R. Accademia dei Lincei* 1887, Fasc. 4.

In Matt. xiii. 49 the angels cast sinners into the furnace of fire. In Rev. ix. we have the four angels bound in the river Euphrates, who are destroyers, but whether good or evil angels it is difficult to say. In Rev. xvi. angels are the direct means of inflicting plagues. The destroying angels of the O. T. correspond to this last class. Familiar instances of these are to be found in 2 Sam. xxiv. 16, 2 Kings xix. 35. A class of angels or spirits created specially for destruction is mentioned in Ecclus. xxxix. 28. In Hermas, Sim. vi. 3. 1, the angel of punishment is a 'just angel.' In the mediaeval visions proper the infliction of torment is the function of demons who are themselves tormented and find their only relief in torturing others. This conception meets us in Dante's *Inferno*.

A good account of the merciless angels of hell is that attributed to R. Jehoshua ben Levi, quoted from *Torath Adam* in Eisenmenger, II. 341.

l. 17. χαρζαναῖς, i.e. thongs or chains. One MS (B) gives ἀλξανες, which seems to be an attempt at χαρζ., and another (D) has θεάφη, which is a late word for brimstone.

A XII. p. 91, l. 1. βιβλίον. The Book or Books of Judgment occur as early as Dan. vii., Enoch xc., Rev. xx., 4 Esdras vi. 20. Two ideas seem to be present in these early books. The record contains either the names of those who are to be saved (Ex. xxxii. 32, Luke x. 20, Phil. iv. 3, Rev. xx. 15), or it contains the register of the works of men, as here (Rev. xx. 12). In the apocalypse of John we have both conceptions side by side.

In another group of books (Jubilees, Prayer of Joseph, Test. XII. Patr., Aseneth) we have a collateral idea. The records are usually called the πλάκες τοῦ οὐρανοῦ, and contain the destinies of our race. Origen explains that these records are the stars.

In our book we meet with two distinct conceptions. First there is the great book of judgment which contains the record of works. Secondly there are the two angels who stand by and record the sins and good deeds. The idea seems to be that these latter register what is happening on earth for future insertion in the book; it might be thought, but for evidence to be adduced later, that the passage represents a somewhat clumsy welding together of two ideas. In Recension B the confusion, if such it be, is absent. We have there two Cherubim who bear two books (for sins and good deeds), and Enoch as the recorder of both.

We must turn once more to the Apocalypse of Zephaniah for an instructive description of the recording angels. In Frag. *a* we have a vision of the Accuser. 'I beheld and saw him with a roll of writing in his hand. He began to unroll it: and when he had unrolled it I saw that it was written in the speech of mine own tongue. I found all my sins which I had committed recorded by him.... When I had not gone to visit a sick man or a widow, I found it written against me in the book as an omission etc.'

In Frag. *b* he saw on mount Seir three men, the wicked sons of the high priest Joatham. Two angels were rejoicing over them. Other two angels were weeping over them. I said, 'Who are these?' The angel said, 'These are the angels of the Lord Almighty, who record all the good deeds of the righteous in their roll, and sit at the gate of Heaven. And they allow me to take the record from them and bear it with me to the Lord Almighty that he may write the names in the book of the living. The angels also of the Accuser, who is upon earth, they also in like manner write all the sins of men in their roll, and sit likewise at the gate of Heaven and deliver the record to the Accuser to write it in his roll and to accuse men when they come hither out of the world.' This passage, I think, shows that Recension A of the Testament is not wrong in the picture it gives us, and that, as was suggested, the great book on the table contains a transcript of the sins and good deeds of men made from the record of the angels in front of the table. It will be remembered that the scene here, as in Zephaniah, is laid at the gate of Paradise.

ibid., l. 7. σάλπιγγα. The trumpet which contains fire is a feature which I do not meet with elsewhere. It is probably meant to convey the idea of a blow-pipe: the flame, celestial in its nature, becomes intensified and tests the souls (or their works) as silver is tried. The connexion of angels with trumpets is usually a different one.

A XIII. p. 92, l. 5. *Abel as Judge of souls.*

Here we have a conception which I do not find recurring in Jewish mythology. At least the storehouses of such matters to which I have had access give no hint of the belief. The root-idea seems to be that Abel, the first victim of human sin, and God's first martyr, is thereby entitled to act as judge of saints and sinners alike. Further, Abel figures as an accuser of sinners even in Biblical writings. 'The voice of thy brother's blood crieth unto me from the ground[1]' says God (Gen. iv. 10), and these words are the subject of an allusion in the Epistle to the Hebrews (xii. 24), καὶ αἵματι ῥαντισμοῦ κρείττονα λαλοῦντι παρὰ τὸν Ἄβελ. I cannot but think that the striking image of Genesis, interpreted after a too literal fashion, has influenced our author in his selection of Abel as judge.

Another explanation is possible. The belief may be due to a tendency resembling that which in early times made Adam, Seth, and Melchizedek the special objects of the devotion of obscure sects. We have seen that the 'Apocalypse of Abraham[2]' was, in the opinion of Epiphanius, a product

[1] It is interesting to notice the tendency to literal interpretation, which is the parent of so many legends, coming out in a mediaeval representation of this scene. In the reliefs of the Chapter-House at Salisbury Abel's blood is shown as a half-length figure emerging from the earth.

[2] That Abraham should be regarded by the later Jews as a recipient of important revelations is only natural. Two facts seem worth mentioning in this connexion. One is the attribution of the Cabalistic books *Sepher Jetzirah* and *Zohar* to Abraham; the other is the tradition reported by R. Manasseh b. Israel in *Nischmath Chajjim* (Eisenmenger, II. 25) that Abraham first learnt and revealed to men the doctrines of the immortality and of the transmigration of souls.

of the Sethians. Some confused belief in an identity of the soul of Abel with that of Seth (cf. Gen. iv. 25) may, as was suggested before, have led members of the Sethian sect to use and to respect a book which paid high honours to the name of Abel.

A xv. p. 95, l. 13. Sarah is here represented as alive. In B xii. she is dead of grief. (See p. 47.)

p. 96, l. 13. 'Ιώβ: he is looked upon in accordance with the traditional Jewish view as a contemporary of Abraham.

A xvi. p. 97, l. 10. ἀρχαγγέλου μορφὴν περικείμενος. Either to this legend or, more probably, to some account of the Fall resembling that in *Apoc. Mosis* 17 (τότε ὁ σατανᾶς ἐγένετο ἐν εἴδει ἀγγέλου) St Paul's words may be held to refer, 'Satan himself is transformed into an angel of light.'

ibid., l. 14. τὴν σιαγόνα αὐτοῦ τῇ χειρὶ κατέχων. The conventional attitude of dejection.

A xvii. p. 98, l. 13. ἠκολούθει δὲ κ. ὁ θάνατος ἕως ἐκεῖ etc.

    sed timor et minae
    scandunt eodem quo dominus, neque
    decedit aerata triremi et
    post equitem sedet atra cura.   Hor. *Od.* iii. 1. 37.

p. 99, l. 3. τοῖς δὲ ἁμαρτωλοῖς. Cf. the accounts of the deathbeds of the wicked in *Apoc. Pauli*, Greg. *Dial.* iv. 18 and 38.

l. 17. Seven heads of dragons: these as is subsequently explained correspond to the seven ages of the world (cf. the 7000 years in B vii.), p. 25, l. 21.

l. 18. Fourteen faces; 'seventeen' in R. The faces or aspects appear to be 1 fire, 2 darkness, 3 viper, 4 precipice, 5 asp, 6 lion, 7 cerastes, 8 basilisk, 9 sword of fire, 10 lightning and thunder, 11 sea, 12 river, 13 three-headed dragon, 14 poison-cup.

p. 100, l. 3. The number of servants who die seems to correspond with the number of death's aspects. In Ar. it is eighteen.

p. 101, l. 4. αὐστηρῷ τῷ προσώπῳ etc. This behaviour of Abraham closely corresponds to that of Moses in the *Phetirath Moshe* (see p. 66), who even goes further and smites Samael with his rod.

p. 102, l. 9. θυμοῦ. I am almost certain that θανάτου must be read here: I have further adopted Mr Robinson's excellent suggestion that the words δρακόντων—βασιλίσκων which in the MSS follow θυμοῦ should be read after ἰοβόλων (l. 17). The blank space of two lines in A shows an omission probably of these very words, which may have occurred twice in the archetype by mistake, and were omitted by the scribe on their repetition.

A xx. *ibid.*, l. 24. 72 deaths. The reason for the selection of this number is not quite obvious; probably it is meant to correspond to the number of nations on the earth as given in Genesis and traditional in all Jewish accounts.

p. 103, ll. 23—28. On the third day Abraham's soul is presented to God and adores him. This agrees strikingly with a spurious Homily or Apocalypse of S. Macarius (Galland, *Bibl. Patr.* III. 237) in which he is described as meeting two angels in the desert, who detail to him the various proceedings of a soul after death. τὰς γὰρ δύο ἡμέρας συγχωρεῖται τῇ ψυχῇ ἅμα τοῖς συνοῦσιν αὐτοῖς ἀγγέλοις πορεύεσθαι ἔνθα βούλεται ἐπὶ τῆς γῆς. This explains Abraham's desire to see the world ἔτι ἐν σώματι ὑπάρχων, see p. 122.

On the third day the angels and the soul go up to heaven. μετὰ οὖν τὸ προσκυνῆσαι τὸν θεὸν γίνεται κέλευσις παρ' αὐτοῦ to the effect that Paradise be shown to the soul. So here the voice of God bids that Abraham be taken to Paradise. καὶ ταῦτα πάντα (i.e. the joys of Paradise) καταμανθάνει ἡ ψυχὴ ἐν ἑξ ἡμέραις: whereat the soul, if it be wicked, laments.

Μετὰ δὲ τὸ θεωρῆσαι πᾶσαν τὴν χαρὰν τῶν δικαίων ἐν ταῖς ἑξ ἡμέραις, πάλιν ἀναφέρεται ὑπὸ τῶν ἀγγέλων εἰς προσκύνησιν τοῦ θεοῦ. It is then conducted over the infernal regions in 30 days. On the 40th it again adores God. Hence it is right to offer the Eucharist for the soul on the 3rd, 9th, and 40th days after death.

Of unbaptized souls it is said that ἀπεινῶς ἄγγελοι ἀπότομοι λαμβάνουσιν τὰς ἀφωτίστους ψυχὰς ἀπὸ τοῦ σώματος, τύπτοντες καὶ λέγοντες, Δεῦρο ἀσεβὴς ψυχή κ.τ.λ., and that they take them only to the first heaven, and show them the Majesty from a distance.

This presentation of the soul to God appears first, as far as I can tell, in 4 Esdras (the 'Missing Fragment' v. 78), 'recedente inspiratione de corpore ut dimittatur iterum ad eum qui dedit, adorat gloriam Altissimi primum.' Again in v. 101 a definite period for this is mentioned, 'septem diebus erit libertas eorum ut uideant qui praedicti sunt sermones.'

Possibly the words of the Psalm 'unto the God of gods appeareth everyone of them in Sion' may have had some influence on the belief.

In the Legend or Apocalypse of Zosimas (contained in Cod. Par. Gr. 1219 and partly also in Bodl. Canon. 19) we have a prolix account of the same matter. The passage in question is the concluding part of the statement drawn up by the 'Blessed ones' of their mode of life, which document they present to Zosimas. When one of them is about to die the angels come to him and say 'καλεῖ σε ὁ θεός.' After the summoned one has bidden farewell to his kindred, the soul departs out of the body, and the angels 'ἁπλώσαντες τὰς στολὰς αὐτῶν δέχονται αὐτήν[1].' Later on we read καὶ ὅτε ἀπέλθῃ εἰς τὸν τόπον ἐν ᾧ δεῖ προσκυνεῖν τὸν θεόν, αὐτὸς ὁ υἱὸς τοῦ θεοῦ μετὰ τῶν ἀγγέλων δέχεται τὴν ψυχὴν τοῦ μάκαρος καὶ προσφέρει πρὸς τὸν ἄχραντον πατέρα τῶν αἰώνων· καὶ πάλιν ὅταν ψάλλωσιν οἱ ἄγγελοι ἄνω, ἡμεῖς ὄντες κάτω ὑπακούομεν αὐτῶν, καὶ πάλιν ἡμεῖς ψάλλομεν, καὶ αὐτοὶ ὑπακούουσιν ἐν τῷ οὐρανῷ ἄνω, καὶ οὕτως ἀνάμεσον ἡμῶν καὶ τῶν ἀγγέλων ἀνέρχεται ἡ δοξολογία τῆς ὑμνολογίας· ὅτε δὲ ἡ ψυχὴ τοῦ μάκαρος πεσοῦσα ἐπὶ πρόσωπον προσκυνῇ τὸν κύριον, τότε καὶ ἡμεῖς πεσόντες προσκυνοῦμεν τῇ αὐτῇ ὥρᾳ τὸν κύριον· ὅτε δὲ ἀναστήσῃ αὐτὴν ὁ κύριος, τότε καὶ ἡμεῖς ἀνιστάμεθα·

---

[1] Compare with this the universal fashion in Christian Art by which angels are represented as carrying souls in a linen cloth.

καὶ ὅτε ἀπέρχηται εἰς τὸν ὡρισμένον τόπον, καὶ ἡμεῖς ἀπερχόμεθα ἐν τῇ ἐκκλησίᾳ, πληροῦντες τὴν εὐχαριστίαν τοῦ κυρίου.

Compare also *Apoc. Pauli* quoted above p. 74, 'adorant primum Dominum Deum,' and *Pass. S. Perpetuae* XI., 'Venite prius, introite, et salutate Dominum.' This last reference I owe to the Editor. In date it comes next to 4 Esdras.

Perhaps these instances will suffice to demonstrate the widely spread character of the belief that the soul was presented to God on its departure from the body.

p. 104, l. 1. ἔνθα εἰσὶν αἱ σκηναὶ κ.τ.λ. These words, as is often the case with the concluding phrases of ancient documents, have had a liturgical turn imparted to them: they closely resemble phrases in Collects of the Burial Services of both Eastern and Western Churches.

The oldest to be found among Western Offices are probably two in the Gelasian Sacramentary.

1. 'suscipi iubeas animam famuli tui *illius* per manus sanctorum angelorum deducendam in sinum amici tui Abrahae patriarchae.' xci.

2. 'collocare digneris in sinibus Abrahae, Isaac, et Iacob.' cv.

Compare, again, this from the Sarum Manual (Maskell, *Monumenta* I. 116), 'eiusque animam suscipi iubeas per manus sanctorum angelorum tuorum deducendam in sinum patriarcharum tuorum, Abrahae scilicet amici tui, et Isaac electi tui, atque Iacob dilecti tui, quo aufugit dolor et tristitia atque suspirium, fidelium quoque animae felici iocunditate laetantur.'

The references to the Three Patriarchs in early Burial Services are very frequent, and have sometimes suggested to me a suspicion that not impossibly the early popularity of the legends connected with the deaths of the Patriarchs might have influenced the composers of the prayers in some slight degree. That there is a connexion in some cases between the language of liturgies and obscure uncanonical works, may, I think, be shown by one instance. In most of the Western Marriage Services the following sentence occurs in one of the Blessings (e.g. Maskell, l. c. p. 58), 'Sit amabilis ut Rachel uiro: sapiens ut Rebecca: longaeua et fidelis ut Sara.' Compare with this the description of Aseneth in the Book of Aseneth (Batiffol, *Studia Patristica*, I. 40) 'μεγάλη οὖσα ὡς Σάρρα, καὶ ὡραία ὡς Ῥεβέκκα, καὶ καλὴ ὡς Ῥαχήλ.' In the Latin (p. 89) it runs: 'eratque magna ut Sarra, speciosa ut Rebecca, et formosa ut Rachel.' The resemblance here seems to me close: and when it is coupled with the frequent allusions made to Joseph and Aseneth in some of the Marriage Rites, it seems to be a possible explanation that the two lines of documents are here independent. 'Aseneth' is not an early book, though I should hesitate to place it as late as the fifth century, with M. Batiffol: it is not impossible, then, that the author of Aseneth was the borrower.

Returning to the Burial Services and the Patriarchal Legends, let us collect a few of the allusions to the Patriarchs. The order in the Sarum Manual yields the following:

NOTES ON THE TEXT. 129

Commendatio Animarum.
1. 'in sinum Abrahae angeli deducant te.'
2. 'adsit ei angelus testamenti tui Michael et per manus sanctorum angelorum tuorum in sinu Abrahae patriarchae tui collocare digneris.'
Cf. *Apoc. Pauli*, the Latin version (and Syriac): the Greek is here abridged. 'Tradatur ergo Michaelo angelo testamenti et perducat eam in paradiso exultacionis ut et ipsa fiat co(h)eres cum omnibus sanctis.'
3, 4, 5 are practically repetitions of 1.
Inhumatio Defuncti.
6. see above, p. 128.
7. 'maneatque in mansionibus sanctorum et in luce sancta quam olim Abrahae promisisti et semini eius.'
8 = 1.
9. 'Benedic Domine locum sepulchri huius sicut benedixisti sepulchra Abrahae, Isaac, et Iacob.'
10. 'qui sepultos Abraham, Isaac, et Iacob in spelunca duplici, in libro uitae ac totius gloriae principes annotasti benedicendos.'
11, 12, 13 = 1.

On 2 it may be noted that a form from a Fleury MS, given by Martene (*de antiq. Eccl. ritibus*, iii. 594) has 'in sinibus Abrahae Isaac et Iacob patriarcharum tuorum,' and similarly on p. 598 the three names occur where in the Sarum Manual the words of 1 only are used.

A Sarum order printed by Martene has 2 in this form (p. 616) 'Assit ei angelus Gabriel, ut per manus......sinibus Abr. Isaac et Iacob.'

It is not, I think, possible to lay very much stress on these allusions: the reasons for their occurrence may very easily be deduced from the Bible. The use made by our Lord of the popular image of 'Abraham's bosom' has inspired the greater part of the phrases here cited. The number of references in Genesis to the burials and burial-places of the Patriarchs has given rise to others (e.g. 9 and 10), and our Lord's mention of Abraham, Isaac and Jacob as still 'living unto God' may be responsible for the occurrence of the three names in some forms of 2 and in 6; the text Matt. viii. 17, is also responsible for something. Yet I have thought well to put the allusions together: for it is not at all impossible that the influence of the Testaments may be present, and, moreover, it is obvious that the Burial Services abound with ideas drawn either from popular belief or from non-biblical sources. The prayer for protection against the princes of darkness, the conception of the angelic escort warding off the evil powers on the passage from the 'land of Egypt' to the 'promised land and the City of Jerusalem': these and others remind the reader forcibly of the prayers in the Apocryphal Acts of the Apostles, e.g. that of John, (Zahn *Acta Joannis*, p. 249) of Thomas, (Bonnet, *Acta Thomae*, p. 91) of Philip, (Tisch. *Acta Apocrypha*, p. 93) of Joseph the Carpenter (*Evang. Apocr.*, p. 127) of the Virgin (Revillout, *Apocryphes Coptes du N.T.*, p. 99). And a further step towards the connexion of these Apocryphal prayers with actual liturgical forms is gained when we find two

J. 9

prayers of S. John in Latin in a book of private devotion (W. de Gray Birch, *An Ancient MS.*, pp. 90, 119). The prayers are taken from the tract of Pseudo-Mellitus (Fabric. *Cod. Apocr. N. T.* iii. 604.) The MSS. containing them are Harl. 2965 and 7653. The provenance of the prayers does not seem to be known to the editor.

The Eastern Offices are not so full of allusions to Abraham's bosom as the Western ones; but there is a near approach to the phrase in the Testament of Abraham of which this note treats. This is in *Const. Ap.*, viii. 41. εἰς κόλπον Ἀβρ. κ. Ἰσ. κ. Ἰακ......ἔνθα ἀπέδρα ὀδύνη, καὶ λύπη, καὶ στεναγμός. The offices in the *Euchologion* yield the phrase εἰς κόλπους Ἀβρ. ἀνάπαυσον.

Lastly, in this connexion, I would call attention to the Κανὼν εἰς ψυχορραγοῦντα in the *Euchologion*. This very striking poem although it makes no definite allusion to Abraham, contains several illustrations of topics treated in the Testament, e.g. the reluctance to die, the chastising angels, the weighing of sins and good deeds, and the fearful spiritual forms which are gathered about the dying man's bed.

M. R. J.

APPENDIX.

THE TESTAMENTS
OF
ABRAHAM, ISAAC AND JACOB.

EXTRACTS TRANSLATED BY

W. E. BARNES, B.D.,
FELLOW OF ST PETER'S COLLEGE, CAMBRIDGE.

PREFATORY NOTE.

THE following extracts are translated from a manuscript containing an Arabic version of the 'Testaments' of Abraham, Isaac and Jacob. An abstract only is given of the Testament of the last named, for it contains little of apocalyptic or ethical interest. In fact it follows the account found in Gen. XLVII—XLIX very closely, but without giving any interpretation of the difficult passages in Jacob's Blessing.

The translation has had the advantage of a revision at the hands of Professor W. Robertson Smith, who, although very unwell and in great pain at the time, went over my work and supplied me with notes and with several conjectural emendations of passages which baffled me. For the loan of the MS my thanks are due in the first place to the Director of the Bibliothèque Nationale, who courteously extended the time for which it was borrowed, and in the second to the Cambridge University Librarian, who made application for the loan and gave facilities for the use of the MS at the Library.

"The MS is 132 of the Catalogue of Arabic MSS of the Bibliothèque Nationale (De Slane, p. 28 seq.); and its contents leave no doubt that it is Egyptian. It was written A.D. 1629 (1345 of the Martyrs). The Arabic is very incorrect and uncultured." (W. R. S.)

The title of the Testaments in the Arabic runs as follows:—"A discourse pronounced by the religious father, our father Athanasius, patriarch of Alexandria, wherein he tells of the departure of the pious fathers, Abraham, Isaac and

Jacob, to their rest on the 28th day of the month Misrâ, from what is found in the Treasury of Sacred Knowledge," etc. The use of *Niyâha*, "departure to rest," in this sense is a Syriacism; cf. Wright Cat. Syr. MSS in B. M., vol. iii, p. 1153, where *tanayyaha*, conj. V, is similarly used in the sense of the Ethpael of the Syriac verb (W. R. S.). "The Treasury of Sacred Knowledge" is probably meant for the title of a book. Two extracts from the Testament of Abraham are here printed. The first is the 'Apocalyptic section' of the book, which is on the whole the most important part of it. The second is selected because it introduces matter not found in the Greek. A somewhat detailed analysis of the Arabic version of the Testament of Abraham, together with a statement of its relation to the Greek, will be found in the Introduction, p. 34 sqq.

W. E. B.

EXTRACTS FROM THE TESTAMENT OF ABRAHAM.

I.

And I say, even I Abraham, he shewed me that place, and in it there was a great door and a little door; and I saw a man clothed in white sitting between the two doors, at one time weeping and at another laughing, but his weeping was more than his laughing twelve times doubled.

Fo. vi. vo.
cf. A, § xi. p. 88—
§ xv. p. 95.
B, § viii. p. 112—§ xii. p. 116.

And I said to the angel Michael, What are these two doors? And the angel said to me, This little door is that which leads to the path of life, and this great door which thou seest to be wide is that which leads to death and destruction; and this man that sits between them is Adam, the first man; GOD hath left him here to watch all the souls that depart from their bodies, as they pass through them in his presence. ‖ Dost thou not see that his weeping is more than his laughing, because he seeth the souls which go forth from their bodies as they pass by him? and those which enter at the wide gate are more than those which enter at the strait gate into eternal life. And because of this his weeping exceeds his laughing.

Fo. vii.

And after this I looked upon many souls and myriads to which their angels refused entrance at the strait gate; and they entered the gate that leadeth to destruction. And the angel Michael said to me, Come that we may look upon these souls, perhaps thou wilt find one who is held worthy to enter into eternal joy.

And our Father Abraham and Michael took counsel between themselves concerning these souls; and they searched and they found between them only a single soul whose sins were counterbalanced by her good works. So they took her into eternal life; and as for the rest of the souls they made them enter into the gate of destruction.

And Michael said to me, Woe to these sinners who attain not to enter into life.

And I answered him, I Abraham, and said to him, And I also am a man who dwells in a material body, and I know not, whether they will let me enter by the strait gate without my suffering tortures for twelve years..........................

And Michael the chief of the angels said to me, Fear not, O Abraham, thou and the saints, (and they who follow thee and whosoever shall thus walk in thy works,) verily they shall enter ‖ into eternal Life. And the angel said to me further, Fear not, O Abraham, verily pleasure and peace and quietness shall be to the soul of him who is in the place in which thou art.

And I said to the angel Michael, These souls which go forth from their bodies, is it God who brings them forth or their angels?

And the angel Michael said to me, Death, which causeth them to depart from their bodies by the command of the Lord, is Michael the holy angel. And I said to him, How many souls go forth from their bodies every day in all the world? and how many souls are born every day? And the angel said, Consider O Abraham that I may instruct thee. And I said to him, Instruct me, O my Lord, for verily I know not. And he said, Hearken, that I may tell thee how many souls go forth from their bodies every day, nine and ninety thousand and nine hundred and nine and ninety.

And while the angel Michael was saying this to me, behold they came with a soul encircling it with opprobrium like a thief and the Judge said, Let us enter into reckoning with it on its works that are written down. So immediately there came forth a man from behind the curtain with a book in his hand, and began to declare the sins of that soul to the end of its actions; and great anguish laid hold of that soul before the righteous Judge, and it denied what was alleged, and said, Not a thing of all this is so, and I have not done it at all. And the unhappy soul thought that all it had done would not be remembered at all. || And GOD the righteous Fo. viii. Judge said, Can there be a lie in this place? Then that soul began saying, O Lord, not one thing of that I am said to have done was so at all. And the righteous Judge gave a glance with His eye and straightway witnesses confronted it. And the first said to it, Look at me, O soul! is it not thou that didst stand and address the spouse of thy daughter with the counsel of women (*or* the counsel of a drunkard), to be with her in place of thy husband, until thou didst kill thy daughter and take her husband from her?

And straightway when that soul heard that it wept and said, Woe is me twice over for my sins, whither shall I flee? I thought that no one knew what I did, and now my deeds put me to silence (*or* rebuke me).

Then a second witness stood up and put her to silence (*or* rebuked her), and said to her, Look, O unhappy soul; while the people of heaven and earth were uttering praises ......and thou didst not regard GOD or remember His name, but wast occupied in eating and drinking and in all the wicked lusts of thy heart.

And the third witness stood up and said to her, Look, O wretched soul, that thou mayest know me. I am he that presideth over thanksgiving, and the angels and the archangels and the cherubim and seraphim are my agents looking upon the race of the children of Adam; and thou in the night didst do works of deceit.

And when that soul heard this it wept saying, Let this be enough for me, O just Judge; not a word remains to me to speak. And she closed her mouth and was cast into || the Fo.viii.vo. lowest part of Gehinnom.

And I said, I Abraham, to the angel Michael, Who is this hoary venerable old man who brings forth to light the deeds of these souls?

And he said to me, Enoch the secret writer. When GOD

saw that he was a trustworthy man, he left him to write good deeds and evil, as often as man doeth them.

II.

Fo. x.
cf. A,
§ xvii. p. 99
—§xx.end,
p. 104.
B, § xiii.
p. 118—
§ xiv. end,
p. 119.

And our Father Abraham said to him, Then present to me thy fearful form and shape that I may behold thee. And Death said to our Father Abraham, Let thy servants go forth from this dwelling, lest they see me and die all of them, verily none seeth my form of fear and liveth.

And our Father Abraham said, Can any die before the completion of his life and the arrival of his time? And Death said to him, Yes, verily, in times of plague and dearth which GOD appointeth and bringeth upon cities and countries because of their sins, while He maketh His anger to dwell upon them and sendeth to bring forth their souls as the Lord pleaseth. Then I go forth, I Death, and my son, whom I have gotten from the treasury of dread and utter fear and name and call Atarlimos. [Verily he is of all the treasuries of fear and dread.] And we go forth together, executing exemplary judgment in wrath, and we destroy from one end of the world to the other. And of those whom we meet in all places we spare neither young nor old, and we respect not the hoary head of an old man and spare not the young man and have no regard for the young one that sucks the milk of his mother, and we leave neither bride nor bridegroom, but bring them forth even from their marriage feast. And my son Atarlimos smites with blains and terror and fear, and I bring forth their souls from their bodies.

And when he said this he began to show his likeness and the foulness of his aspect and the semblance of his form.

Fo. x. vo. ‖ And behold many heads, some of them with the face of serpents, and some of them breathing flames of fire, until through fear of him eighteen of the servants of Abraham our Father died, and those who were present with his servants fell on their faces, and the shadow of death overshadowed them, until the angel Michael raised them up (I mean the servants of our Father Abraham), and set them on their feet; and Death and his companion departed to their places. Then Michael, chief of the angels, took the soul of our Father Abraham, and received it in garments like white snow, and bore it away on his fiery chariot, after the hosts of the angels had met it with praises and thanksgivings, until they laid it up in the regions of refreshing and rest and eternal delights for ever.

EXTRACTS FROM THE TESTAMENT OF ISAAC.

[AFTER a homiletic preface of the usual kind the story begins as follows.]

It came to pass when the days of our Father Isaac the Father of the Fathers drew nigh that he should depart from this world and go forth from this body, the Compassionate, the Merciful sent to him the chief of the angels, Michael, whom He had sent to his Father Abraham, on the morning of the eight and twentieth day of the month Misri.

He said to him "Peace be unto thee, O Elect Son!" Then he came to the faithful old man our Father Isaac, (for the Holy Angels used to converse with him every day.) And he fell on his face and saw that he was like his Father Abraham, and he opened his mouth and cried with a loud voice and said with exultation and praise, Verily I see thy face as if I saw the face of the Creator the Merciful.

Then said the Angel to him, O my friend Isaac, I have been sent to thee from the presence of God the Living One, that I may take thee up to heaven to be with thy Father Abraham and all the saints, because thy Father Abraham expecteth thee, and he hath come to thee, and he hath prepared for thee the throne ‖ with thy Father Abraham, even for thee and thy beloved son Jacob, and ye shall be above every one in the Kingdom of the heavens in the glory of the Father and of the Son and of the Holy Ghost, and ye shall be called by this name to all future generations, "The Fathers;" and ye shall be Fathers to all the world, O faithful old man our Father Isaac.

He answered saying to the Angel, Verily I marvel because of thee; art thou not my Father Abraham? And the Angel said to him, I am not thy Father Abraham, but it is I who minister to thy Father Abraham. And now rejoice and let thy face shine and be not dismayed, for thou shalt not be taken with pain, but with gladness, and thou shalt attain to delight and rest for ever, and thou shalt go forth from straitness into enlargement, and thou shalt depart to the joy that has no ending, and to the light and the joy without bound, and to the praise and exultation that cease not.

And now make thy testament and set in order thy house, for thou goest to rest; and withal blessed be thy father who begat thee, and blessed thy seed which cometh after thee.

And when our Father Jacob heard them conversing in this colloquy one with another, he began to conceal himself from them without speaking. And our Father Isaac said to the Angel with patience and submission, What shall I do this day with the light of my eye, Jacob my beloved? I fear for him because of Esau, and thou knowest all.

And the Angel said unto him, O my beloved Isaac, all the peoples which are in the world, if they were gathered together to one place, would not be able ‖ to cancel (lit. untie) (Fo.12.vo.) thy blessing upon Jacob, because at the time when thou didst bless him, He Who holds all and the Son and the Holy Spirit and thy Father Abraham all answered saying, Amen. His neighbour shall not prevail against him, but he shall be exceeding strong and shall exercise lordship. And he shall be father of many peoples, and twelve tribes shall proceed from him.

And Isaac said to the Angel, Verily thou hast taught me and given me knowledge of good tidings; nevertheless let not Jacob hear, for he will be grieved and dismayed, and I verily have never once grieved his heart.

And the Angel of the Lord said, O my friend Isaac, blessed are all the righteous who depart from their bodies, blessed are they when they see God the Compassionate, the Merciful. Woe, woe, three times to the sinner when he begetteth children upon the earth, for verily for him are many sorrows. Thou shalt teach thy sons thy ways and all the precepts of thy father which he commanded thee (and fear not at all for Jacob) that they may be a memorial for future generations afterwards, that the faithful may do them and attain by them to the life that endureth, that is eternal. Nevertheless I will observe thy injunction. And verily I come to thee with joy, speedily. The peace which the Lord hath given me I give to thee and go quickly to Him that sent me.

And when the Angel said this he arose from the bed of our Father Isaac and departed from him; and he looked upon him and was filled with wonder at what he had heard and seen and began to say, I shall not see the light until they ask for me.

Fo. 13. And while he was thinking, ‖ Jacob had come to the door of the sleeping-place of his father: and the angel had cast slumber upon him that he should not hear them. And when he entered the sleeping-place of his father he said, Father, with whom wast thou talking? And his father Isaac said to him, You seem to hear me, O my son; they have sent to thy aged father to take him from thee, O my son Jacob. Then he fell on his father's neck and wept and said to him, My strength is departed from me, wilt thou make me an orphan, O father, and today I shall be of no account? And he fell on the neck of our Father Isaac and kissed him and they both wept until they were outworn and weary, while Jacob said, Father, I will go with thee and I will not part from thee. And he said to him, O my son, this is not in my power, O my son and my beloved Jacob. Nevertheless I thank God that thou also art become a father, and thou shalt remain until they ask for (? $ἀπαιτοῦσι$) thee, because I know the day on which they came forth into the world that vanisheth. [*Here occur some corrupt words which defy translation.*] As my father Abraham told me, I cannot turn aside anything of the decree which is determined for every man, and so it shall be, because that which is written shall not be shaken.

EXTRACTS FROM THE TESTAMENT OF ISAAC. 143

Howbeit God knoweth, O my son, that my heart is grieved for thy sake, though I myself am glad because I go to the Lord. And now thou shalt be established in the Spirit; and put from thee this weeping and lamenting. Hearken, O my son, that I may tell thee and give thee understanding concerning the first man, I mean our Father Adam, who was created, whom God created with His hand, and our mother Eve. Verily Abel and Seth and our Father Enoch, and Mahalaleel the father of Methuselah, and Lamech the father of Jared, and Enosh the father of our father Noah, and his sons || Shem and Ham and Japheth, and after them Phinehas and Cainan and Noah and Eber and Reu and Terah and Nahor and my Father Abraham and Lot[1], these all death took away except our Father Enoch the only perfect one, who ascended to heaven.

And hereafter twelve mighty ones shall come forth, and Jesus the Messiah shall come of thy seed of a virgin whose name is Miriam, and God shall abide upon him till a hundred years be fulfilled.

And Isaac used to fast all the day, not breaking his fast until the evening. And he used to offer sacrifices for himself and for all the people of his household, for the salvation of their souls, and they used to rise up for prayer in the middle of the night, and in the day time he would pray to God. And he did this for many years, and he fasted for three periods of forty days, every time the forty days' fast came round, and he ate no flesh and drank no wine for the length of the days of his life, and he never touched fruit nor slept upon a couch, because he was occupied with prayer every day and with supplication before GOD for the length of his life.

And when the multitudes heard that a man of God had appeared, they were gathered together to him from every country and from every place that they might hear his instructions and his life-giving precepts, that he might teach them, because it was the Spirit of God which spake in him. Then the great men who were gathered together

---
[1] These names are restored from the E.V.

to him said to him, What is this wisdom which has rested upon thee since the time that the light of thine eyes departed from thee, and how is it that thou seest now?

And as for the faithful old man, he smiled and said to them, Verily them ‖ who are present I will tell: God healed me when He saw that I had drawn near to the gate of death: he hath appointed for me this consolation in my old age that I should be a priest of the Lord. Then one said to him, Begin me a discourse that I may receive consolation and keep it in mind.

And our Father Isaac said to him, When thou speakest in anger keep thyself from defaming, and beware of vainglory. See that thou speak not of thyself alone[1]; take care that there proceed no corrupt word out of thy mouth. Keep thy body that it may be pure, for it is the temple of the Spirit of Holiness that dwelleth in it. Take heed to thy "vile" body that it may be pure and sanctified. Beware that thou sport not with thy tongue lest a corrupt word proceed from thy mouth. Beware of stretching out thine hand to that which thou dost not own. Do not present thine offering when thou art not clean. Bathe in water when thou wouldest draw near to the altar. Do not mingle thy thoughts with the thoughts of the world. What time thou standest before Him, thy most meritorious offering is to make peace between men. When thou desirest to bring thy offerings to God, when thou drawest near to come before the altar, thou shalt pray to God a hundred times without remission.

At the beginning thou shalt say this thanksgiving, even this, to God Who is not comprehended, Who cannot be searched out, the Lord of Might, the Treasury of Purity. Cleanse me by Thy mercy, of thy free bounty upon me, for I am a thing of flesh and blood fleeing to Thee. And I

---

[1] Probably a deep-seated corruption. Transpose the words "When thou speakest in anger" to a position behind "See that thou speak not" at the same time striking out "Of thyself alone" as a corrupt doublette. The opening words of the discourse will then run as follows:—"Keep thyself from defaming and beware of vainglory and see that thou speak no word in anger." (From W. R. S.)

know my filthiness and do Thou cleanse me, O Lord! || For Fo. 14. vo.
lo! my cause is committed unto Thee, and to Thee I flee for
refuge. I know my sins, so cleanse me, O Lord, that I may
enter into Thy presence with modesty. Now are my sins
heavy. I am near to the fire that burneth. Thy mercy is
upon all things; take away all my trespasses! forgive me,
even me the sinner! And forgive all Thy creatures whom
Thou hast created who obey not and have not the faith;
and as for me, I am grieved for everyone bearing Thine
image who meets me[1], and towards him are my eyes. I have
come to Thee, and I am Thy servant, and I am the son of
Thy handmaid, the sinner; And Thou art the forgiving One,
forgive me of Thy free bounty, and hear my request that I
may be deemed worthy to worship at Thy holy altar. Let
this burnt offering be acceptable with Thee. Give me not
over to mine ignorance because of my sins; receive me like
a lost sheep. The God Who led our father Adam and Abel
and Noah and our Father Abraham shall be with thee, O
Jacob, and shall be with me again; receiving (?) my
offering from me.

And when thou hast drawn near and hast done this
before ascending the altar, then offer thy offerings. And
beware and take heed that thou grieve not the Spirit of the
Lord, for the priest's office is not easy and it is required of
all priests from this day till the last of the generations is
finished and the world comes to an end, that they be not
filled with drinking wine, and be not satisfied with eating
bread, and speak not of matters of the world, and listen not
to him who speaks of them, but spend all their activities and
their life in prayer || and watching and perseverance in the Fo. 15.
religious life, that he may make request to the Lord in peace.
And it is required of every man upon the earth, be he
miserable or be he fortunate, that he keep the testimonies
that are appointed. Because after a little time they shall
be removed from this world and from its grievous anxieties,
and shall be engaged in holy angelic service, because of their
purity, and stand in the presence of the Lord and His angels

[1] The text of the preceding three lines is doubtful.

because of their pure offerings and angelic service, because their earthly service resembles their occupation in the heavens, and the angels shall be their companions because of their perfect faith and purity. And great is their honour in the presence of the Lord, and there is neither small nor great to whom the Lord will not give increase, desiring that he be without fault and without sin.

And now be humbling yourselves to God with repentance for your sins; and sin no more. Thus, thou shalt not kill with the sword, thou shalt not kill with the tongue, thou shalt not commit adultery with thy body, thou shalt not keep anger until the setting of the sun, and thou shalt not take to thyself vain praise. Thou shalt not rejoice at the fall of thine enemies nor of thy brethren; thou shalt not revile; beware of slander. Look not upon a woman with thine eye with lust; beware of these sins and what resembles them; take ye heed that ye may be delivered every one of you from the wrath which shall be revealed from heaven.

And as for the multitudes that surrounded them, when they heard this they cried out all together, saying, Verily right and true is all which this righteous old man hath spoken.

He was silent, and the cloak was returned to him, and they covered his face. And as for the assembly and the priest who was present, they were silent and said, || Let him rest for a little.

Then came to him the Angel of God, and took him to the heavens and shewed him things in fear, and many wild beasts having left sides, and all their sides were joined (as brethren) so that they could not look one upon another,[1] and their faces were as the faces of camels; others had as it were the faces of dogs, and others as it were the faces of lions and hyænas and leopards, and others had only one eye.

[1] "I saw terrible things and many kinds [*Here some words must have dropped out*] making signs to one another on every side like brethren, (but) unable to wait for one another" (ex emend. w. r. s.)

He said, I saw and behold they brought in a man hurrying him along. And when they came to the lions, those who were conducting him departed from him. Then the lions turned upon him and rent him in the midst and divided him limb by limb and gnawed him and swallowed him. And after this they cast him forth from their mouths and he returned to his former state. And after the lions the other beasts came and they did the same to him. They took him one after the other, and everyone of them gnawed him, swallowing him and casting him forth and he returned each time to his former condition.

Then I said to the Angel, What is the sin, O my Lord, which this man hath sinned that they have done thus unto him? The Angel said to me, This man whom thou seest offended his neighbour five hours ago and he died without being reconciled to him. So he is delivered to five of the tormentors that they may torment him a whole year for each hour of the five during which he remained in enmity with his fellow.

Then the Angel said to me, O my beloved Isaac, look Fo. 16. upon these 60 demons (DEWA) who torment for every hour that a man remains at enmity with his neighbour. And he is brought hither to these who torment him each one for an hour until a whole year is fulfilled, any man who has not made peace and repented of his sin before his departure and separation from his body.

And he brought me to a river of fire, and I saw its waves beating and rising higher than 30 cubits, and the voice thereof was like rushing thunder. And I looked upon many souls sinking in it to a depth of more than nine cubits, and they who were in that river were weeping and crying out with a loud voice and deep groaning. And the river had intelligence in the fire thereof that it should not hurt the righteous but the sinners only, burning them. And it burnt everyone of them because of the stinking and loathsome odour which enwrapt the sinners.

And I considered the deep river whose smoke ascended up before me, and I saw a number of men in the bottom thereof, crying out, weeping every one of them and groaning. And the Angel said to me, Look into the lowest part that thou mayest see those whom thou wilt see in the lowest depth; these are they that have committed the trespass of Sodom; verily they endure a grievous punishment.

And I looked upon him who was set over the torment, and he was of fire all of him, and he was smiting the satellites of the Infernal Fire and saying to them, Kill them outright and they shall know that God is for everlasting.

Fo. 16. vo. And the Angel said to me, Lift up thine eyes and look ‖ upon all the punishments. Then I said to the Angel, My sight cannot contain them because they are so many, but I desire to know how long these are to continue in this punishment. And he said to me, Until the God of mercy be merciful and have mercy on them.

And after this then the Angel took me to Heaven, and I saw Abraham and worshipped him and he kissed me, he and all the pious ones. And they were all gathered together and did me honour for my Father's sake, and they gave me the hand and brought me to the pulpit of the curtain of the Father. And I prostrated myself to Him and worshipped with my father and all the saints, and we praised and cried aloud saying: Holy, Holy, Holy is the Lord the Sabaoth, the Heaven and the Earth are filled with Thy hallowed Glory.

And the Lord said to me from the top of the sanctuary, Every one who names his son after Isaac my beloved, my blessing shall rest upon him and upon his house for ever. Good is thy coming, O Abraham, and good is thy stock and the presence of the blessed stock. And now whatsoever thou shalt ask in the name of thy beloved son Isaac shall be to thee this day as a covenant for ever. Then answered my Father Abraham and said, Thine is the sovereignty, O Lord, Ruler of the Universe. And the Lord said from the top of the sanctuary to my Father Abraham, Every man who shall name his son by the name of Isaac my beloved, or shall write his testament, shall have a blessing which shall not come to an end, and my blessing in his house shall not cease;

or if he shall give a poor man to eat on the day of the feast of my beloved Isaac, verily I will give him to you in my Kingdom. Then said my Father Abraham, Oh divine Father, Ruler of the Universe, even if he cannot write his testament or his will, let thy blessing and mercy enfold him, for thou art the Merciful. And the Lord said to Abraham, Let him give the hungry bread to eat, and I will give him a place in my Kingdom and he shall be present with you at the first hour of the banquet of the thousand years.

Fo. 17.

And the Saviour said to our Father Abraham, And if he is poor and cannot find bread in his house, then let him keep vigil for a whole night in memory of my beloved Isaac without slumbering, and I will give him inheritance in my kingdom. My Father Abraham said, And if he is weak and cannot keep vigil, let thy mercy and compassion enfold him still. And the Lord said to him, Then let him bring a little incense in my name on the memorial day of my beloved Isaac thy son. And if so be that he cannot read, then let him go that he may hear the reading from one who can read it. And if he do not any one of these things, then let him enter his house and shut the door upon him and pray with a hundred prostrations, I repent; then I will give him to you as a son in my Kingdom; but better than all this let him bring an offering on the memorial day of my beloved Isaac. And all who shall do all that I have said, even they shall obtain the inheritance, the Kingdom in my Heavens. And of all who shall take pains and transcribe his will and his testament and his story, and shew mercy even by giving a cup of cold water, and believe from all their heart, my strength and the spirit of my holiness shall be with them for their prosperity in this world, and there shall be no wavering in their religion, and I will give you them in my Kingdom, and they shall be present the first hour at the banquet of the thousand years. Peace be upon you, O my beloved, the saints.

And when He had finished this discourse the Heavenly Ones began to cry out, saying, Holy, Holy, Holy is the Lord Sabaoth, the Heaven and the Earth are full of thy hallowed

Glory. The Father who holdeth all answered from His hallowed place and said, O Michael my faithful servant, call together all the Angels and all the Saints. And ride upon the chariot of the Seraphim, and command the cherubim to go before. And when He had said this, Jacob was carried beyond himself, and he clung to his father and kissed him weeping. Then our Father Isaac made him stand upright and made signs to him, glancing with his eyes, Be silent, O my son.

Then said Abraham to the Lord, O Lord, likewise remember my son Jacob. And the Lord said to him, My strength shall be with him and he shall glorify my name, and he shall be lord of the land of promise, and the enemy shall not have dominion over him. And our Father Isaac said to Jacob, O my son, keep my dying charge, that I make known to thee this day for the safe keeping of my body. Thou shalt not injure the image of GOD in that which thou doest, for the image of man was made in the image of GOD; and thus will GOD do to thee at the time when thou meetest Him and beholdest Him. And this is the beginning and the end as our Father hath said. And when he had said this the Lord took his soul from his body white as snow, and He received it and carried it with Him upon His sacred chariot and went up with it || to the heavens, while the Cherubim sang praises before it and His holy Angels, and He gave to him the Kingdom of heaven and all those graces that give satisfaction which our Father desired. GOD gave him them, and the fulfilment of His covenant is for ever.

Such was the decease of our Father Abraham and our Father Isaac son of Abraham on the 28th day of the month Misri, on this selfsame day; and him we regard as holy and as a prophet. And on the day on which our Father Abraham brought the offering to GOD on the eight and twentieth day of the month Amshir, the Heaven and the Earth were filled with the sweet savour of his walk before the Lord.

And our Father Isaac was as silver that is burned, that is melted, that is purified from dross, made pure by fire; and in like manner, whosoever shall display the bounty of our Father Isaac (i.e. give alms in his honour) Father of the Fathers, on the day on which Abraham the Father of the Fathers brought him as an offering to GOD, the sweet savour of his offering shall ascend toward the inner curtain of Him Who holds all. Happy are all who shall shew mercy on the day of the memorial of the Father of the Fathers Abraham and of our Father Isaac, for they shall have a dwelling in the Kingdom of the Heavens, because our Lord hath brought them into His sure covenant for ever. And He will keep it for them and for those who shall come after them, saying to them, All who do mercy in the name of my beloved Isaac, verily I will give them to you in the Kingdom of the Heavens.

And He shall be present with them at the first hour of the feast of the thousand years, that they may keep festival in everlasting light in the Kingdom of our Lord and our GOD and our King and our Saviour Jesus the Christ. This is He to Whom is due glory and majesty and strength and dominion and reverence and honour and praise and worship, with the Merciful Father and the Spirit of Holiness, now and for all times to the ages of the ages and to everlasting of everlasting. Amen.

The story of the decease of our Father Isaac is finished; and the thanks and the praise be to GOD for ever and aye!

TESTAMENT OF JACOB.

(ABSTRACT.)

After the ascription of praise, and a short preamble, the story begins.

When the time of Jacob's death drew near, Michael was sent to him, and bade him write his 'dogmatic and didactic testament.' Jacob, whose custom it was every day to converse with angels, agreed, saying, 'Let the will of the Lord be done.'

A short recapitulation of God's dealings with Jacob follows. After this it is said that Jacob was very old, and the angel of the Lord came to him, seemingly, in the semblance of Isaac (just as in the Testament of Isaac, the angel appears in the likeness of Abraham). Jacob was afraid, but the angel reassured him, reminded him of God's goodness to him in the past, and promised blessings to those who should observe the day of his feast, or give alms in his name; finally bidding him make ready for death, and bid farewell to his household. Jacob's household were accordingly assembled, and wept over him, while he comforted them.

Here follows an extract from Genesis, narrating shortly the last interview of Jacob with Joseph, the blessing of Ephraim and Manasseh, and the assembling of Jacob's sons (Gen. xlvii. 29—xlix. 1). The Blessings in Gen. xlix. are not given.

Immediately after this we have what seems to be a short abstract of a vision seen by Jacob, corresponding to those in the two preceding Testaments, in this form:

'And after this one caused him to pass through the heavens, that he might see the places of rest. And, behold, he came to those who were punishing many who were perverted to idolatry, and they were accustomed to punish sinners, namely, adulterers and adulteresses (various forms of impurity are enumerated), astrologers, oppressors, idolaters, tale-bearers, double-tongued. And as for all these sinners, their punishment was fire unquenchable, where shall be weeping and gnashing of teeth.'

A short account of Jacob's burial follows, taken from Gen. l. 4 sqq. It is then said that the narrative is taken from the 'spiritual books of God,' and the 'holy Treasury of knowledge belonging to our fathers the holy and pure Apostles.'

After a further homiletic passage, we find a quotation from Genesis (xlviii. 3, 4).

Then: 'This have we heard, O my beloved brethren, from our ancestors the patriarchs.... These are they whose names are the Holy Fathers. And Jacob instructed his sons concerning the punishment and called them (*sic*) the Sword of the Lord, which is the river of fire, which punished (?) in order that it might separate the transgressors and the polluted.' (Comp. Test. of Isaac, p. 147.)

An ethical exhortation of some length follows, of which the main heads are these:

Pay attention to prayer and fasting...and ye are they who shall drive out the Satans. Shun the wickedness of this world, a sharp tongue and adultery and all evil works, because the unjust shall not inherit the kingdom of God (the text of part of 1 Cor. vi. 9, 10 follows). Praise the saints, for they are they who shall intercede for you. Practise hospitality and ye will be recompensed as were Abraham and Isaac. Give bread to the poor and God will give you to eat of the tree of life. Clothe the naked, and God will clothe you with the garment of praise, and ye shall rest with Abraham, Isaac, and Jacob. Read the word of God, and remember those who write holy books, and ye shall be written in the book of life.'

This is said to be taken from the 'ancient book concerning

APPENDIX.

our holy Fathers.' After a further exhortation, the Testament finally concludes. It has plainly been much worse treated than even the Testament of Isaac; but enough remains to show that it is a companion document constructed on the same principles as the other two Testaments. We have, first, the appearance of Michael to Jacob; next, the summoning of the household, then the scanty remains of a vision of Paradise and Hell; and lastly, displaced, as I take it, the ethical discourse, or Testament proper, which, wholly wanting in the story of Abraham, is so prominent in the Testament of Isaac, and in those of the Twelve Patriarchs. It is prefaced, in the document before us, by a slight reference to the vision of torment.

ON THE TESTAMENTS OF ISAAC AND JACOB.

The following short essay is intended to do duty alike as Introduction and Notes to the two documents whose names stand at its head. The resources at my command do not allow me to hope that I can throw much light on them; and in particular, the ethical element is one which I am forced to leave almost entirely untouched. However, the few facts which I have been able to collect may as well be set down at once.

The existence of books under the names of Isaac and Jacob is hardly noticed by any ancient writer. On p. 11 of this volume will be found a passage from the Apostolic Constitution which speaks of books attributed to the 'Three Patriarchs,' and on p. 12 is a passage from Priscillian's writings which might imply that he knew books under the names of Isaac and Jacob, but which more probably does not imply such knowledge.

Besides this, there is an item in the so-called Gelasian lists of Apocryphal books, which has been cited, though erroneously, in this connexion. It intervenes between the 'Liber Ogiae' (probably identical with a book used by the Manichaeans under the name of ἡ τῶν γιγάντων πραγματεία), and the 'Poenitentia Origenis.' As it stands in our present texts, the entry in question reads thus:

"Liber qui appellatur Testamentum Iob; apocryphus." But Fabricius (*Cod. Pseud. V. T.* I. 438) read 'Iacob' for 'Iob.' As there is an extant Testament of Job (printed by Mai, *Scriptt. Vett. Nova Collectio*, VII. 180) it seems unnecessary to adopt the reading of Fabricius.

The same writer (l. c. p. 437) conjectured that the 'Ἀναβαθμοὶ 'Ιακώβου described by Epiphanius (*Haer.* xxx. 16) had reference to the vision of Jacob in Gen. xxviii., and accordingly renders the title as *Scala Iacobi*. The blunder is a strangely gross one for Fabricius; for the book is an Ebionite production referring to James the brother of the Lord, as Epiphanius plainly tells us[1].

A third conjecture must be mentioned, that of Cotelier on *Const. Apost.* vi. 16, that the entry Πατριάρχαι in the synopsis of Pseudo-Athanasius refers to the Testaments of the Three Patriarchs. But in all probability the Testaments of the Twelve Patriarchs are meant.

Again, a phrase in the Testament of the Twelve Patriarchs has been thought to imply the existence of Testaments of the Three Patriarchs. The passage is *Zabulon* ix., ἔγνων ἐν γραφῇ πατέρων μου ὅτι ἐν ἐσχάταις ἡμέραις ἀποστήσεσθε ἀπὸ κυρίου, κ.τ.λ.; and a similar reference has been suspected in *Benjamin* x. Both are unreliable. It is well known that the numerous references to writings of Enoch in the Testaments of the Twelve Patriarchs find no support from our extant Book of Enoch. And just in the same way the vague references to writings of Abraham, Isaac, Jacob are most likely meant only to add local colour and a certain verisimilitude to the prediction of their descendants.

Two entries in Catalogues of MSS have seemed likely to throw further light on our subject. The first was of a Carshunic History of Isaac the Patriarch, in the Bodleian Catalogue of Syriac MSS (Cod. 140 ff. 341—6). This, through the kindness of the Bodleian authorities, I was able to have photographed, and Professor W. Robertson Smith was so good as to read it for me. But it was a disappointment to find that the tract was merely an exaggerated paraphrase of the story of the sacrifice of Isaac: some apocryphal details were added, and in particular the colours of the ram, which was the substitute for Isaac, were dwelt upon. But the document is hardly an Apocryphon in the

---

[1] See Lightfoot, *Galatians*, p. 330, etc.

accepted sense, and certainly has nothing to do with the Testament of Isaac.

The second of the entries referred to was of a Διαθήκη 'Ιακώβ in a Paris MS (Coislin 296. of cent. XII. f. 5). This on examination proved to be merely a transcript of Gen. xlix. But it is interesting to find any document under this title, and the existence of such a thing goes a little way towards confirming the idea that a Testament of Jacob did at one time exist in Greek.

The Testaments here translated exist in other copies and in at least one other language, viz. Ethiopic (see p. 6), while other MSS of the Arabic are in the Vatican library (Mai, *Scriptt. Vett. Nov. Coll.* iv. cod. 171. Assem. *Bibl. or.* i. 986, ii. 285).

The few illustrations of the text which I have been able to collect had better be subjoined here in their order.

Michael is sent to Isaac as he had been sent to Abraham, and comes in the form of Abraham, p. 140. This feature implies that the writer, whether identical or not with the author of the Testament of Abraham, was acquainted with that book; and indeed the general plan of the second Testament inevitably leads us to that conclusion.

'*From straitness into enlargement,*' p. 141. *Test. Abr.* B § vii. p. 111. This probably indicates that the phrase quoted is one belonging to the original form of the Testament of Abraham.

'*Till a hundred years be fulfilled,*' p. 143. It is not clear what the meaning of the number a hundred can be in this connexion. Most probably the number is corrupt, and the prophesied interval was in its true form meant to extend to the time of the end of the world. The Christian prophecy of which this forms part may be easily paralleled from the Ascension of Isaiah (xi.) and the Testament of Adam.

Isaac offered sacrifices for his household. Cf. Job i., and Abraham's sacrifice in Jubilees xvi.

Isaac fasted for three periods of 40 *days in the year, and abstained from flesh, wine, and fruit, and from sleeping on a couch,* p. 143. It is tempting to see in the latter part of this

158   APPENDIX.

description a trace of Essene influence. The three periods of forty days are possibly the three '$\tau\epsilon\sigma\sigma a\rho a\kappa o\sigma\tau a\iota$'[1] of the Greek Church, those of Lent, of the Nativity, and of the Virgin; or something corresponding to the 'three Lents' of the Montanists, in which they practised a $\xi\eta\rho o\phi a\gamma\iota a$, very like that ascribed to Isaac.

When the multitudes heard that a man of God had appeared, p. 143. The meaning seems to be that the rumour of the appearance of Michael had been spread abroad. It seems plain that all the events narrated are supposed to take place immediately before the death of Isaac.

'*Do not present thine offering when thou art not clean. Bathe in water when thou wouldest draw near to the altar*,' p. 144. Cf. Test. Levi, ix. 8, Jubilees xxi. (tr. Schodde) 'At all times be clean in thy body and wash thyself with water before thou goest to sacrifice upon the altar.' The speech of Abraham to Isaac, in which this phrase occurs, supplies to some extent the want of any ethical or hortatory element in the Testament of Abraham. The dying speech of Isaac to Esau and Jacob (Jub. xxxvi.) is of less general application. It is possible to imagine an Essene influence in the passage which heads this note.

'*I am near to the fire that burneth*,' p. 145. Cf. Is. xxxiii. 14, and the *agraphon* quoted by Origen and Didymus (Resch, p. 98), ὁ ἐγγύς μου ἐγγὺς τοῦ πυρός.

'*I am grieved for every one bearing Thine image who meets me, and towards him are my eyes*,' p. 145. Cf. p. 150. "Thou shalt not injure the image of God in that which thou doest, for the image of man was made in the image of God." It seems from this that 'I have compassion upon' would here be a better rendering than 'I am grieved for.'

Injunction to reverence the priests, p. 145. So, in Test. Ruben vi., Juda xxi., Iss. v., Dan vi., Neph. viii., etc., reverence for Levi is enjoined.

The comparison between the priesthood and the angelic

---

[1] Cf. Anastasius Antiochenus, *de tribus quadragesimis*.

hierarchy finds its fullest development in the works of the Ps.-Dionysius the Areopagite.

Beware of these sins and what resembles them, p. 146. Cf. *Didache* c. 3 Τέκνον μου, φεῦγε ἀπὸ παντὸς πονηροῦ καὶ ἀπὸ παντὸς ὁμοίου αὐτοῦ. That this is a characteristically Jewish saying has been shewn by Dr Taylor, *Lectures on the Teaching &c.* (1886) pp. 23 ff. The moral precepts should throughout be compared with the *Didache* cc. 1—6.

The Vision of Torment, p. 146. Here the employment of the first person is specially noticeable, in connexion with its occurrence in the corresponding sections of the Testament of Abraham. Obviously, again, the vision is much abridged. The Three Testaments concern themselves, seemingly, with different departments of eschatology. Whilst Abraham sees the power of judgment, Isaac sees the torments of Hell, and Jacob is shown the 'places of rest' as well as the torments.

The episode of the lions, p. 147. A striking parallel to this is found in a Jewish book. Eisenmenger and, following him, Stehelin (*Traditions of the Jews*) quote a passage from the *Torath Adam*, f. 97. " R. Jehoshua ben Levi hath said: 'Upon measuring the first house of the dwellings of Hell I found it to contain a hundred miles in length and fifty miles in breadth; in it are many caverns, and in them are fiery lions, and when a man falls into one of these caverns the lions devour him, and when he is consumed he appears again as perfect as if he had not been touched by the fire, and then are they who are thus restored thrown again into the fire of every cavern in the first division of Hell....The angel Kushiel smites them with a fiery scourge (cf. p. 123 of our book)." The Rabbi describes in monotonously similar terms each one of the seven mansions of Hell. For the duration of the torment, *a whole year for every hour*, cf. Hermas, *Sim.* vi. 4. 4.

The fiery river, p. 147. It would be difficult to name any vision of Hell in which this feature does not appear. The 'fiery stream' of Dan. vii. is not there conceived of as an instrument of punishment, it would seem; yet this is its use in the minds of the later Rabbis[1]. Whether it takes the form of lake or river, the feature is wellnigh universal in Apocalyptic literature. The distinctive trait of the description before us is the statement that 'the river had intelligence in the fire thereof, that it should not hurt the righteous but the sinners only[2].' I am inclined to bring this into connexion with a phrase which occurs in Clem. Alex. *Cohort.* p. 47 (Potter), πῦρ σωφρονοῦν. *Paed.* iii. 8, p. 280, *Ecl.* 25, p. 985, φρόνιμον πῦρ. Tertullian and Minucius Felix, speaking of fire which destroyed heathen temples, as Clement does in the first passage cited, call it 'sapiens ignis.' In the third of these passages Clement speaks of the fire as φθαρτικὴ τῶν χειρόνων καὶ σωστικὴ τῶν ἀμεινόνων, and he adds διὸ καὶ φρόνιμον λέγεται παρὰ τοῖς προφήταις τοῦτο τὸ πῦρ. To what prophet he alludes I cannot discover; he may well be drawing on an apocryphal source. Elsewhere (*Exc. Theod.* 81. *Ecl.* 8) he dwells on the double nature of fire, and uses the epithet νοητόν, though in a different sense.

The idea that souls are plunged to various depths in the river of fire according to the nature of their sin is one found in several visions, e.g. *Apoc. Pauli* 31.

The pulpit of the curtain of the Father, p. 148. Cf. 'the inner curtain of Him who holds all.' In Clem. Alex. *Exc. Theod.* 38, we find mention both of the river of fire and of the curtain before the throne. Ποταμὸς ἐκπορεύεται πυρὸς ὑποκάτω τοῦ θρόνου τοῦ τόπου, καὶ ῥεῖ εἰς τὸ κενὸν τοῦ ἐκτισμένου, ὅ ἐστιν ἡ γέεννα...καὶ αὐτὸς δὲ ὁ τόπος πυρινός ἐστι. διὰ τοῦτο, φησί, καταπέτασμα ἔχει, ἵνα μὴ ἐκ τῆς προσόψεως ἀναλωθῇ τὰ πράγματα.

Holy, Holy, Holy is the Lord the Sabaoth, the Heaven and the Earth are filled with Thy hallowed Glory, p. 148 (cf. p. 149). The form of this Doxology is exactly that of the Liturgy of S. Mark (Swainson, p. 48): Ἅγιος, ἅγιος, ἅγιος Κύριος Σαβαώθ· πλήρης ὁ οὐρανὸς καὶ ἡ γῆ τῆς ἁγίας σου δόξης. Two points are to be noted: (1) 'Heaven and Earth,' as in the Liturgies and the *Te Deum*, but not in

---

[1] See also Clem. Alex. *Exc. Theod.* 38.
[2] Cf. Commodian *Instr.* ii. 2. 10. *Carm. Ap.* 996.

Isaiah vi. ('the whole earth'); and (2) the addition of ἁγίας, which seems to be peculiar to the Alexandrian Liturgy. It may also be observed that there would seem to be a Christian Liturgical element in the Prayer before offering Sacrifice on pp. 144 f., and in the paragraph which follows it.

'Then said my father Abraham, O divine Father...even if he cannot write his testament, let thy...mercy enfold him, &c.,' p. 149. This petition and those that follow are closely modelled on the intercession of Abraham in Gen. xviii. A clause has plainly dropped out before the words 'And the Saviour said,' p. 149. The supplement required is 'And my father Abraham said, And if he is poor and cannot find bread in his house, let thy mercy and compassion enfold him still.'

With the conditions imposed and the blessings promised in this paragraph should be compared a passage in an Egyptian apocryphal book which I have already had occasion to cite, the History of Joseph the Carpenter, c. xxvi. "Whatever man shall pay heed to the offering on the day of thy memorial, I will bless him and reward him in the congregation of virgins. And whosoever shall give good to the wretched, the poor, the widow, and the orphan from the labour of his hands, on the day when thy memorial is celebrated, and in thy name, he shall not be in want all the days of his life. And whosoever shall give a cup of water or wine to the widow or the orphan in thy name, I will give him to thee, that thou mayest go in with him into the banquet of the thousand years....And whosoever shall write the story of thy life and of thy labour and thy departure from this world, and this word that is spoken by my mouth, I will put him under thy protection as long as he liveth."

M. R. J.

INDEX I.

OF GREEK WORDS.

ἀδημονέω A 84
ἄλυπος A 87
ἁμαξηγέω A 87
ἀνάπηρος A 77
ἀνασπάω A 90
ἀνάστημα A 88
ἀνύπαρκτος A 101
ἀνυποφόρος A 101, 102
ἀποκάλυψις A 83
ἀποφυσόω A 102
ἀροτριασμός AB 78, 105

βορβορόω A 101

δαμάζω A 79
διέλαιος A 80
διχάζω A 88
δουλίς A 95

ἐναγκαλίζω B 105
ἐξιλεόω B 116
ἐπιβαρής AB 82, 106, 108, 109, 116
ἐπιξενίζω AB 80, 82, 83, 110
ἐπίξενος A 78, 80
ἐρηκινός B 107

ζεῦμα B 110, 121
ζοφερός A 99
ζοφώδης A 99
ζυγοστάτης A 93

ἡλιόμορφος A 84, 92, 93, 97, 99
ἡλιόρατος A 78, 90, 97

θεάφη A 90, app. crit.
θεόπνευστος A 103
θεοϋφαντός A 103

ἰσοζυγέω B 114

καθυπουργέω A 91
κακοφρονέω A 94
κλινάριον A 80
κοχλάζω A 99, 101

ληθαργέω B 115

μετεωρίζομαι AB 79, 107

νεόνυμφος A 87

ξενισμός B 117

οἰκονομία B 112
ὁμόσκηνος A 97
ὀψικεύω A 87, 103

παμφάγος A 81, 91
πανάρετος A 82
πανίερος A 77
παραμύθιον B 117
παραφέρω (καὶ λέγω) B 110
παρεδρεύω A 78
πληροφορέω A 78
προπάτωρ A 85
προχαιρετίζω A 78
πυθμήν A 101

σαπρότης B 118
σκύλλω B 107
στειράω A 85
συλλήπτωρ A 97
συνόμοιος B 113
συντομία B 109
σωματικῶς B 112

ταλανίζω A 103
ταμεῖον B 109
τετραόδιον A 77
τρικέφαλος A 99
τρίκλινος A 80, 97, 98
τρομάζω A 96

ὕπανδρος B 116
ὑπείκω A 86
ὑποβρύχιος A 102
ὑφαπλόω A 80

φλογέστατος A 99
φωταγωγέω A 84
φωτοφόρος A 84, 91, 94

χαρζανή A 90

INDEX II.

TO THE INTRODUCTION AND NOTES.

A

Abel 28, 125 sqq.
Abraham
  Apocalypse of; see *Apocalypse*
  book attributed to him 125
  his bosom 72 sqq., 128 sqq.
Acta Pilati 1, 127
Acts
  of Andrew 1
  of Andrew and Matthew (Matthias) 2, 3, 75, 123
  of Andrew and Peter 33, 123
  of John 4, 129
  of John, by Ps-Mellitus 130
  of Matthew 123
  of Peter and Paul 4
  of Philip 129
  of Simon (Sahidic) 123
  of Thomas 2, 3, 24, 123, 129
Adam
  at gate of Paradise 123
  Apocalypse of; see *Apocalypse*
  books of 5, 8, 9, 121
  Testament of 121
  tract on 3
Adoration of God by souls 126
Alban's Abbey, S. 31
Aleatoribus, de 26
Alexander, Romance of 60 sqq.
Anaphora Pilati 1
Andrew, S.; see *Acts*
Angelology 55
Angels
  chastening 123
  of death 55
  Origen on 14
  recording 124
Apocalypse
  of Abraham 6, 9, 14, 27, 28, 125
  of Adam 121
  Anonymous, in Coptic 71
  of Bartholomew 75
  of Baruch 9
  of Elias 8, 9

Apocalypse
  of Esdras (= 4 Esdras) 8, 9, 10, 12, 71, 124, 127
  of Esdras (ed. Tischdf.) 9, 24, 32, 65 sqq.
  of Methodius 2, 5
  of Moses 3, 4, 9, 34, 121, 123, 126
  of Paul 15, 20 sqq., 44 sqq., 49, 71, 74, 121, 126, 128, 129, 160
  of Peter 23 sqq.
  of Sedrach 31 sqq., 66
  of the Virgin 3, 122
  of Zephaniah 8, 21, 25, 74, 122, 123, 124
  of Zosimas 127
Apollonius Mathematicus 121
Apostles, as judges 52 sqq.
Apostolic Constitutions 11, 130
  do. do. Coptic 121
Arles Cathedral 73
Aseneth, Book of 31, 120, 124, 128
Assumption of Moses 8, 9, 15 sqq., 34, 68, 122
Assumption of the Virgin
  Coptic 58, 129
  Greek 1, 33, 58, 123
  Syriac 122
Atarlimos 41, 49
Athanasius 7
Athanasius, Synopsis of 7 sqq.

B

Bahayla Mikhael, Abba 63
Ballad, modern Greek 68, 69
Barlaam and Josaphat 59
Barnabas, Epistle of 14
Barontus, Vision of S. 73
Baruch, rest of words of 2, 4, 59
Bedargon 57
Blastares, Matthew 28
Bodleian, MSS in the 2, 17, 18, 31, 156
Bourges, window at 74
Burial offices, references to the Patriarchs in 128

INDEX.

C

Callisthenes, Pseudo- 61
Canonician MS 2
Cedrenus, George 9, 121
Charon 56, 68
Christian element in Testament of Abraham 50 sqq.
Clement of Alexandria 18, 123, 160
Commodian 160
Cross, history of the 61
Cypress, the 60 sqq.
Cypriote Ballad 68

D

Date of the Testament of Abraham 51
David, History of 11
Death, personified 39, 40, 41, 55 sqq.
Didache 14, 159
Dives and Lazarus 73
Dokiel 40, 45
Doukas, a scribe 7

E

Egypt 29, 76
Eldad and Medad, Book of 8
Eliezer 35, 48, 120
Enoch, Book of 8, 11, 122, 123
Epiphanius, S. 13 sqq.
Esdras; see *Apocalypse*
Esther, Targum Sheni on 63
Eton College, MS at 7
Euchologion 130
Eurippus, tract on S. John Baptist 1, 2
Evodius, S. 58

F

Fear of Death 64 sqq.
Fiery river 159

G

Gale's MSS 5
Gaster, Dr M. 6, 16
Gates, the two 38, 46, 50, 52, 123
Gaulmyn, Gilbert 64, 121
Gelasian Decree 155
Gelasian Sacramentary 128
George, a scribe 1
Glycas, Michael 61
Gregory, Dialogues of 23, 126

H

Harleian MSS 130
Heemskerck, Martin 74
Hell, description of 159
Hermas 14, 124, 159
Hesychius 121
Hippolytus, S. 123
Horace 126
Hours of the day and night 121

I

Isaac
  Testament of; see *Testament*
  History of 156
  Vision of 44
  Writings of 13
Isaiah, Ascension of 8, 9, 55, 157

J

Jacob; see *Testament*
James, Ascents of 156
Jehoshua ben Levi 159
Jerome, S. 12
Jerusalem, MS at 2
Job; see *Testament*
John Baptist, S., tract on 1, 2
John Evangelist, S.; see *Acts* and *Assumption*
Joseph of Arimathaea, story of 1
Joseph the Carpenter, History of 34, 57, 65, 129, 161
Joseph the Patriarch, Prayer of 8, 13, 15, 124
Jubilees, Book of 17, 125, 157, 158

L

Lamech, Book of 8, 10
Language of the Testament of Abraham 51
Laodiceans, Epistle to the 12
Lincoln Cathedral 74
Lions of Hell 159
Liturgies, 128, 160

M

Macarius of Egypt, S. 19, 126, 127
Macarius Magnes 120
Maccabees, Fourth Book of 73
Mapes, Walter 69
Marriage Offices 128
Masek, sons of 35, 120
Matthew, S.; see *Acts*
Matthew Paris 30
Methodius, S. 24; and see *Apocalypse*
Michael, S. 55 sqq., 70 sqq.
Mohammedan beliefs cited 62, 72
Montpellier, MS at 4
Moses, Tracts on his death 64, 66 sqq.; and see *Apocalypse*, *Assumption*, *Testament*

N

Nicephorus, Stichometry of 7 sqq.
Nicetas, Catena of 17
Noah, book of 13

O

Oceanus, river of 38, 45, 46
Og, Book of 155
Origen 14 sqq.
Orphica 60

P

Paradise
  the Patriarchs in 72 sqq.
  trees of 59 sqq.
Paradosis of Pilate 1
Paris, MSS at 1, 2, 3, 4, 7, 21, 121, 157
Patriarchs; see *Testament*
Paul, S.; see *Apocalypse*
Perpetua, S., Passion of 59, 128
Peter, S.; see *Acts* and *Apocalypse*
Philip, S.; see *Acts*
Pilate; see *Acts*
Pistis Sophia 58, 122
Primasius 59
Priscillian 12 sqq.
Protevangelium 2, 4, 121, 123
Psellus, Michael 121
Puruel 40, 45

R

Rebekah 36 sqq., 48
Resch, Agrapha 158
Rheims Cathedral 73

S

Saints, lives of various 1, 2, 3, 4, 5
Salisbury, sculpture at 125
Samael 58, 67
Sarah, death of 43, 47
Sarum Manual 128
Sethians 13 sqq., 28, 125
Severus of Antioch 15 sqq.
Sibylline oracles 13, 21, 23, 24
Simon, S.; see *Acts*
Sixtus of Siena 16, 68
Sixty Books, list of the 7 sqq.
Solomon, Psalms of 8, 10; and see *Testament*
Souls
  exodus of 19 sqq., 57, 76
  weighing of 70 sqq.
Sozomen 10, 23
Stichometries 7 sqq.

T

Tartaruchus 22
Temeluchus 22, 24
Testament
  of Abraham *passim*
  of Adam 121, 157
  of Hezekiah 9
  of Isaac 133, 140 sqq.
  of Jacob 133, 152 sqq.
  of Job 9, 120, 155
  of Moses 8
  of Solomon 9
  of the Three Patriarchs 11, 133 sqq.
  of the Twelve Patriarchs 8, 31, 120, 156, 158
Thanatos; see *Death*
Theophilus, Itinerary of 31
Thomas, S.; see *Acts*
Thurchill, Vision of 30 sqq.
Tobit, Book of 12, 13, 55, 76, 120
Trees, speaking 59 sqq.
Trumpet 39, 125

U

Unwillingness to die 64 sqq.

V

Versions of the Testament of Abraham 1, 6, 33 sqq.
Vienna, MSS at 2, 4

W

Ways, the two 14, 38
Weighing of souls 70 sqq.; of sins 130

Y

Yule, Col., on fabulous trees 61

Z

Zahn, on Stichometries 7
Zechariah, Apocryphal Book of 10
Zephaniah; see *Apocalypse*
Zosimas; see *Apocalypse*

www.ingramcontent.com/pod-product-compliance
Lightning Source LLC
Chambersburg PA
CBHW051933160426
43198CB00012B/2129